THE
FRENCH AND ITALIAN
COMMUNIST PARTIES

Cass Series: Totalitarian Movements and Political Religions

Series Editors: Michael Burleigh and Robert Mallett
ISSN: 1477-058X

This innovative new book series will scrutinise all attempts to totally refashion mankind and society, whether these hailed from the Left or the Right, which, unusually, will receive equal consideration. Although its primary focus will be on the authoritarian and totalitarian politics of the twentieth century, the series will also provide a forum for the wider discussion of the politics of faith and salvation in general, together with an examination of their inexorably catastrophic consequences. There are no chronological or geographical limitations to the books that may be included, and the series will include reprints of classic works and translations, as well as monographs and collections of essays.

International Fascism, 1919–1945
Gert Sørenson and Robert Mallett (eds)

Faith, Politics and Nazism: Selected Essays by Uriel Tal
With a Foreword by Saul Friedlander

Totalitarian Democracy and After: International Colloquium in Memory of Jacob L. Talmon
Yehoshua Arieli and Nathan Rothenstreich (eds)

The French and Italian Communist Parties: Comrades and Culture
Cyrille Guiat

The Italian Road to Fascism
Emilio Gentile, translated by Robert Mallett

THE
FRENCH AND ITALIAN
COMMUNIST PARTIES

Comrades and Culture

CYRILLE GUIAT

Heriot-Watt University, Edinburgh

FRANK CASS

LONDON • PORTLAND, OR

First published in 2003 in Great Britain by
FRANK CASS PUBLISHERS
Crown House, 47 Chase Side
London N14 5BP

and in the United States of America by
FRANK CASS PUBLISHERS
c/o ISBS, 5824 N.E. Hassalo Street
Portland, Oregon, 97213–3644

Website: www.frankcass.com

British Library Cataloguing in Publication Data

Guiat, Cyrille
   The French and Italian communist parties: comrades and
   culture. – (Cass series. Totalitarian movements and
   political religions)
   1. Parti communiste francais 2. Partito comunista italiano
   3. Communist parties – Cross-cultural studies 4. Communist
   parties – France – Ivry-sur-Seine 5. Communist parties –
   Italy – Reggio Emilia
   I. Title
   324.2′44075

ISBN 0-7146-5332-2 (cloth)
ISSN 1477-058X

Library of Congress Cataloging-in-Publication Data

Guiat, Cyrille, 1968–
   The French and Italian communist parties: comrades and culture/Cyrille Guiat.
      p. cm. – (Cass series–totalitarian movements and political religions,
      ISSN 1477-058X)
   Includes bibliographical references and index.
   ISBN 0-7146-5332-2 (cloth)
   1. Parti communiste français–History. 2. Partico comunista italiano–History.
   3. Comparative government. I. Title. II. Series.

   JN3007.C6 G83 2002
   324.244′075–dc21

2002026784

Typeset by Tradespools, Frome, Somerset
Printed in Great Britain by MPG Books Ltd, Bodmin, Cornwall

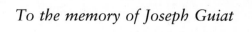

To the memory of Joseph Guiat

Contents

Figures

Foreword

This book is a study in comparative communism and it is rich detail derived from fieldwork conducted in two countries over seven years. Although the research was conducted in France and Italy it integrates those findings into the scholarship of the English-speaking world. There are few such ambitious undertakings and the primary research in both these countries is at the same time thorough and original. It is a work that will add more to the growing post-communist study of communism and help the understanding of the twentieth century communism phenomenon – something far from complete.

This book reports on research done in two cases but it is not a 'descriptive monograph'. One key feature of this book is methodological. It is a comparative study of cases selected for their common attributes. These two communist communes are not, of course, statistical samples but cases that justify systematic comparisons and contrasts. In the social sciences great claims are made for comparative approaches as they – to some small extent – make up for the inability of the human sciences to do experiments or conduct controls. If social situations cannot be repeated then comparing cases and filtering out variables can make advances. Hence in political studies, for these reasons, more than a little lip service is paid to the notion of comparative work but unfortunately few studies are rigorously comparative. There is the problem of 'non-additivity' which bedevils case studies. 'Comparative' works are often collections of case studies and in some these may be no more than Cook's Tours of different countries without any attempt to measure the variables against each other (one purpose of comparison).

This research is different. In the first place the two comparative cases have been carefully chosen to provide a rough equivalence and in the second case they take very similar institutions (that is the Communist Parties) and look at the outcomes. The differences between the Communist Parties of France and Italy were often noted during the

Cold War and frequently (for political reasons) their approaches were contrasted.

This book takes up the question of their differences and asks what the practical outcome was. Local government has been selected and the communes of Ivry-sur-Seine and Reggio Emilia. In social composition and Party domination these two were similar enough to make a meaningful comparison almost as if some unseen hand had placed the Parties in position for comparative purposes. Perfect equivalence cannot be achieved but enough of a yardstick has been constructed to make the results meaningful and valuable. Within the local societies the cultural policies and their outcome in the municipalities have been compared. Cultural policy is one of the areas of local government in both countries that has scope for autonomy and where the central government's interference is less than in, for example, health and welfare. Both Parties had definite cultural policies of which they made much but the outcomes were, as the study shows, very different.

After filtering out a multitude of factors the research shows that the distinguishing quality was the activity of the Communist Parties. These were, by the 1970s, distinct organisations and the speculations of the students of comparative communism are confirmed by this research. The argument of this book is that the Parties had distinctive political approaches and that these led to different outcomes. The hypothesis is confirmed by the comparative study.

This is a rather bald way of summarising an intricate argument and a forcefully written book that takes the reader through aspects of Italian and French local and cultural policy. It is a contribution to the study of culture and of politics as well as of local government and of communism. There are many reasons for reading this study and the rigorous methodological background is in that sense a support. However, those interested in ideology, political parties and country studies will all find this book of great value.

D.S. Bell
University of Leeds
June 2002

Series Editor's Preface

Cyrille Guiat's *The French and Italian Communist Parties* adds new vigour to the lively and controversial debate on post-war communism. As he points out in his Introduction, the publication of Stefan Courtois' *Le livre noir du communisme (The Black Book of Communism)* in 1997, sparked a major discussion on the very nature of communist ideology. But had Courtois and his team, in demonising the various communist regimes, simply exposed the true perniciousness of communism in power, or were they pursuing other, political ends? More specifically, what does this wider debate mean in terms of Communist Party policy in France and Italy?

Guiat begins with the premise that the Parti Communiste Français (PCF) and the Partito Comunista Italiano (PCI) were not dissimilar entities in their formative years, but that they, albeit as satellites of the Stalinist edifice, gradually diverged from one another in the wake of the Second World War. As the PCI drifted further away from Moscow, the PCF remained more closely connected to Stalin. If, Guiat argues, one concentrates on both parties as 'primarily national, societal' forces, as many scholars have done, then the association with both Moscow and other international communist parties is not patently apparent. Yet an examination of the PCF/PCI role within the Comintern and beyond demonstrates, with some clarity, their respective relationships with the Kremlin. In broad terms, the PCF remained a 'tool' of Soviet foreign policy, whereas their Italian comrades, while remaining allies of Moscow, focused more keenly on 'national/societal factors'.

Hence Guiat's excellent case study of PCF/PCI cultural policy in Ivry-sur-Seine and Reggio Emilia respectively exposes this subtle divergence in attitudes. The PCF in Ivry pursued a cultural policy based on 'indoctrinating' the local population with ideas about the superiority of Sovietism. In short, the PCF in this region were 'a Leninist revolutionary force irrevocably linked to international communism'. This by no means suggests that their counterparts in Reggio Emilia had lost their connection with the world of global communism. The PCI leadership, made up of more bourgeois elements, was principally concerned with strengthening communist identity through social and cultural activity at local level. Nevertheless, the PCI never renounced its links with the Soviet Union, even if these links were never as strong as those of the PCF. This subtle distinction is what gives Guiat's book its unique, masterful quality in assessing functional communism at work. His open invitation to the scholarly community to undertake similar comparative analysis will, if undertaken, only contribute still further to our understanding of Soviet ideology, and its implications for western European politics.

Robert Mallett
Series Editor

Acknowledgements

In the production of this book, I have benefited from so much help and support in three different countries that it is difficult to begin this acknowledgement. The foremost places are probably Ivry-sur-Seine and Reggio Emilia, where during my research trips I was very fortunate to meet many people who helped me in a number of different ways. My sincere gratitude goes to them all, but some cannot be allowed to pass without more specific mention.

In Ivry, several PCF members and officials were kind enough to answer my questions: I should mention particularly André Minc and Fernand Leriche for their time. The staff of the municipal archive also provided me with dedicated assistance in finding relevant materials, and I would like to record my warmest thanks to them.

With regard to my stay in Reggio Emilia, I must start by expressing the huge debt I owe to my friends Francesca and Roberto Zelioli for being so generous in inviting me to stay in their home in the beautiful Emilian countryside during my stay in Italy. Above all, their kindness went far beyond the provision of a 'home away from home', as they introduced me to a number of PDS members and officials whose insight proved indispensable to my work. I am very grateful to them all, especially Antonio Canovi, Maurizio Festanti, Giuseppe Gherpelli and Antonio Zambonelli.

Closer to my adopted home, the United Kingdom, I cannot but express my thanks *du fond du coeur* to David S. Bell (University of Leeds) whose advice and enthusiasm about this piece of research have been truly invaluable and a source of constant inspiration. I am also very grateful to John Gaffney (Aston University), Edward Gouge (University of Leeds) and Robert Mallett (University of Birmingham) for their precious comments on earlier drafts of my manuscript, and to Andrew Humphrys at Frank Cass, whose help and editorial expertise in seeing this book through to its final form have been immense.

Closer to my new home still, in Edinburgh, I have for the past ten years enjoyed in the School of Languages at Heriot-Watt University the generous support of many colleagues and friends. Sincere thanks are due to my three successive Heads of School who provided guidance as well as support in the form of funding for research and teaching relief: Ian Mason, Anthony Stanforth and, above all, Margaret Lang. My heartfelt, special thanks go to Colin Grant and Chris Ross for their stimulating advice on various aspects of this book. Isabelle Perez also deserves a personal acknowledgement for her support and friendship.

In a way, this book sends me back to my first home, across the Channel. During what has now been a long time in Scotland, my parents have progressively come to accept the idea of my being a fair way away from France. I can only hope that they find here a token of my love and gratitude to them. Finally, I remain eternally grateful to my wife, Catherine Durand, whose help and support have been a source of constant sustenance.

Abbreviations

ANPI	National Association of Italian Partisans
CERM	Centre d'Etudes et de Recherches Marxistes
CGIL	Confederazione Generale Italiana del Lavoro
CGT	Confédération Générale du Travail
CGT-FO	Force Ouvrière
CLN	(Italian) National Liberation Committee
CNE	Comité National des Ecrivains
CPSU	Communist Party of the Soviet Union
DCI	Democrazia Cristiana Italiana
FNSP	Fondation Nationale des Sciences Politiques
MRP	Mouvement Républicain Populaire
PCF	Parti Communiste Français
PCI	Partito Comunista Italiano
PDS	Partito Democratico della Sinistra
PSI	Partito Socialista Italiano
SFIO	Section Française de l'Internationale Ouvrière
SPD	(German) Social Democratic Party

Introduction

As one of the key historical and political phenomena of the twentieth century, communism has attracted and continues to attract a prolific literature which is at the heart of numerous controversies: 'it [communism] has always aroused the passions of its opponents as well as those of its advocates'.[1] A recent example of such a passionate debate was the publication in France, in November 1997, of *Le Livre noir du communisme* (The Black Book of Communism) by a team of historians led by Stéphane Courtois.[2] This publication gives a graphic, detailed account of the crimes committed by communist regimes in the twentieth century and offers a macabre estimate of the total number of victims of repression at about 85 million. It was fiercely challenged by a number of French intellectuals and triggered an unprecedented media controversy between Courtois and a number of historians close to or members of the French Communist Party, who argued that Courtois' motives for orchestrating this major work were more political than academic.[3] In a television debate he was in fact accused by Communist Party historian Roger Martelli of attempting to 'assimilate' communism with Nazism and to advocate a 'Nuremberg trial of communism' which would echo, more than 50 years later, the series of trials of Nazi leaders held in 1946.[4]

As the two largest non-ruling communist parties in the world, the French Parti Communiste Français (PCF) and its Italian counterpart, the Partito Comunista Italiano (PCI), have also been for a long time the subject of a very substantial and polemical body of literature (see Chapter 1). Notwithstanding all these controversies, an idea which is commonly found in the comparative literature on these two parties is that there exists a contrast between them. Thus, it is often claimed, the PCF remained a very orthodox, Bolshevik revolutionary party whose aim was to create a Soviet-style society in France, while its unconditional fealty to Moscow was a key characteristic of its identity and strategy. The PCI, on the other hand, is often depicted as a more independent political force which rejected the Soviet model in the 1950s and progressively embarked on a strategy veering towards Western-style democracy and reformism.[5]

In a stimulating comparative study of these two parties, French historian Marc Lazar uses an original metaphor to illustrate this contrast. Writing about their strategies in the years 1945–47, he suggests that they could be compared with two satellites which, having been launched simultaneously, started to follow increasingly diverging trajectories. This was because of minimal differences in the launching process, which in the end resulted in the two satellites following distinct orbits.[6] Lazar's metaphor is revealing for various reasons. First, it implies that these two parties were not substantially different in their early years (both were created in the winter of 1920–21), but that their divergence emerged in a subtle form in the years following the Second World War and that, from then on, it progressively increased. Second, and more importantly, it suggests that they were not radically different in nature: they were both satellites revolving around the same planet, that of the international communist movement, with the Soviet Union as their centre of gravity. Being in different orbits simply meant that one of the two parties, the PCI, was further away from Moscow than the other, the PCF. This in turn leads to our third, crucial remark, namely that these two parties are eminently comparable as phenomena of a similar nature.

While there obviously exists a substantial body of comparative literature on these parties (see Chapters 1 and 2), it is claimed here that there is a niche for a new approach to the comparative study of the PCF and the PCI for at least two reasons.

The first is that most comparative studies tend to be somewhat general, consider these parties from the macro-political level, and embrace a great number of aspects of these parties. This leads in turn to the second reason, namely that a number of these studies fail to provide a clear, structured framework of analysis that would enable a productive comparison of these parties. Moreover, these reasons are compounded by the fact that the overwhelming majority of comparative studies on these parties are distorted by political motives (see Chapter 1).

Accordingly, this book is a comparative study (in a strong sense) of the PCF and the PCI based on two carefully designed municipal case studies (see Chapter 2). This structured, comparative framework is used to study in detail the cultural policies of the PCF in Ivry-sur-Seine (France) and of the PCI in Reggio Emilia (Italy) in the period extending approximately from the early 1960s to the early 1980s.

The aim of this new approach is to adopt the hypothesis that there is a contrast between the French and Italian Communist Parties and to test this hypothesis from a micro-political angle. In other words, the two case studies are used as a kind of laboratory to establish whether this general contrast identified by the literature is visible on the ground. It is also hoped that, by adopting such an approach based on policy outcomes at the local level, a less politically distorted view of these parties will emerge.

One of the difficulties in using such a focused approach is that this study inevitably touches upon a wide number of concepts and/or fields of political science, such as local government in France and Italy, the use of comparison and/or case-study design in the social sciences, culture and cultural policy-making, and of course the full range of concepts used in the study of communist parties. As a result, the discussion of the literature used in this study might appear fragmented. This is justified, however, by the fact that it was felt preferable, for heuristic reasons, to divide the review of literature and the discussion of the concepts across the various chapters rather than have a very substantial review presented in a single, cumbersome chapter at the beginning of this work.

The first part of this book (Chapters 1–4 inclusive) is devoted to the overall design and presentation of the comparative framework for the two case studies on Ivry-sur-Seine and Reggio Emilia (Chapters 5 and 6 respectively). Chapter 1 is a discussion of the controversial literature on the French and Italian Communist Parties and introduces a number of key concepts for the study of these parties, such as their societal and teleological dimensions. In Chapter 2 it is argued that a combination of both the comparative and case-study methods, despite some of the shortcomings of each of these methods taken individually, can provide a structured, focused framework for the study of the two parties. A presentation of the design of the case-studies, including a discussion of the main reasons for selecting the cultural policies of the two towns as a primary object of investigation, is also found in this chapter. In Chapter 3 it is contended that, notwithstanding the view that France and Italy are highly centralised states, the municipalities in these two countries enjoy a similar degree of local autonomy in cultural policy-making, which enables a revealing comparison of the action of two communist municipalities in this field. A number of concepts relevant to the study of the cultural policies of the two parties are discussed in Chapter 4, which completes the comparative framework of this study.

The two case studies of Ivry-sur-Seine and Reggio Emilia are found in Chapters 5 and 6 respectively. Last, but not least, Chapter 7 revisits the historical contrast between the PCF and the PCI by reviewing a number of potential factors which could account for the emergence of this divergence and suggests that, in the last instance, international factors prevailed. The conclusion provides a summary of the findings of the research, namely that on the ground, at municipal level, there was a contrast between the PCF and the PCI, and suggests potential research areas in the hope that further investigation in the comparative study of these two parties will follow in the near future.

NOTES

[1] M. Lazar, 'Le communisme est-il soluble dans l'histoire?', *L'Histoire*, 223 (1998), p. 70. (Unless otherwise indicated, all translations of excerpts in other languages are my own.)

[2] See S. Courtois, (ed.), *Le Livre noir du communisme: Crimes, terreur, répression* (Paris: Laffont/Bouquins, 1998).

[3] See A. Chemin, 'L'histoire du communisme redevient un enjeu politique', *Le Monde*, 9–10 November 1997, p. 7.

[4] Ibid., p. 7.

[5] See, for example, R. Tiersky, *Ordinary Stalinism: Democratic Centralism and the Question of Communist Political Development* (London: Allen & Unwin, 1986).

[6] M. Lazar, *Maisons rouges: Les Partis communistes français et italien de la Libération à nos jours* (Paris: Aubier, 1992), p. 53.

1

The French and Italian Communist Parties: A Critical Review of the Literature

The French and Italian Communist Parties, which were the two largest non-ruling communist parties in western Europe, have attracted substantial academic and media attention, mostly from French, Italian and English-speaking scholars. While a thorough discussion of this considerable body of work would go far beyond the scope of this study – and would indeed require a substantial volume in its own right – the present chapter aims to provide an outline of the main aspects of the literature concerning the French and Italian Communist Parties. In an attempt to classify these studies, and for heuristic reasons, this chapter is divided in three sections which review different schools of thought pertaining to the literature on French and Italian communism. However, it is recognised that these categories are, like any, somewhat arbitrary, and that they do not therefore claim to be comprehensive or watertight.

Accordingly, the first section of this survey discusses a number of studies which tend to emphasise the national, societal dimension of these parties by focusing on their interactions with the French and Italian political and social systems. These studies include the works published by scholars sympathetic to their object of research, such as communist historians.

Acknowledging the fact that these studies tend to neglect the international dimension of these parties, that is to say their constitutive and cast-iron tie to international communism and the Soviet Union, the second section examines what could be called the critical historiography of these parties. This is a body of works published by historians and political scientists who claim that communist parties were indissolubly linked to the Soviet model. They argue that these parties remained a foreign 'transplant' or a 'counter-society' dedicated in the long term to the promotion of a worldwide revolution embodied by the Soviet Union, the so-called 'Fatherland of socialism', which they defended at all costs, sometimes to the detriment of their domestic social integration and political success.

Yet, while these controversies have pitted scholars writing on either the PCF or the PCI against each other, it is argued in the third section that most comparative studies involving these two parties claim that there is a contrast between them. The French Communist Party, it is claimed, always remained more Leninist, revolutionary, sectarian and internationalist (or teleological) than its Italian counterpart, which is often described as a more pragmatic, reformist and societal force. The magnitude of this contrast is in itself a controversial matter. Some scholars see in it only a mere difference in style, while others systematically play one party against the other to produce a marked difference. It is concluded in this chapter, however, that there is sufficient evidence to confirm the existence of a contrast, which is tested empirically through the two case studies which form the core of this study.

COMMUNIST PARTIES AS PRIMARILY NATIONAL AND SOCIETAL PHENOMENA

A great number of studies published in French, Italian and English argue that the French and Italian Communist Parties were largely independent political parties whose strategies were determined by their respective national socio-political environments. It is possible to discern three broad categories of research here. The first two are suggested by Lazar. Writing about the PCF, he distinguishes between two groups of communist historians, official Party historians on the one hand, often paid, commissioned and published by the PCF, and university scholars not tied to the Party whose research was often conducted and published outside the Party, but who were PCF members or backers.[1] The third proposed category is less clearly defined and includes studies by non-communists (although some might have been close to the Party) which tend to echo or develop the view that the PCF (or the PCI) was first and foremost a national political force deeply rooted in its socio-political environment.

The PCF as a primarily national, societal force

Several studies highlight the highly political nature of PCF historiography.[2] This political function, largely based on a teleological dimension stemming from the self-proclaimed status of Marxism as the science of history, is best summarised by Courtois and Lazar in the introduction to their *Histoire du PCF* (History of the PCF):

The PCF, more than any other party, attributes decisive importance to history and to its own history, of which it always strives to give an official version: in 1964 this led it to publish a *Manuel d'histoire du PCF* [Manual of the History of the PCF] and to issue directives and injunctions to its historians. Claiming to be a Marxist, or more precisely a Marxist–Leninist party ..., it sees itself as the bearer of a scientific and eschatological theory of history; in other words, everything in history had to demonstrate that the Communist Party was the party of the proletariat ... whose mission and ultimate objective was to establish a communist society. But the PCF has also become its own historian for political and ideological reasons. Not only does it conscript the past in the service of its present strategy; but also, Marxism being erected into the science of history, it offers, from the Party's viewpoint, the opportunity to justify in irrefutable fashion the past, the present and the future of the Party.[3]

This obsession with history led to the publication of a Party historiography which was often 'manichaean, simplistic, manipulative, constantly rewritten according to the imperatives of the day', based on a few sacred texts and placed under the control of the Party's highest authorities.[4] Among the sacred texts produced were the autobiography of Maurice Thorez, *Fils du peuple* (Son of the People), in fact written by a PCF ghostwriter, Jean Fréville, and published for the first time in 1937, and the *Manuel* of 1964, which echoed in format and orthodoxy the *History of the Communist (Bolshevik) Party of the Soviet Union* first published under the auspices of Stalin in 1938.[5] The PCF also published orthodox studies on particular aspects of its history, such as *Le PCF dans la Résistance* (The PCF in the Resistance).[6] To this official PCF historiography, one could add the numerous books of memoirs of orthodox PCF leaders such as Etienne Fajon, Gaston Plissonnier or André Wurmser, to name but a few.[7] Most of these accounts play the general, hagiographic function summarised by Courtois and Lazar above, that is to say they echo, through personal testimonies, the official version of Party history.

Some official historical publications, however, play a more specific role. This is for instance the case of François Billoux's *Quand nous étions ministres* (When We Were Ministers), an account by a PCF leader of the three post-war years (1944–47), during which the Party formed a coalition government with other left-wing forces.[8] This was published at the time when the PCF had just entered an official electoral alliance with the French Socialist Party on the basis of a Programme Commun de Gouvernement, and served to demonstrate that French communists could be trusted as a democratic, government party on the basis of their positive contribution to the reconstruction of France 25 years earlier. In his preface to Billoux's account, Georges Marchais, then Secretary-General of the Party, was keen to underline that this account played a key political role:

> This book, although it deals with an experience which took place 25 years ago, is of direct relevance to the current political situation. It constitutes an element of the vast, nationwide campaign led by our Party on the theme of a programme of a democratic government of popular union.[9]

This admission that history was used for reasons of political expediency further illustrates that to PCF leaders history was not an independent endeavour. As a result, the historical production of communist historians was closely monitored, at least until the 1970s.

The communist historiography of French communism started to evolve in the 1970s, as a result of two factors. First, PCF official historiography, which had until then enjoyed in France a quasi-monopoly or at least a 'hegemonic' (as Gramsci would have said) status, was strongly challenged in the mid-1960s by the publication of Annie Kriegel's thesis on the origins of the PCF, which emphasised the 'accidental' creation of this party and its 'foreign' nature vis-à-vis the traditions of the French working-class movement (see below). This challenge prompted PCF historians to fend off Kriegel and her followers by emphasising the national and societal dimension of French communism through the detailed study of its strategy and implantation into the French socio-political environment, as discussed below.

The second factor is that communist historians, in the context of the relative relaxation of Party control upon its social scientists which followed the Argenteuil meeting of 1966 (see Chapter 4), were starting to attempt to 'win their independence from the Party leadership, through research carried out in universities but also in specialised research centres funded by the PCF such as the Maurice Thorez Institute'.[10] This changing approach to historical and political research was advocated in a number of books published in the 1970s and early 1980s. Thus, in the opening sentences of his study of the PCF, Jean Elleinstein wrote: 'This book is a result of my own work, I have not sought any authorisation from anyone prior to writing it, and I have not asked anybody to read it', implying that he had not been submitted to any Party control or censorship.[11] By the same token, the team of PCF historians who published *Le PCF, étapes et problèmes* (Key Dates and Issues in the History of the PCF) in 1981 claimed that the notion of 'official history' was outdated and argued that they had produced genuine, rigorous historical research.[12] A very similar claim to have moved beyond official historiography and towards a critical approach was made by Burles, Martelli and Wolikow in their 1981 book on the strategy of the PCF.[13]

It should be argued that this autonomy was only very relative: for instance, historians were not allowed access to PCF archives which could have shed some light on controversial aspects of its history. However, the main argument here is that the need to fend off the emerging view that French communism was mainly an imported, foreign phenomenon and the process of relative freeing of PCF scholars resulted in a number of stimulating studies whose quality is widely acknowledged, even by historians who are highly critical of French communism such as Lazar.[14] These studies can be gathered under two main concepts or variations – implantation and strategy.

The first, the implantation approach, emerged in the 1970s under the influence of Jacques Girault, PCF member and professor of history at the University of Paris-I, and had a clear, self-proclaimed goal: 'We intend to react against the classical historiography [Kriegel and her followers] which places unwarranted emphasis on the role of the International.'[15]

Accordingly, in this collective work, Girault and his colleagues focused on the implantation of French communism in its socio-economic context, particularly in the red suburbs of Paris, between the two world wars, in order to outline its diversity. The main features of this approach, as found for instance in Bernard Chambaz's chapter on PCF implantation in Ivry, contain a thorough emphasis on local conditions through a detailed study of the local economy and population, the local political situation, the organisation of the Party at the local level, its electoral results and the actions of the communist municipal authority in the field of welfare, and the conclusion that French communism in Ivry was quite unique.[16] This societal approach, focusing on the study of the local terrain on which the PCF blossomed, held that communism was rooted in French society and tradition, and led to a series of detailed studies on red municipalities.

One such monograph is Annie Fourcaut's study of Bobigny, a bastion of French municipal communism, published in 1986. In this major work, Fourcaut argues that suburban communism was successful in creating a form of collective identity, of social integration for local populations which had been uprooted from rural areas and had flocked to the Paris area: 'The communism found in the suburbs [of Paris] between the wars appears much more to be a form of popular culture than a political opinion ... Its [the PCF's] strictly political role was relatively minor.'[17]

Furthermore, Fourcaut attributes the success of French communism on this particularly fertile terrain to its ability to understand and harness 'the expectations of the society in which it inserted itself'.[18] In other words, what Fourcaut argues in substance is that there was a strong symbiosis between a particular socio-economic context (the Paris suburbs in the 1920s and 1930s) and a political party which successfully addressed numerous problems (housing, loss of identity, striking poverty) stemming from the crisis of the rapid, somewhat uncontrolled development of the suburbs in the Paris area.

A similar approach based on communism as an identity is developed by Michel Hastings in his doctoral thesis on Halluin, a mining town situated on the Franco-Belgian border. Indeed, while acknowledging that there exists in the case of the PCF a 'fundamental contradiction between the international vocation of its revolutionary strategy and its embodiment in a French society with a rich working-class history',[19] he claims that the local, societal dimension of French communism was prevalent: 'communism in Halluin is not defined by directives coming from Paris [the PCF national leadership] or the International'.[20] He also attributes the success of the PCF in Halluin to the existence of a 'symbiosis between the political organisation and its implantation terrain on the basis of a response to social demands',[21] or, in other words, 'an encounter, that is to say the circumstantial equation between a social demand and a satisfactory response'.[22]

Since the implantation thesis sought to establish the societal dimension of French communism, it did not concern itself with its political and/or ideological dimension. In fact, this became the main function of the second PCF historiographical variation which emerged more or less simultaneously, in the late 1970s, and was headed by a team of historians including Jean Burles, Roger Martelli and Serge Wolikow whose research efforts focused on the strategy of the PCF.

In two books published in 1981, these historians, while acknowledging the role played by the Comintern in the shaping of the PCF strategy in its early years (from the 1920s to the early 1930s), argue that the Party played an increasingly important and active role in this field, especially from the mid-1930s and the Popular Front era:

> [In studying the strategy of the PCF], one immediately encounters the role of the International, which cannot be ignored if one seeks to understand the shaping and implementation of the strategy of the PCF. At the time this was an integral part of a worldwide revolutionary strategy, designed and co-ordinated by the Communist International. The intervention of the Comintern was in many respects decisive, even if it does not explain entirely the strategy of the PCF which, as we shall see, was at times different from that of other communist parties, because of the balance of forces and of the concrete situation faced by the Party.[23]

This quotation is a good summary of this view which, while it pays lip service to Kriegel's theories, aims at establishing that the PCF progressively became the master of its own strategy which evolved according to its changing national environment. This point is best illustrated by a brief presentation of the accounts of two particularly significant strategic eras for the PCF, namely the Popular Front (1934–38) and the Liberation and Reconstruction of France (1944–47).

In a study devoted to the PCF and the Popular Front, Wolikow argues that the decision of 1934 to drop the Comintern strategy of fighting the Socialist Party, which had meant that socialists had to be denounced as 'social-traitors' or even 'social-fascists', and to start building a wide anti-fascist alliance with other left-wing forces (Popular Front) was the result of a two-way PCF/Comintern process in which the French Party played an increasingly crucial role:

> The origins of the Popular Front are found in the policy and influence of the PCF as well as in the analysis and thinking of the International. At the start, the initiatives, fortunate or unfortunate, probably came from the Comintern leadership, but from 1934 onwards this tendency was at least partially reversed and the PCF played a decisive part in the design of the new orientation, a design which was explicitly geared towards the national level.[24]

However, and significantly, in Wolikow's conclusion to this study, the role of the Comintern is totally eclipsed and the PCF is depicted as a democratic, national force:

> By then [1938] the Communist Party, in France, had succeeded in rooting itself in national soil ... The Popular Front policy is an unprecedented example in twentieth-century France of an historical initiative: it demonstrated the ability of the PCF to ... grasp the specific features of national reality in a given political context in order to alter this context to the advantage of the working class and of the struggle for political democracy.[25]

By the same token, the strategy of the PCF in 1944–47 is described by Jean-Paul Scot as anti-fascist, democratic and in the interest of France, and he strongly rejects Kriegel's claim that the PCF successively adopted three strategies of 'direct conquest of power' (a Bolshevik-style revolution), 'defence of the interests of the socialist camp' and eventually alliance with other political forces.[26]

The two approaches found in PCF historiography, implantation and strategy, undoubtedly complement each other, and create the image of a national, societal party which managed to win a great deal of leeway from Moscow. In a more recent work (1995), Roger Martelli attempts to merge both approaches in a book entitled *Le Rouge et le bleu* (The Red and the Blue). In this study, he focuses on what he calls the 'polymorphism' of French communism. There are, he claims, many forms of communism in France – *les communismes* – shaped by local conditions.[27] He also insists that there was a process of 'syncretism' between imported Bolshevism and French political traditions, which resulted in *le stalinisme à la française*,[28] hence rejecting the notion that communism was merely an import (Kriegel). In a few words, Martelli reasserts the essential Frenchness of the PCF: 'The success of the PCF is attributable to the fact that it succeeded in merging a worldwide ambition with nationally rooted realities, by creating a communist territory which has characterised French society for a number of decades.'[29]

Thus, these two approaches combine to present the PCF as a national party largely independent of Moscow and drawing on French political traditions such as working-class radicalism and protest to create a diversity of local communisms which successfully addressed the specific socio-economic and cultural problems faced by some segments of the French population. While this national, societal dimension tends to be emphasised to a greater degree by communist scholars, it is echoed in a number of studies by non-communist researchers.

While some of these studies are more or less faithful mirrors of PCF orthodoxy (see Jacques Fauvet's *Histoire du PCF* [History of the PCF], below), others insist on its function as a 'tribune', harnessing and organising working-class discontent (Lavau), or on its ability to act as a government party at the local level (Lacorne, Schain).

In his two-volume *Histoire du PCF* first published in 1964–65, Jacques Fauvet, who was then chief editor of *Le Monde*, claimed to have written an objective, independent account of the history of the PCF, unlike the team of Party historians who had just published the 1964 *Manuel*, which he called a 'catechism'.[30] However, his interpretation of the strategy of the PCF during crucial historical eras such as the Popular Front and the Liberation of France systematically neglects the role of Moscow and focuses on the national environment to which the Party had to adjust. For instance, he neglects the international dimension of French communism when he describes the PCF's decision to dismantle its potentially revolutionary armed militias (*milices patriotiques*) in January 1945 as a 'realistic' decision based on a pragmatic assessment of the balance of power in France which led the Party to play the card of legality by joining other political forces, including de Gaulle, in order to form a provisional government.[31]

8

This idea that the PCF is first and foremost a French political party interacting with its national environment is also at the core of a number of studies by scholars such as Frédéric Bon, Georges Lavau, Nicole Racine or Jean Ranger, followed in the 1980s and 1990s by Bernard Pudal and Marie-Claire Lavabre, who all worked under the auspices of the Fondation Nationale des Sciences Politiques (FNSP), a leading political research institution in France. While the FNSP strongly rejects the idea that the PCF is a foreign implant on French soil, a revolutionary 'counter-society' seeking to implement a new, Soviet-style polity in France, this school of thought has made a highly regarded contribution to the knowledge of French communism through the study of the communist vote in France (Jean Ranger), the sociology of PCF membership (Bernard Pudal) or the creation of a communist 'collective memory' (Marie-Claire Lavabre).[32]

One of the leading scholars in this school was undoubtedly Georges Lavau, whose main analyses can be found in his contribution to a landmark, collective volume published in 1969 and in his *A quoi sert le Parti communiste français?*, published in 1981.[33] Lavau focuses primarily on the interaction between the PCF and the French political system by discussing the following questions: what is the role of the PCF in France (*A quoi sert le Parti communiste français*)? Is it opposed to the French political system (in other words, is it a revolutionary, anti-system party)? And does it contribute to the working of this system? His reply is unequivocal: 'Since at least 1936, the French Communist Party has, in its own way, made a "positive" contribution to some elements of the French political system.'[34] This contribution of the PCF to French political life was that it had played the role of a 'tribune', in the Roman sense of the word, namely that its main function had been to:

> organise and defend plebeian social categories, that is to say categories that are excluded or feel excluded from the process of participation in the political system, and from the benefits of the economic and cultural systems, and to give them a feeling of strength and of self-confidence.[35]

Thus, Lavau argues that the PCF ceased to be a revolutionary party during the Popular Front era, when it greatly contributed to the political integration of the French working class into the French socio-political system, and goes on to demonstrate that after this period (mid-1930s), the PCF was a moderate, legalistic political force rejecting any 'adventurous' (revolutionary) temptation.[36] Far from being a Leninist 'counter-society' opposed to the existing system:

> From 1935 at least, the PCF borrowed virtually nothing from the strategy assigned to the [Bolshevik] Party by Lenin in *What Is To Be Done?* In other words, the PCF did not seek to remain outside the political system, and it did not systematically seek to oppose this system.[37]

By adopting a functionalist approach focusing on the integrative role of the PCF, Lavau totally neglects the international dimension of the PCF, and indeed the Comintern or the international strategy of the Soviet Union are hardly mentioned in his works. While some of his arguments on Leninism go against communist historiography (the PCF always claimed to follow Lenin's model), his overall analysis of the PCF as a 'tribune' of the working class strengthens the claim that the PCF is first and foremost a national party fully integrated into the French system.

Other studies, broadly based on the same claim, focus on more specific aspects of French communism, such as its electoral strategy or its action in local government. In *Les Notables rouges* (The Red Notables), Denis Lacorne uses organisational sociology concepts to study the enforcement of Party line in the context of the municipal elections of 1977, and focuses on the complex, at times conflictual, nature of intra-party relationships, thereby challenging the assumption that the PCF is a highly centralised, monolithic bureaucracy.[38] One of his major findings is that local PCF leaders, far from being sectarian revolutionaries, behave like *notables* from any other political party, that is to say that they succeeded in becoming integrated into the French politico-administrative system.[39] Another finding is that there exists a fair amount of latitude vis-à-vis the Party line, insofar as local conditions often led local PCF cadres to be increasingly flexible in the negotiations with the Socialist Party prior to the elections.[40]

In another study of the PCF, also based on the idea that local communist leaders tend to be pragmatic and flexible politicians, Martin Schain focuses on communist mayors as policy-makers and on the PCF as a government party.[41] In his chapter on PCF electoral support at the local level, Schain echoes Lavau's analysis of the Party as a 'positive tribune' and rejects the view that a communist vote equates to a mere protest vote.[42]

There are, among these scholars, a number of differences in interpretation, which makes it difficult to regroup them in a united, watertight school of thought. For instance, while PCF historians claim that the Party remained a revolutionary force committed to socio-economic change, non-communist ones tend to argue that the PCF has become a fully integrated, non-revolutionary, government party like any other. Nonetheless, all these studies by communist or non-communist scholars have one factor in common: by focusing on the implantation of the PCF, its strategy, its electorate, its membership or its municipalities, they systematically underestimate the international dimension of this political party. This dimension was, as argued below, central to every aspect of its very existence. A comparable, albeit not identical, approach to the Italian Communist Party is characteristic of the historiography of this party.

The PCI as a primarily national, societal force

Like its French counterpart, the PCI has been the subject of a wide-ranging historical and political literature produced mostly by Italian, French, German and English-speaking scholars. However, any discussion of this literature must start with two preliminary remarks.

First, as Lazar argues, PCI historiography was much more subtle, much less ideological and orthodox than the PCF one, even if it also played a crucial political role.[43] As a result, the boundary between the two categories of communist scholars (Party historians and independent ones) is even more difficult to draw than in the French case.

Second, the depiction of the PCI as a primarily Italian (national), societal phenomenon has over the years acquired a quasi-hegemonic status among students of this party in Italy and abroad, among communists and non-communists alike, and it was only recently, in the mid-1990s, that a strong challenge to this view emerged, based on a thorough study of Comintern and Soviet archives (see below). This has resulted in a striking imbalance in the literature which is not found in the case of the PCF: while numerous scholars, following Kriegel, have challenged the national and societal pretensions of the French party, only a small number have proposed the view that the PCI was a mere outpost of the international communist movement, a totalitarian, counter-society party paving the way for a revolutionary process of socio-economic and political change. In other words, while in the case of the PCF there exists a well-established 'Kriegelian' school which includes a number of foreign scholars, in the case of the PCI only a few scholars have challenged the overwhelming, conventional picture of the PCI as a societal, Italian party.

According to Lazar, the PCI never wrote an 'official history' similar to that found in the PCF's *Manuel* of 1964 and historical research undertaken by PCI historians enjoyed a 'real degree of autonomy' which resulted in an 'historical production of a generally high quality'.[44] By the same token, such overtly hagiographic publications as *Fils du peuple* by Thorez have no equivalent in PCI literature, and PCI leaders or former leaders have only rarely published their memoirs.[45]

This contrast, however, does not mean that historical publications by PCI scholars did not perform a particular function. As argued by Kertzer in 1996, the PCI used history to construct symbols (see Chapter 4) and to legitimate its post-war strategy of an 'Italian road to socialism'.[46] Accordingly, one of the focal points of PCI historiography is the role of the Party in the struggle against fascism, a key tenet of post-war PCI identity. For instance, the five-volume *Storia del partito comunista italiano* (History of the PCI) published by communist historian Paolo Spriano between 1967 and 1975 describes the struggle of the Party against the fascist regime in its years of clandestinity (1922–43), thus portraying it as the first Resistance nucleus in fascist Italy.[47] In the words of Bosworth, Spriano's *Storia del PCI* depicts 'a shadow of that better Italy, which communists and anti-fascists alike had kept alive despite the fascist tyranny'.[48] Spriano's massive work also emphasises the role played by two great leaders, Antonio Gramsci and Palmiro Togliatti, who he claims paved the way for the post-war course of the PCI. In fact, it has been argued that Spriano was part of the process of harnessing Gramsci's intellectual legacy which started in the 1950s in order to give Italian communism a primarily independent, national façade.[49] Bosworth summarises Spriano's contribution to PCI history as follows: 'Spriano thus embodied a communist historiography which certainly honoured the Party's past, but which did agree that there were issues to debate and research to be done.'[50]

A substantial number of scholars, many of them non-PCI members, were to follow in Spriano's footsteps in describing the PCI as a national, anti-fascist force committed to a democratic process of change, to the extent that the view that the PCI progressively became a party rooted in Italian society and master of its own strategy was virtually hegemonic in Italian academic and media circles in the 1970s and 1980s.[51]

This view was widely echoed abroad. In France, in particular, the PCI generated a high level of political sympathy and even fascination from left-wing scholars and journalists alike.[52] For instance, Marcelle Padovani, the Italian affairs specialist working for the French weekly *Le Nouvel Observateur*, published in 1976 a study of the PCI in which she presented the Party in a very sympathetic light as a progressive, democratic party which had long gained its freedom from Moscow.[53] Similarly, in 1977 French left-wing sociologist Henri Weber edited a book on the PCI and eurocommunism, in which he wrote:

> Of all the communist parties of western Europe, the PCI is the one which moved first and farthest towards independence of the Soviet party-state. Not a week goes by without *Unità* denouncing the acts of repression or arbitrary measures in Eastern countries.[54]

He then drew an explicit parallel between the PCI in Italian society and the German SPD (Social Democratic Party) in pre-1914 German society by writing that it was 'a bureaucratic, working-class party seeking to rationalise existing society, not to revolutionise it'.[55]

The enduring fascination surrounding the PCI is also found in English-language publications by scholars such as Donald Sassoon or Joan Barth Urban, to name only two. Unlike students of the PCF who systematically neglect the international dimension of the Party (see above), these scholars thoroughly investigate the relationship between the PCI and Moscow, and conclude that this party progressively managed to conquer a substantial degree of ideological and strategic latitude from the centre of world communism.

In his *The Strategy of the Italian Communist Party*, Sassoon argues that this process began in the Resistance years (1943–45), when the PCI gave priority to its national objectives:

> It appears here that ever since the days of the Resistance Italian communists were constructing and defending those pluralistic elements which would be characteristics of post-war Italy. The 'new party' thus emerged from the ruins of fascism … If, on the one hand, there can be no doubt as to the positive effects of such 'conquest' not only for the PCI but for the whole of Italian society, one should not forget that this 'conquest', as all others, was not an easy one, nor could it be complete, nor could it be definitive. What has been called '*doppiezza*' has continued to play its role in the strategy of the PCI.[56]

Thus, while acknowledging the survival of the *doppiezza*, that is to say of a revolutionary agenda hidden behind a legalistic façade, Sassoon appears to reproduce the picture of the PCI as a 'new party' (a mass-party, as opposed to the Leninist model of a small army of professional revolutionaries) committed to Western democracy and not to a Soviet-style polity.

In her major study of the relationship between the PCI and the Soviet Union, Joan Barth Urban goes further, dating the beginnings of this process of increasing independence back to the early years of the PCI in the 1920s and 1930s. For instance, she portrays Togliatti, Secretary-General of the PCI from the mid-1920s to his death in 1964 and key figure of the Comintern in the 1930s, as a 'moderate, non-sectarian' leader in the late 1920s.[57] As tokens of his autonomy from Moscow and Stalin, she argues that Ercoli (Togliatti's Comintern alias) 'had been in Stalin's disfavour in the late 1920s and again in the late 1930s',[58] and that

'Togliatti was, by the early 1930s, the only European communist leader whom the Stalinists had not placed in power'.[59]

Similarly, Urban holds that the PCI 'deviated from Moscow's policy'[60] during the Resistance when it adopted a strong republican stance of alliance with other anti-fascist forces at the time of the creation of the CLN (National Liberation Committee) in September 1943, whose 'pluralistic structure differed sharply from the monistic national front envisaged by the Comintern'.[61] In fact, Urban claims that there was a strong continuity in PCI strategy throughout the history of this party:

> One of my central arguments is that the PCI leaders from Togliatti to Berlinguer [from the 1920s to the early 1980s] posited reformist alliance policies that, while not breaking with the capitalist order, would – so they hoped – facilitate an eventual transition to socialism.[62]

Whereas such studies endeavour to explore the changing relationship between the PCI and Moscow, if only in an attempt to demonstrate the ever-growing divergence between them, many other English-speaking scholars ignore this key aspect of Italian communism and focus on particular aspects of the PCI, such as the internal debates which seem to have taken place inside the PCI in the 1960s,[63] the failure of the 'historic compromise' strategy of a broad alliance with the Christian Democrats in the 1970s which might have resulted in the PCI entering a coalition government at the national level,[64] or the effects of this strategy on the PCI at the local level in Turin.[65]

There is no direct equivalent in the case of the PCI to the implantation outlook developed by a number of French historians in the case of the French Party. Nonetheless, the identity, political culture, symbols and social interactions of the PCI have been thoroughly studied by anthropologists such as David Kertzer and Cris Shore.

In his *Comrades and Christians*, Kertzer studies the PCI in Albora, a district of Bologna and bastion of Italian communism, with a clear emphasis on its social context. Indeed, his premise is that, in most studies of the PCI, 'the social context of communist allegiance has been remote or absent'.[66] Through the detailed case study of local PCI sections and associations, he reaches the conclusion that PCI identity and allegiance were primarily societal and associational in nature: 'membership has become a badge of social identity rather than an expression of political militancy'.[67] Another of his contentions is that the ideology of the Party had become secondary to its local members: 'little attention is paid to the ideological outlook of new recruits'.[68] He therefore rejects earlier views of communist membership as a social and psychological pathology by claiming that, in Albora, it was normal behaviour to join the PCI, 'a key to in-group status'.[69] Finally, Kertzer also provides a detailed study of the construction and use by the Party of symbols such as the Resistance and lay rites (communist funerals, for instance) which became major pillars of communist identity, whereby the PCI became a kind of secular church competing with the Catholic Church in Italian society.

He further develops this research into the function of rites and symbols in his *Politics and Symbols*, in which his central claim, in somewhat provocative fashion, is that symbols were at the core of politics: 'politics depends heavily – indeed, integrally – on symbolism, and that symbolic change has important political and material consequences'.[70] While this study of PCI symbolism at work includes useful insights into the role played for instance by history-writing in the creation and consolidation of the Italian communists' mental universe and identity, Kertzer can be criticised for overlooking other fundamental dimensions of Italian communism, such as ideology, leadership, strategy and, inevitably, internationalism.

Another anthropologist who studies PCI identity is Cris Shore. In his *Italian Communism: The Escape from Leninism*, he claims that the PCI's long-lasting success in Italian society was due not only to its disengagement from the Soviet Union in the 1960s or to its national, independent strategy of an 'Italian road to socialism', as is commonly argued, but also to its overwhelming social role:

> The PCI's survival and expansion in postwar Italy is owing above all to its success in establishing itself as an entrenched part of the fabric of community life. This has been achieved largely by creating a 'communist culture' in Italy: a powerful social movement based around the Party itself, one that in many respects rivals the Catholic Church in strength and influence.[71]

In another publication, he uses the model of ethnicity to describe the process of communist identity-making, based on a number of cultural markers, such as the sharing of myths (Gramsci, Togliatti, the Resistance), of rites, of a common language ('PCI-speak') and behaviour ('communists have clean hands', they are not corrupt).[72]

Thus, as in the case of the PCF, the bulk of this national, societal literature tends to portray the PCI as a political force which conquered its independence from Moscow quite early in the post-war years (or even before, as Urban argues) to become a 'new party', that is to say a mass-party which was committed to the creation of a strong communist culture based on a number of key symbols such as anti-fascism and the Resistance. This 'new party', which progressively departed from the

Leninist model of a vanguard army of revolutionaries, abandoned most of its revolutionary tenets before scrapping them altogether in 1991 when it became a social-democratic force (the Partito Democratico della Sinistra, or PDS), an event which many interpret as the logical conclusion of a process started under Togliatti and continued by his successors. From a strategic point of view, it is claimed that the Party always pursued as its aim a broad alliance of democratic, republican forces while asserting its legitimacy as a government party through the efficient management of the Italian regions and municipalities it controlled.

While the contribution of many of these studies to the knowledge of Italian communism is beyond doubt, their almost systematic neglect of the international nature of this phenomenon, as in the case of many writings on the PCF, is highly questionable. Accordingly, the next section of this chapter examines a more critical approach to communism which insists on the crucial significance for both the French and Italian Communist Parties of their international dimension.

COMMUNIST PARTIES AS PRIMARILY INTERNATIONAL PHENOMENA

In a seminal article published in the mid-1980s, after a decade which had seen the publication of numerous studies of Western communist parties marked by a growing fascination for eurocommunism,[73] Tony Judt wrote: 'It is an enduring characteristic of writings about the left that they are consistently sympathetic to their material.'[74] He then criticised the commonly found emphasis on the so-called 'national' strategies of the communist parties of western Europe by claiming that, if strategy there was, then it had to be seen as an integral part of worldwide Soviet geopolitical strategy and that specific national circumstances were external to the projects of these parties.[75] In fact, his arguments were part of a methodological plea to find a balance between the 'interior' (domestic) and 'exterior' (international) histories of these parties.

Yet, while his challenge on what he implicitly considered as the quasi-monopolistic view of communist parties as national entities might have appeared as a controversial – and in some ways provocative – one, it was not unprecedented, especially in France where a highly critical historiography of the PCF had emerged two decades earlier.

The PCF as a primarily international phenomenon: Annie Kriegel and her disciples

A critical historiography of communism in general, focusing on the role played by the Comintern, emerged very early in France, with the works of a number of anti-communist 'precursors'.[76] Among them were Boris Souvarine, a former Bolshevik and Comintern leader who published the first critical biography of Stalin in France in 1935 and was behind the creation of the *Est-Ouest* journal (a well-documented, critical periodical) during the Cold War, and Hungarian émigré François Fejtö who published a seminal *Histoire des démocraties populaires* (A History of the People's Democracies) in 1952.[77] However, as argued by Lazar, these precursors based in France were systematically denigrated by the PCF and by French universities, and, as a result, their audience was marginal.[78]

This situation was to change drastically with the publication in 1964 of Annie Kriegel's doctoral thesis on the origins of the PCF, issued in paperback in 1969. In this landmark work, based on impressive documentary sources, Kriegel argues that the birth of the PCF was the result of a series of historical accidents and that it marked a clear departure from the working-class and socialist traditions of France, following the 'betrayal' of the French socialists who had turned their backs on pacifism in 1914 and joined in the war effort and the failure of a number of strikes in 1920. In other words, she claims that the PCF is irrevocably foreign, an import or a 'transplant' that only managed to survive on French soil through a process of active 'bolshevisation' of its cadres imposed by the Comintern.[79] After this pioneering study, Kriegel went on to describe the PCF as a 'counter-society' fundamentally external to French society, shaped by its Leninist birth and its Stalinist style and subjected to Moscow's international strategy.[80] In the same study, she discerns two different levels or dimensions of French communism. First is the level 'exposed to all eyes', 'the communist plan as it appears in everyday political life', the 'battle against established society', oscillating between tactics of co-operation with other forces and a relentless struggle.[81] In other words, this is communist presence in the 'real world', in French society.[82] Beneath this first level, Kriegel discerns a second, hidden one, a 'basic strangeness', the 'exteriority of the [French] communist world' in relation to established society, as she calls it, which encompasses the inherent link of the PCF to Leninist legacy and to the Soviet model, its secretive operations as a 'counter-society', and so on.[83]

In spite of the fierce opposition of the PCF, which launched an impressive programme of research explicitly aimed at fending off Kriegel (see the two approaches discussed above), and of a number of established scholars (see Lavau and the FNSP), Kriegel's work exerted a growing appeal both in France and abroad.

In France, a number of scholars embarked on studies which clearly emphasised the international and secretive dimensions of the PCF. This was for instance the case of Philippe Robrieux, also a former PCF leader (he had been head of the communist students' union in the early 1960s), who published in the 1970s a very critical biography of Maurice Thorez before publishing his massive four-volume *Histoire intérieure du Parti communiste* (PCF: The History from the Inside) in the early 1980s.[84] While Robrieux was fiercely criticised by communists and 'Kriegelians' alike for his alleged over-reliance on private sources and for his penchant for conspiracy theories, his work remains to date a useful insight into the sectarian working of the PCF as a secretive organisation controlled by the Soviet authorities.[85]

Other French historians who followed in Kriegel's footsteps in the early 1980s were Stéphane Courtois and Jean-Jacques Becker. In his book on the PCF during the war, Courtois, who has since become the leading disciple of Kriegel, challenges the widespread view of the PCF as a primarily patriotic force adjusting its strategy to national circumstances. He claims that it was a faithful follower of Stalin's directives throughout the war, to the detriment of its strategy of alliance with other left-wing forces:

> This constant preoccupation [the international dimension] of the PCF has bit by bit killed off its governmental ambitions ... The power of the USSR and of the socialist camp having become the determining factor of the Party's accession to power, the class alliance (workers, peasants, middle classes) and the political alliance with other left-wing forces has lost all its relevance. It is on the contrary the fulcrum position of France between the USA and the USSR which has become decisive for the communists.[86]

Thus, what Courtois argues in substance is that the PCF acted at the end of the Second World War as a mere tool in the Soviet geopolitical game. This explains in turn the subsequent policy of *rapprochement* with de Gaulle, whose outlook on the independence and sovereignty of France was seen as a very useful means to neutralise American influence in western Europe.[87]

In a similar fashion, Jean-Jacques Becker tackles the view of PCF historians on the Party's strategy. In his *Le PCF veut-il prendre le pouvoir?* (Does the PCF Seek to Take Power?), he argues that the strategy of the PCF was in fact primarily determined by non-domestic factors and openly criticises others for neglecting this aspect:

To explore the relationship between the Communist Party and power without acknowledging that its activity was decided by international circumstances would have about as much historical relevance as to undertake an analysis of the history of the Roman Catholic Church in France while ignoring the existence of the papacy.[88]

In strategic terms, he claims that the so-called 'Popular Front turning point' of 1934 was in fact part of an international Soviet move, and that the 1945 decision to abandon short-term insurrectional tactics (the dismantling of the *milices patriotiques*) and to join forces with de Gaulle was 'intended to ensure that France would maintain a foreign policy which favoured the socialist bloc'.[89] However, this did not mean that the PCF had abandoned its revolutionary credentials in the long run: it simply meant that it prepared a future revolutionary process by playing a double game combining a legal mask and a hidden agenda, as the Bolsheviks had done between February and October 1917, in order to be ready when the international situation was ripe for a revolution in France.

A further stage in the development of the 'Kriegelian' school was the creation in 1982 of *Communisme* by Kriegel and Courtois. This journal was to attract a number of scholars such as Marc Lazar, and to promote a pluridisciplinary approach embracing both the international and national/societal dimensions of communism, with a clear emphasis on the former.

However, historical research into the international links of the PCF faced a major obstacle, that is to say that most archives on the Comintern and on Western communist parties were kept secret in Moscow. With the collapse of the Soviet Union in 1991 and the subsequent opening of some of the Comintern archives to Russian as well as Western historians, further research into this dimension of French communism was undertaken as a result of which it was possible to substantiate most of the earlier claims made by Kriegel and her disciples.

Such recent publications based on Russian archives include the seminal *Histoire du Parti communiste français* by Courtois and Lazar, and the remarkable *Eugen Fried: Le grand secret du PCF* (Eugen Fried: The Big Secret of the PCF) by Kriegel and Courtois.[90] The history of the making of this book is in itself worth mentioning: it was started by Kriegel and Courtois in 1983, provisionally abandoned due to lack of access to primary sources, restarted in the early 1990s following the opening of the Comintern archives and completed by Courtois after Kriegel's death in 1995. It provides an insight into the crucial role of Eugen Fried, a Hungarian communist sent to France by the Comintern to organise the PCF into a disciplined, obedient structure. Among other things, this publication demonstrates that Thorez, who became Secretary-General of the PCF in 1930, owed his position to Fried, who was in fact the real leader of the French Party until the late 1930s.

Other critical accounts of the PCF which do not explicitly claim to be inspired by Kriegel's approach and which are more journalistic than academic in style and purpose but which are nonetheless of use to students of French communism include Dominique Desanti's *Les Staliniens* (The Stalinists), an autobiographical account of a former communist journalist during the Cold War, Jean Montaldo's books, which shed some light on the dubious activities of the PCF in its municipalities and on its mysterious financial resources, and Denis Jeambar's *Le PC dans la maison* (The PCF in Government), an exposure of the PCF's strategy of infiltration of French institutions during its period in government (1981–84).[91]

As mentioned earlier, Kriegel's emphasis on the foreign nature of the PCF also found an echo among English-speaking scholars. The main proponents of this approach are Ronald Tiersky, a former student of Annie Kriegel, and David Bell and Byron Criddle.[92] The latter authors summarise their views on the PCF in the following terms:

> The PCF has been in essence a totalitarian party, dedicated to the success of Soviet-type systems ... The French Communist Party was, until 1991, an outpost of a communist world revolutionary movement ... The broad strategies (as distinct from the local application of these) were not undertaken for electoral reasons but for Soviet foreign policy purposes.[93]

The Kriegelian view of the PCF could therefore be summarised as follows: the Party was in essence the product of the international communist movement, the Comintern, and its key objectives, as dictated by Comintern *missi dominici* until 1943 or by Stalin and his successors thereafter, were to defend and promote the interests of the Soviet Union as an international power.

This is why, for instance, the PCF scrapped its revolutionary tactics in early 1945, when it became clear that a revolution in France would have undermined Stalin's project of securing eastern Europe by turning the countries liberated by the Red Army into people's democracies. This is substantiated, with strong documentary evidence, by Buton and others.[94]

This also resulted in the PCF double game of May 1981, when PCF leader Georges Marchais, after the first ballot of the presidential election, publicly appealed to the communist electorate to vote for Mitterrand, the socialist candidate, in the second ballot and at the same time secretly instructed seasoned PCF members to cast a so-called 'revolutionary vote' for Giscard d'Estaing in a bid to have Mitterrand defeated, because Giscard enjoyed the favour of the USSR.[95]

Thus, the 'Kriegelian' school strongly suggests that the PCF consistently remained a tool in Soviet foreign policy, even when such strategic behaviour was detrimental to its membership and electorate. From the point of view of its organisation, the Leninist legacy remained in place in the PCF until the mid-1990s, as the Party consistently functioned as a top-down bureaucracy, constantly purging itself of its 'deviant' elements, namely members and leaders who dared to oppose the line,[96] and as a close, secretive counter-society slowly paving the way for a revolution in France.

However, this strong emphasis on the international dimension of French communism did not amount to total neglect of its national/societal face. In fact, in 1975, Kriegel herself argued that the two dimensions had to be taken into account when studying the PCF, and that the domestic interests of the Party and the geopolitics of the USSR either converged, in which case the Party flourished at the national level (e.g. the Popular Front, the Liberation of France) or diverged, in which case the PCF would always sacrifice its domestic position on the altar of its allegiance to Moscow.[97]

This bi-dimensional approach is further developed by Tiersky, who proposes a quadripartite model of the PCF integrating two faces (each comprising two aspects), namely a 'hard' face including its Leninist organisation and its secretive nature (a 'counter-society') and a 'soft' face encompassing its role as a 'tribune' for the defence of the interests of the working class (see Lavau), and its pretensions as a governing party.[98]

Courtois and Lazar also propose a comprehensive bi-dimensional model intended to take on board the many 'branches' of the literature on the PCF. This model is probably best summarised by these two historians themselves:

> We hold that communism comprises two dimensions. The first is teleological and arises from the universal revolutionary project stemming from the founding experience of the victory of Bolshevik communism in Russia after the revolution of October 1917. It includes a doctrinal corpus elaborated by Lenin and codified by Stalin, Marxism–Leninism; an organisational model, the party of revolutionary professionals and ruled by democratic centralism; a strategic principle based on the unconditional defence of the USSR and of the socialist camp and which results in the adoption of a strategy and tactics meeting Soviet interests and ideology, but also dependent upon power struggles within the USSR. The other dimension, the societal one, includes everything that, in the life of

the PCF, stems from global society – and not only from the political system – in which the Party is inserted. The first dimension is marked by the drive, with the impulse from the 'centre', Moscow, to impose homogeneity, cohesion and unity on all communist parties; the second dimension is marked by the diversity which arises from the various social, cultural and political configurations facing a given communist party. The PCF is at the junction of these two variables which can either function in harmony or on the contrary may be in conflict with each other. In this last case, it is always the teleological dimension which wins at the expense of the societal dimension.[99]

The PCI as a primarily international phenomenon: a recent challenge to the hegemonic, national/societal view

As argued before, few scholars have challenged the predominant view of the PCI as an essentially national/societal entity, and there is no direct equivalent of Kriegel or her disciples in Italy. However, a number of historians and political scientists have studied the international dimension of the PCI, and some, especially in the 1990s, have published detailed studies which have shed new light on Italian communism.

One of the first significant attempts to assess the extent of the international ties of the PCI came, quite tellingly, from an American specialist of Soviet foreign policy, Donald Blackmer. In his *Unity in Diversity: Italian Communism and the Communist World*, 'he paid equal attention to both the continuity and change in the Party's relationship with the international communist movement generally, and with Moscow specifically' and explained 'the maintenance of this relationship as only one of the Party's basic interests (together with the maintenance of its influence over other organizations and the search for political and social alliances that would constitute the core of the so-called *via italiana al socialismo*)'.[100]

Thus, while his main conclusion was that the PCI was not primarily driven by international considerations, he nonetheless acknowledged the strength of this dimension as a variable interacting with other, domestic ones in a two-way, bi-dimensional model, even if he was later to conclude that the national dimension had become its primary interest.[101] Also, the fact that he co-authored a small volume with Annie Kriegel on *The International Role of the Communist Parties of Italy and France* can be seen as an indication that the international dimension of the PCI should not have been underplayed.[102]

Other studies stressing the teleological face of Italian communism have been published more recently, in the 1990s, in Italy and abroad. These include for instance a book by Luciano Pellicani, who considers that until its last days the PCI remained a truly 'revolutionary party', thus rejecting the view that it had undergone a process of social-democratisation.[103] He also strongly challenges the widespread, hagiographic view of Gramsci as a precursor of the 'Italian road to socialism' by claiming that he had in fact been a totalitarian thinker who had advocated the dictatorship of the PCI over the working class.[104]

A more general challenge to PCI hegemony over its own history came as a strong criticism of the Party's monopoly on the historiography of the Resistance, and of the harnessing by the Party of this era to create the myth of a national, pluralist force. This came in particular from Italian historian Claudio Pavone, who in 1991 published a book entitled *Una guerra civila* (A Civil War), which was to trigger a massive, nationwide controversy.[105] In fact, the bulk of his argument is that, contrary to PCI claims that the Resistance was primarily a patriotic war of liberation waged against Nazism and fascist collaborators, there existed in Italy in 1943–45 a three-dimensional conflict, namely a patriotic war, a civil war during which the communists settled old scores with fascists or alleged fascists and which went on in such areas as Emilia-Romagna until 1949, and a class war.[106] While the full historiographical debate which ensued goes far beyond the scope of this study, its relevance here is that it reintroduced the international dimension of the PCI into the study of its strategy during those years – hence the vehement reactions by post-communist (PDS) historians and leaders.

This breach of the PCI monopoly over the interpretation of the Resistance was exploited by another leading historian, Renzo de Felice. His outlook can be summarised as follows:

> The most basic [conclusion] was that Italian communists ... could not credibly claim a usable anti-fascist past. The pretensions of the Communist Party to have led the Resistance, and thus to have acquired national and moral credentials which might separate its history from the worst aspects of the Soviet revolution, were peremptorily refuted: 'The Communist Party of Togliatti had always been a Stalinist party. It was neither revolutionary, nor reformist, but part of the world system of power of the USSR.'[107]

Thus, through these new approaches to the history of the Italian Resistance, the international dimension of the PCI – faithful compliance with Stalin's directives – became apparent after decades of deliberate neglect.

The PCI's relationship with Moscow in Stalin's era is the main subject of a very detailed study published in 1997 by two historians working in Italian universities, Elena Aga-Rossi and Victor Zaslavsky. This book, based on extensive research in Moscow, challenges what the authors call the 'persistent myth of the Marxist-oriented historiography', which was to 'interpret the history of the PCI as one of a constant trend towards an ever-increasing degree of independence from Moscow'.[108] In fact, through a thorough study of a number of historical episodes, they claim that the PCI was no more than a tool in Soviet foreign policy, and that this international tie between the PCI and Moscow prevailed, sometimes to the detriment of the Italian communists' national interests. Two such historical episodes can be discussed briefly to substantiate the overall argument – the issue of Trieste and that of the fate of Italian prisoners of war in the Soviet Union.

The city of Trieste, in north-east Italy, was at the core of international tensions and territorial disputes in 1945–48: while Italy claimed that it was irrevocably Italian, and was supported by the USA, Tito's Yugoslavia had ambitions to take over this city, and was backed up by Stalin, who saw in Tito's territorial claims an opportunity to expand the Soviet sphere of influence (this was before the rift between Stalin and Tito). The issue was to create an almost intractable dilemma for Togliatti's PCI: was it going to support Tito's claims and Stalin's foreign policy, at the risk of running against the tide of Italian public opinion, which was massively opposed to such claims? Or was the Party going to strengthen its national credentials – these were the years in which Togliatti was trying to assert the Italian nature of his party – by opposing Tito, in which case it would have incurred Stalin's ire? Which of the two dimensions of Italian communism would prevail?

Aga-Rossi and Zaslavsky claim, based on substantial historical evidence, that Togliatti, in the face of this dilemma, was much inclined to follow Stalin's directives. To give but one example, when Tito's army 'liberated' Trieste in May 1945, Togliatti launched an appeal to the 'workers of Trieste' in which he urged them to welcome Tito's troops as a liberation army.[109] Thus, the Trieste affair can be seen as a perfect, textbook test of Togliatti's post-war national pretensions, which reveals that they were in fact only secondary to the defence of Soviet interests.

Another example of Togliatti's full compliance with Soviet foreign policy priorities is the tragic story of thousands of Italian POWs detained in Soviet camps during the Second World War.[110] It is estimated that, out of 85,000 wartime POWs, only 2,000 survived and were sent back to Italy after the war. This tragedy prompted the Italian government to ask the Soviet Union for an explanation regarding such casualties. In what became one of Italy's major public concerns for a number of years, the

PCI's outlook was again questionable. While a genuinely national PCI could have been expected to intervene in favour of Italian POWs during and after the war (after all, the PCI would have been in an ideal position), it did nothing. On the contrary, in a 1943 letter to an Italian comrade who had asked for such an intervention, Togliatti revealed his allegiance to Stalin as well as a profound cynicism:

> Our political position with regard to the armies which invaded the Soviet Union has been defined by Stalin, and there is nothing more to say. In practice, if a large number of prisoners die as a result of these harsh conditions [of detention] we have absolutely nothing to say ... The fact that for thousands and thousands of families Mussolini's war, and above all the expedition against Russia, has ended with a tragedy, with personal grief, is the best and most effective of antidotes.[111]

These two examples (Trieste and the tragedy of Italian POWs) clearly substantiate the claim that the international dimension of Italian communism prevailed in those years, and help underpin a challenge to the traditional outlook on the PCI as a national force.

On a less specific level, foreign scholars have also stressed the existence of an enduring tie between the PCI and the international communist movement until the late 1980s. This is for instance the case of Stephen Gundle who argues that, even if the PCI 'had a distinctive political tradition of its own and [had] not since the far-off days of the 1950s relied heavily on the external sponsorship of the Soviet Union for its legitimisation and internal cohesion',[112] its ties to the Soviet model remained fairly central to its identity into the 1980s, thus explaining the disarray of many of its activists in 1991. Thus, Gundle describes the PCI as a party which, in spite of all its efforts to disengage from the Soviet model, never carried this process to its logical conclusion, namely a clear rift with international communist organisations.[113]

This more critical literature on the PCI requires some comment. In spite of stimulating works (Blackmer), it never reached the status and scope of the 'Kriegelian' school in France, and remained a minority view unable to mount a strong challenge to the national outlook on the PCI, at least until the mid-1990s (see Aga-Rossi and Zaslavsky).

It is possible to argue that, as in the case of the PCF, the two dimensions, teleological and societal, have to be borne in mind when studying the PCI, especially in the light of recent developments in the historiography of these two parties.

However, it is possible to argue that, whereas in the case of the PCF the teleological dimension always prevailed, in the case of the PCI the national/societal factors became prevalent after the 1950s. In fact, the assumption that there exists a contrast between these two parties is commonly found in the literature and is discussed in the next section.

CONTRASTING THE TWO PARTIES: THE COMPARATIVE LITERATURE ON THE PCF AND THE PCI

In spite of the numerous controversies and debates which divide scholars writing on French and/or Italian communism, an almost universal idea is that there exists a contrast between the two parties. This contrast was probably best summarised by Blackmer and Tarrow who wrote in 1975:

> The *Parti Communiste Français* (PCF) had always appeared to most observers more dogmatic, more sectarian, more closely tied to the industrial working-class, more dependent on the Soviet Union, in sum, less open than the *Partito Comunista Italiano* (PCI) to the pressures and influences of the bourgeois society surrounding it.[114]

Two explanatory remarks can be made about this contrast. First, it is indeed found in 'the overwhelming majority of studies, whatever their viewpoint and their author'.[115] For instance, comparative studies which tend to agree on the increasing independence of these parties in the 1960s and 1970s usually argue that the PCI had disengaged from the Soviet model much faster than its French counterpart.[116] By the same token, studies by authors who are much more critical of these parties also acknowledge that there is a contrast relating to some aspects of the PCF and the PCI. This is, for example, the case of Neil McInnes who, while stressing overall the 'uniformity and continuity' which characterise the communist phenomenon,[117] concedes nonetheless that there are differences between the two parties concerning their ties to the working class. Thus, he describes the PCF as 'the most dogmatically proletarian in its approach', by contrast to a more 'interclassista' PCI.[118] He also identifies a contrast in the role of communist intellectuals in France and Italy: 'the PCI had never gone as far in zhdanovism as the French Party, which had its own Zhdanov in the person of Laurent Casanova'.[119]

A sharper contrast is drawn by Tiersky, a known 'Kriegelian' and therefore a proponent of the primacy of the international dimension of communism.[120] Even the late François Furet – a staunch critic of communism as a totalitarian phenomenon – acknowledges this contrast when writing about the two parties' reactions to Khrushchev's Secret Report in 1956.[121]

The second remark is in fact an attempt at explaining the emergence and long-lasting success of this contrast in the literature. In the introduction to his seminal *Maisons rouges* (Red Houses), Marc Lazar writes about his frustration at what he calls the systematic, 'insidious' contrast established between the two parties by scholars.[122] He goes on to trace the origins of this systematic opposition to the historiography of the PCI, which he claims used the PCF as an 'inverted mirror' conferring increased credibility to the view of the PCI as a national phenomenon: 'the discourse on the originality of the Italian Party is much strengthened by a comparison with its French counterpart'.[123] A recent example of the use of this contrast by an expert on Italian communism can be found in Gundle's seminal study of the relationship between the PCI and culture:

> In contrast to a party like the French Communist Party (PCF), which was always reluctant to risk diluting its purity by mixing too freely in the waters of the mainstream of society, the Italian Communists sought, while remaining faithful to their basic purposes, to penetrate Italian society and become a force in every sphere of national life.[124]

The same use of an 'inverted mirror' is made by critics of the PCF, who use the PCI as an example of a communist party which managed, unlike the PCF, to win some degree of independence from Moscow and to diverge from the original Leninist model that the two parties shared as a common legacy.[125]

Thus, the more-or-less systematic use of this contrast for argumentative purposes has fuelled the passionate and politically motivated literature on the French and Italian Communist Parties. This situation has led scholars such as Lazar to advocate a more detached, 'disenchanted' approach to these parties without resorting to what has become a stereotype, namely that there was a good party (the PCI) and a bad one (the PCF).

CONCLUSION

In the substantial literature on the French and Italian Communist Parties, it is possible to discern two main approaches. The first one, called the national or societal one, insists on the rooting or implantation of these parties in their domestic socio-economic environments and emphasises the role they played in their respective political systems. In so doing, it systematically neglects, deliberately or not, the second dimension of communism, which is its international or teleological one, that is to say the cast-iron link of these two parties to the Soviet Union, a country which was for decades seen as a model to emulate.

It is argued by Courtois and Lazar that both dimensions are needed to understand these parties, and that in the case of the PCF the international dimension always prevailed.[126] It has been suggested in this chapter that such a two-dimension model could equally be applied to the study of the PCI, especially in the light of recent studies which have clearly confirmed that this party also had a prevalent international facet in the post-war years. This new shedding of light means that the hegemonic view of the PCI as a party which would have become a reformist, national force as early as 1944–45 has to make way for a more nuanced, dispassionate approach.

NOTES

[1] Lazar, 'Le communisme est-il soluble dans l'histoire?', pp. 71–2.

[2] See G. Lavau, 'L'historiographie communiste, une pratique politique', in P. Birnbaum and J.M. Vincent (eds), *Critique des pratiques sociales* (Paris: Gallimard, 1978), pp. 121–64.

[3] S. Courtois and M. Lazar, *Histoire du PCF* (Paris: Presses Universitaires de France, 1995), p. 13.

[4] Lazar, 'Le communisme est-il soluble dans l'histoire?', p. 70.

[5] See M. Thorez, *Fils du peuple* (Paris: Editions Sociales, 1937); PCF, *Histoire du Parti communiste français (Manuel)* (Paris: Editions Sociales, 1964).

[6] See PCF, *Le PCF dans la Résistance* (Paris: Editions Sociales, 1967).

[7] Amongst a vast body of literature, see, in particular, E. Fajon, *Ma vie s'appelle liberté* (Paris: Laffont, 1976); G. Plissonnier, *Une vie pour lutter* (Paris: Messidor, 1984); A. Wurmser, *Fidèlement vôtre: Soixante ans de vie politique et littéraire* (Paris: Grasset, 1979).

[8] See F. Billoux, *Quand nous étions ministres* (Paris: Editions Sociales, 1972).

[9] Ibid., p. 10.

[10] Courtois and Lazar, *Histoire du PCF*, p. 15.

[11] J. Elleinstein, *Le PC* (Paris: Grasset, 1976), p. 9.

[12] R. Bourderon (ed.), *Le PCF, étapes et problèmes, 1920–1972* (Paris: Editions Sociales, 1981), pp. 10–11.

[13] J. Burles, R. Martelli and S. Wolikow, *Les Communistes et leur stratégie: Réflexions sur une histoire* (Paris: Messidor/Editions Sociales, 1981), pp. 60–1.

[14] Lazar, 'Le communisme est-il soluble dans l'histoire?', p. 71.

[15] J. Girault (ed.), *Sur l'implantation du Parti communiste français dans l'entre-deux-guerres* (Paris: Editions Sociales, 1977), p. 11.

[16] B. Chambaz, 'L'implantation du Parti Communiste Français à Ivry', in Girault (ed.), *Sur l'implantation du Parti communiste français dans l'entre-deux-guerres*, pp. 147–77.

[17] A. Fourcaut, *Bobigny, banlieue rouge* (Paris: Editions Ouvrières/Presses de la FNSP, 1986), p. 15.

[18] Ibid., p. 18.

[19] M. Hastings, *Halluin-la-Rouge, 1919–1939: Aspects d'un communisme identitaire* (Lille: Presses Universitaires de Lille, 1991), p. 10.

[20] Ibid., p. 13.

[21] Ibid., p. 9.

[22] Ibid., p. 214.

[23] Burles, Martelli and Wolikow, *Les Communistes et leur stratégie*, p. 67.

[24] S. Wolikow, 'Le PCF et le Front populaire', in Bourderon (ed.), *Le PCF, étapes et problèmes*, p. 105.

[25] Ibid., p. 197.

[26] J.P. Scot, 'Stratégie et pratiques du PCF, 1944–1947', in Bourderon (ed.), *Le PCF, étapes et problèmes*, pp. 234–6.

[27] R. Martelli, *Le Rouge et le bleu: Essai sur le communisme dans l'histoire française* (Paris: Editions de l'Atelier, 1995), p. 18.

[28] Ibid., pp. 100–14.

[29] Ibid., p. 127.

[30] J. Fauvet, *Histoire du Parti communiste français (vol. 2): Vingt-cinq ans de drames, 1939–1965* (Paris: Fayard, 1965), pp. 8–9.

[31] Ibid., p. 148.

[32] See J. Ranger, 'L'évolution du vote communiste en France depuis 1945', in F. Bon (ed.), *Le Communisme en France* (Paris: Armand Colin, 1969), pp. 211–54; and also J. Ranger, 'Le déclin du Parti communiste français', *Revue française de science politique*, 36, 1 (1986), pp. 46–63; B. Pudal, *Prendre Parti: Pour une sociologie historique du PCF* (Paris: Presses de la FNSP, 1989); M.C. Lavabre, *Le Fil rouge: Sociologie de la mémoire communiste* (Paris: Presses de la FNSP, 1994).

[33] G. Lavau, *A quoi sert le Parti communiste français?* (Paris: Fayard, 1981). See also G. Lavau, 'Le Parti communiste dans le système politique français', in Bon (ed.), *Le Communisme en France*, pp. 7–81.

[34] Lavau, 'Le Parti communiste dans le système politique français', p. 8.

[35] Ibid., p. 18.

[36] Ibid., pp. 18–21.

[37] Ibid., p. 38.

[38] D. Lacorne, *Les Notables rouges: La construction municipale de l'union de la gauche* (Paris: Presses de la FNSP, 1980).

[39] Ibid., p. 94.

[40] Ibid., pp. 181–95.

[41] M. Schain, *French Communism and Local Power: Urban Politics and Political Change* (London: Pinter, 1985), pp. 1–2.

[42] Ibid., pp. 32–3.

[43] Lazar, *Maisons rouges*, p. 18.

[44] Ibid., p. 18.

[45] Some PCI leaders have written detailed accounts of their political career, but they are not books of memoirs *stricto sensu*. See, for instance, G. Ceretti, *A l'ombre des deux T: 40 ans avec Palmiro Togliatti et Maurice Thorez* (Paris: Julliard, 1973), and G. Pajetta, *Le crisi che ho vissuto: Budapest, Praga, Varsovia* (Rome: Editori Riuniti, 1982).

[46] D. Kertzer, *Politics and Symbols: The Italian Communist Party and the Fall of Communism* (New Haven, CT: Yale University Press, 1996), pp. 16–40.

[47] See the massive work by P. Spriano, *Storia del partito comunista italiano* (Turin: Einaudi, 1967–75. Five vols).

[48] R.J.B. Bosworth, *The Italian Dictatorship: Problems and Perspectives in the Interpretation of Mussolini and Fascism* (London: Arnold, 1998), p. 189.

[49] Ibid., pp. 188–91.

[50] Ibid., p. 191.

[51] Amongst these numerous studies, see particularly G. Mammarella, *Il partito comunista italiano, 1945–1975* (Florence: Vallechi, 1976); R. Mieli (ed.), *Il PCI allo specchio* (Milan: Rizzoli, 1983); L. Paggi and M. D'Angelillo, *I comunisti italiani e il riformismo* (Turin: Einaudi, 1986).

[52] A fine example of such academic work is the volume published by FNSP scholars: J. Besson (ed.), *Sociologie du communisme en Italie* (Paris: Armand Colin/Presses de la FNSP, 1974).

[53] See M. Padovani, *La Longue Marche: Le PC italien* (Paris: Calmann-Lévy, 1976).

[54] H. Weber, *Le Parti communiste italien: aux sources de l'eurocommunisme* (Paris: Christian Bourgois, 1977), p. 31.

[55] Ibid., p. 35.

[56] D. Sassoon, *The Strategy of the Italian Communist Party from the Resistance to the Historic Compromise* (London: Pinter, 1981), p. 243.

[57] J. B. Urban, *Moscow and the Italian Communist Party from Togliatti to Berlinguer* (London: I.B. Tauris, 1986), p. 79.

[58] Ibid., p. 10.

[59] Ibid., p. 85.

[60] Ibid., p. 148.

[61] Ibid., p. 168.

[62] Ibid., p. 16.

[63] See G. Amyot, *The Italian Communist Party: The Crisis of the Popular Front Strategy* (London: Croom Helm, 1981).

[64] See J. Ruscoe, *The Italian Communist Party (1976–1981) on the Threshold of Government* (London: Macmillan, 1982).

[65] See S. Hellman, *Italian Communism in Transition: The Rise and Fall of the Historic Compromise in Turin, 1975–1980* (Oxford: Oxford University Press, 1988).

[66] D. Kertzer, *Comrades and Christians: Religion and Political Struggle in Communist Italy* (Cambridge: Cambridge University Press, 1980), p. xvi.

[67] Ibid., p. 48.

[68] Ibid., p. 55.

[69] Ibid., p. 62.

[70] Kertzer, *Politics and Symbols*, p. x.

[71] C. Shore, *Italian Communism: The Escape from Leninism* (London: Pluto Press, 1990), p. 10.

[72] C. Shore, 'Ethnicity as Revolutionary Strategy: Communist Identity Construction in Italy', in S. Macdonald (ed.), *Inside European Identities: Ethnography in Western Europe* (Oxford: Berg, 1993), pp. 27–53.

[73] A good example is H. Machin (ed.), *National Communism in Western Europe: A Third Way for Socialism?* (London: Methuen, 1983).

[74] T. Judt, '"The Spreading Notion of the Town": Some Recent Writings on French and Italian Communism', *The Historical Journal*, 28, 4 (1985), p. 1012.

[75] Ibid., p. 1016.

[76] Lazar, 'Le communisme est-il soluble dans l'histoire?', p. 71.

[77] On Boris Souvarine, see J.L. Panné, *Boris Souvarine, le premier désenchanté du communisme* (Paris: Laffont, 1993); F. Fejtö, *Histoire des démocraties populaires* (Paris: Le Seuil, 1979).

[78] Lazar, 'Le communisme est-il soluble dans l'histoire?', p. 71.

[79] A. Kriegel, *Aux origines du communisme français* (Paris: Flammarion, 1969), pp. 423–39.

[80] A. Kriegel, *The French Communists: Profile of a People*, trans. E. Halperin (Chicago, IL: University of Chicago Press, 1972).

[81] Ibid., p. 357.

[82] Ibid., p. 362.

[83] Ibid., pp. 362–4.

[84] See P. Robrieux, *Maurice Thorez, vie secrète et vie publique* (Paris: Fayard, 1975) and P. Robrieux, *Histoire intérieure du Parti communiste* (Paris: Fayard, 1980–84. Four vols).

[85] Robrieux gives his own version of the controversy surrounding his *Histoire intérieure du Parti communiste* in P. Robrieux, *La Secte* (Paris: Stock, 1985), pp. 232–51.

[86] S. Courtois, *Le PCF dans la guerre: De Gaulle, la Résistance, Staline ...* (Paris: Ramsay, 1980), p. 483.

[87] Ibid., p. 483.

[88] J.J. Becker, *Le Parti communiste veut-il prendre le pouvoir? La stratégie du PCF de 1930 à nos jours* (Paris: Le Seuil, 1981), p. 12.

[89] Ibid., p. 164.

[90] See Courtois and Lazar, *Histoire du PCF*, and A. Kriegel and S. Courtois, *Eugen Fried: Le grand secret du PCF* (Paris: Le Seuil, 1997).

[91] See D. Desanti, *Les Staliniens: Une expérience politique, 1944–1956* (Verviers: Marabout, 1976); J. Montaldo, *La France communiste* (Paris: Albin Michel, 1978) and J. Montaldo, *Les Finances du parti communiste* (Paris: Albin Michel, 1977); D. Jeambar, *Le PC dans la maison* (Paris: Calmann-Lévy, 1984).

[92] See R. Tiersky, *French Communism, 1920–1972* (New York: Columbia University Press, 1974); D.S. Bell and B. Criddle, *The French Communist Party in the Fifth Republic* (Oxford: Clarendon Press, 1994).

[93] Bell and Criddle, *The French Communist Party*, Preface and p. 1.

[94] See P. Buton, *Les Lendemains qui déchantent: Le Parti communiste français à la Libération* (Paris: Presses de la FNSP, 1993).

[95] Courtois and Lazar, *Histoire du PCF*, p. 392.

[96] On the history of PCF internal purges, see M. Dreyfus, *PCF, crises et dissidences* (Brussels: Complexe, 1990). On one of the most famous of these purges, see C. Tillon, *Un 'Procès de Moscou' à Paris* (Paris: Le Seuil, 1971).

[97] See A. Kriegel, 'The French Communist Party and the Fifth Republic', in D. Blackmer and S. Tarrow (eds), *Communism in Italy and France* (Princeton, NJ: Princeton University Press, 1977), pp. 69–86.

[98] Tiersky, *French Communism*, p. 369.

[99] Courtois and Lazar, *Histoire du PCF*, pp. 17–18.

[100] See D. Blackmer, *Unity in Diversity: Italian Communism and the Communist World* (Cambridge, MA: MIT Press, 1968); S. Serfaty and L. Gray (eds), *The Italian Communist Party Yesterday, Today and Tomorrow* (London: Aldwych Press, 1981), pp. 234–5.

[101] See D. Blackmer, 'Continuity and Change in Postwar Italian Communism', in Blackmer and Tarrow (eds), *Communism in Italy and France*, pp. 21–68.

[102] D. Blackmer and A. Kriegel, *The International Role of the Communist Parties of Italy and France* (Cambridge, MA: Harvard University, Center for International Affairs, 1975).

[103] L. Pellicani, *Gramsci, Togliatti e il PCI: Dal moderno principe al post-comunismo* (Rome: Armando Editore, 1990), pp. 7–8.

[104] Ibid., pp. 24–60.

[105] C. Pavone, *Una guerra civila: saggio storico sulla moralità nella Resistenza* (Turin: Bollati Boringhieri, 1991). For a detailed analysis of the controversy and of Pavone's work, see Bosworth, *The Italian Dictatorship*, pp. 180–204. See also, on these controversies, S. Neri Serneri, 'A Past to be Thrown Away? Politics and History in the Italian Resistance', *Contemporary European History*, 4, 3, November (1995), pp. 367–81, and P. McCarthy (ed.), *Italy since 1945* (Oxford: Oxford University Press, 2000), pp. 1–5.

[106] Bosworth, *The Italian Dictatorship*, pp. 180–204. See also R. de Felice, *Les Rouges et les noirs: Mussolini, la République de Salo et la Résistance, 1943–1945* (Geneva: Georg Editeur, 1999).

[107] Bosworth, *The Italian Dictatorship*, p. 18.

[108] E. Aga-Rossi and V. Zaslavsky, *Togliatti e Stalin: Il PCI e la politica estera staliniana negli archivi di Mosca* (Bologna: Il Mulino, 1997), p. 20.

[109] Ibid., pp. 131–55.

[110] Ibid., pp. 157–80.

[111] Togliatti's letter of 15 February 1943 is quoted extensively in Aga-Rossi and Zaslavsky, *Togliatti e Stalin*, p. 165.

[112] S. Gundle, 'The Italian Communist Party: Gorbachev and the End of "Really Existing Socialism"', in D.S. Bell (ed.), *Western European Communists and the Collapse of Communism* (Oxford: Berg, 1993), p. 15.

[113] Ibid., pp. 15–30.

[114] Blackmer and Tarrow (eds), *Communism in Italy and France*, p. 6.

[115] Lazar, *Maisons rouges*, p. 17.

[116] See, for instance, P. Lange and M. Vannicelli (eds), *The Communist Parties of Italy, France and Spain: Postwar Change and Continuity* (London: Allen & Unwin, 1981), p. 7; R. Tannahill, *The Communist Parties of Western Europe: A Comparative Study* (Westport, CT: Greenwood Press, 1978), p. 221; K. Middlemas, *Power and the Party: Changing Faces of Communism in Western Europe* (London: André Deutsch, 1980), p. 90.

[117] N. McInnes, *The Communist Parties of Western Europe* (Oxford: Oxford University Press, 1975), p. 46.

[118] Ibid., p. 60.

[119] Ibid., p. 79.

[120] See Tiersky, *Ordinary Stalinism*.

[121] F. Furet, *Le Passé d'une illusion: Essai sur l'idée communiste au XXe siècle* (Paris: Le Livre de Poche, 1996), p. 757.

[122] Lazar, *Maisons rouges*, p. 17.

[123] Ibid., p. 19.

[124] S. Gundle, *Between Hollywood and Moscow: The Italian Communists and the Challenge of Mass Culture (1943–1991)* (Durham, NC: Duke University Press, 2000), p. 5.

[125] Bell and Criddle, *The French Communist Party*, p. 226.

[126] Courtois and Lazar, *Histoire du PCF*, pp. 17–18.

2

Designing the Study: A Comparative Framework Based on Two Municipal Case Studies of the PCF and the PCI

As established in Chapter 1, there is already a copious body of literature on communism in general and on the PCF and the PCI in particular, since these were the strongest communist parties in western Europe. In view of this, the need for yet another study of these two parties might seem questionable. However, as mentioned in the Introduction, it is contended here that comparative studies of these two parties, with a few notable exceptions, tend to remain very general and macro-political and fail to provide a structured comparative framework for their study. Moreover, as argued in Chapter 1, a number of studies are pervaded by political motives and systematically play one party against the other in order to produce a strong, term-for-term contrast between the PCF and the PCI.

In view of these two observations, the purpose of this methodological chapter is to fill the gap by proposing a carefully structured comparative approach based on two case studies of these parties at the micro-political level, that is to say at the municipal level. This approach will combine two methods which are traditionally used in political science, the comparative method and the case study. While some criticisms of both methods are justified, it is argued here that these two approaches can be used in a complementary fashion, each offsetting the main shortcomings inherent in the other.

The first section of this chapter reviews some of the problems often associated with the comparative method in social science research, such as the lack of a carefully designed framework. It is argued that a number of works often presented as comparative approaches are in fact mere compilations of country-specific monographs which offer little comparison. The second section identifies the shortcomings and merits of the case-study approach in political science and presents the case for a combined approach using the positive features of each method, offsetting, it is hoped, their respective shortcomings. This structured, comparative approach takes the form of two carefully selected, representative municipal cases, one in France and one in Italy. These are presented in the third section. It is claimed that such an approach constitutes in effect a 'laboratory' to test the postulated contrast between the PCF and the PCI.

THE COMPARATIVE METHOD IN POLITICAL SCIENCE: ADVANTAGES AND POTENTIAL SHORTCOMINGS

As an instrument of investigation, comparison is well established in the social sciences, and many political scientists since Aristotle have demonstrated the benefits of comparing various political objects. A useful synthesis of the intellectual, heuristic and even moral benefits of the comparative approach can be found in a book on comparative politics by Bertrand Badie and Guy Hermet, two French political scientists.[1] In their introduction, they highlight four functions of the use of comparison in the social sciences.

First, comparison fosters better knowledge of other countries' political systems and cultures, overcoming stereotypes and clichés in the process, and thus improves knowledge of one's own culture through comparison with different cultures. This is a point made by Gabriel Almond and Sydney Verba in the opening chapter of *The Civic Culture*:

> By far the greatest amount of empirical research on democratic attitudes has been done in the United States ... Our five-country study offers us the opportunity to escape from American parochialism and to discover whether relations found in the American data are also encountered in democratic countries whose historical experiences and political and social structures differ from one another.[2]

Second, according to Badie and Hermet, the comparative method facilitates understanding of the specific nature of a particular political system – especially by using the method of 'dramatic contrasts' or 'maximum differences' – and invalidates any claim that political phenomena or so-called 'political science laws' are universal. Third, comparison can help overcome the researcher's own determinisms and analytical frameworks and eliminates any historical determinism. For instance, comparative studies have shown that the Industrial Revolution was not a universal process: thus, the use of the comparison enables the scholar to challenge paradigms constructed by others. Finally, it reduces the temptation to ethnocentrism.[3]

In fact, it can safely be argued that some of the most seminal works in political science over the past 40 years or so are systematic, wide-ranging, comparative and, in most cases, collaborative studies based on very extensive research. In a long list of such classics, one must start with the previously mentioned *Civic Culture*, by Almond and Verba, which examines political attitudes and cultures across five highly different nations (Britain, Germany, Italy, Mexico and the USA). In a discussion of the long-lasting influence of this milestone study, Arendt Lijphart writes:

> The more important contribution of *The Civic Culture* is its painstakingly careful description and analysis of the details of five political cultures. Its purpose is not only hypothesis testing at the macro level but also, more significantly, exploration and discovery of patterns of attitudes at the micro level.[4]

Building on concepts and methods found in *The Civic Culture*, Sydney Verba co-edited in the late 1970s another cross-national survey of participation and political equality.[5]

This type of very systematic comparative research can also be found in the stimulating book by Robert Putnam on the beliefs and attitudes of British and Italian political elites, based on hundreds of interviews with politicians from both countries, and in the equally fascinating and insightful work by Sydney Tarrow on French and Italian politicians at the local level.[6] In his more recent landmark study, *Making Democracy Work*, Putnam revisits the influence of civic culture or traditions on the working of political institutions (in this case, the Italian regional governments formed in the early 1970s), and his research is based on breathtaking empirical data collection spanning six selected Italian regions and 20 years of institutional and political development (1970–89): it includes four waves of interviews with councillors in these regions, totalling in excess of 1,700 interviews, three waves of interviews with community leaders (entrepreneurs, bankers, etc.), six specially commissioned nationwide surveys, a careful examination of statistical measures of institutional performance, and a detailed study of the legislation produced by the six regions over the period of study![7] As Putnam himself puts it: 'In short, we came to know these regions and their protagonists well.'[8]

More specifically, the use of the comparison approach in communist studies has also been advocated by several scholars. In his book on the history of communist countries since 1945, Jean-François Soulet develops the following argument. Communism was by definition an attempt to impose a single political and economic model to a variety of countries: the so-called laws of Marxism–Leninism were always presented as scientific, and therefore universal. With its universal claims, communism was based on a framework of concepts, such as the dictatorship of the proletariat and the leading role of the Communist Party, which were shared by all communists across the world. Thus, the Soviet Union was presented as a universal model – and accepted as such by hundreds of thousands of communists. All these common elements, according to Soulet, invite comparative studies aimed at confirming the universality of this model or at identifying the degree of deviance of particular cases from the general model.[9]

However, notwithstanding the methodological value of comparison in political science in general and in communist studies in particular, one should be aware of the potential shortcomings of the comparative approach. In fact, in so doing, it is possible to identify the features which are needed to produce a structured approach combining the benefits of the comparison and of the case study.

The French political scientist Georges Lavau once wrote that comparison was merely a 'typical exercise for trainee political scientists'[10] devoid of any originality. This was a clear expression of a condescending, if not hostile, attitude towards the use of the comparative method in the social sciences, an attitude shared by many scholars. This attitude has remained widespread in the fields of political science and history to the extent that virtually all scholars publishing a comparative study feel compelled to start their book or article by an explicit justification of the use of comparison in their approach. For instance, the introduction to Soulet's book contains such a justification, as does the introduction to Marc Lazar's *Maisons rouges*.[11]

This compulsory self-justification from scholars who write truly comparative studies, as well as the criticisms of the comparative method, probably stem from the fact that a number of works which claim to be comparative are in fact only comparative by name. There is thus a plethora of comparative books which display significant shortcomings in their approach. What is often presented as a comparative study is usually a collective publication edited by one or two scholars who also contribute the introduction, the conclusion and sometimes one of the chapters. The core of the book is usually in the form of a series of country-specific chapters of a monographic nature, written by country specialists. Such a format is of course justifiable and often unavoidable, for no single scholar can be expected to be an expert on, for example, five or more communist parties. However, the problem with this approach often lies in the fact that no overall comparative framework is provided.

Each contributor provides an analytical framework which is designed for the purpose of the specific phenomenon or case being studied, but there are few, if any, explicit parallels between the various contributions in the form of cross-references.[12] In other words, there is often no structure common to all monographs which would enable a genuine comparison based on non-country-specific concepts.

These criticisms are well encapsulated by historian Nigel Copsey who, in an article on the extreme right in France and Britain, argues:

> Except for a small number of recent studies, existing literature on the contemporary extreme right tends to follow a quite rigid country by country-based approach which fails to develop common theoretical perspectives. The key weakness of these specialised multi-country studies is neglect of a genuine comparative framework which often results in collections of 'descriptive' essays.[13]

An example of such a study in the field of Western communist parties is the book edited by Waller and Fennema. In its introduction, this book claims comparative status: 'the treatment is overall comparative'.[14] Yet, the reader cannot but be struck by the disparity in structure and emphasis of the various contributions. For instance, the contribution on the PCF is primarily concerned with the issue of decline (sub-headings include 'the electoral collapse', 'crisis of militancy', 'the Party's public standing falls', 'the crisis of leadership') and uses the two-dimensional model (societal and teleological) discussed in Chapter 1 to explain the demise of French communism.[15] The chapter on the PCI, on the other hand, focuses on different factors (sub-headings include 'parliamentary representation', 'politico-administrative power') and barely touches upon the central question of decline. It also neglects to mention the teleological dimension of Italian communism and its role in the process of adaptation undergone by the Party.[16] Moreover, the few cross-references between chapters are at best anecdotal, and the overall study, in spite of the opening and concluding chapters by Waller and Fennema respectively, clearly lacks a structured comparative framework.

The frequent occurrence of such collections of country-specific monographs is probably a result of the many difficulties inherent in comparative research, which can be subsumed under the expression 'sources of non-comparability'.[17]

First of all, for reasons pertaining to the fragmented nature of academic training and research, it can be difficult for the same researcher to be equally expert in the various fields (history, politics, sociology, socio-linguistics) needed in order to give a sound comparison the multidisciplinary approach it might require. This is why wide-ranging comparative studies are usually collective works calling on various specialists, with the resulting problems mentioned above.

Similarly, while it is possible to be a specialist on two, possibly three, countries' political systems and cultures, any scholar embarking on a comparative study of more cases will undoubtedly come under the fierce criticism of single-country specialists (see, for instance, Soulet's anticipation of such reactions).[18] Even a comparison of two countries will pose many problems, for linguistic and principally cultural reasons. Some translation problems will also inevitably arise, since some political concepts can prove virtually impossible to translate for reasons of lack of cultural equivalence.[19]

Moreover, the researcher has to confront other problems when comparing two different realities: for instance, the statistical sources available for two different countries will come from different categorisations, some archives will be available for one of the parties studied but not for the other. Thus, Lazar mentions the fact that the PCI opened some of its archives – until 1956 – much earlier than the PCF.[20]

Another crucial problem with genuine comparative projects, to which critics of the comparative method are only too keen to draw attention, is that by seeking mostly to compare different, sometimes highly contrasting realities, the comparative inquiry only produces very general findings which do not apply to any of the particular cases discussed. This is what Feldman calls 'comparison without cases'.[21] In a way, this returns the researcher to the dilemma between the specific and the general identified some 30 years ago by Sydney Verba, that is to say that the increase in 'more explicitly comparative works' induced the emergence of a 'kind of literature [which] provides us with many generalisations that do not seem to fit many or any of the relevant cases'.[22]

There are, however, examples of studies which are truly comparative in approach from the outset. In the literature on the PCF and the PCI, three examples are worthy of mention. First, the pioneering article published in 1968 by Thomas Greene[23] was, according to Lazar, one of the first attempts to use a common framework in an attempt to identify some of the elements which distinguish these two parties.[24] This was followed a few years later by what is now considered a milestone in this field, Blackmer and Tarrow's *Communism in Italy and France*, first published in 1975. This is admittedly a series of monographs, but it applies a systematic, topic-based approach common to both objects of comparison. For instance, it examines in chapters specific to the PCF and the PCI the role of these two parties in local government and their relations with Moscow *inter alia*.[25] The main advantage of this book is to render the comparison between the two parties explicit. A scholar interested in, for instance, the respective memberships of the two parties would find in this book two parallel chapters dealing with this issue.

In the final analysis, the best example of a systematic comparison between the two parties is to be found in Lazar's *Maisons rouges*, published in 1992, which adopts a resolutely comparative approach. The book is organised in two parts. The first one is a comparative history of the two parties since the end of the Second World War organised in periods (1945–47, 1947–56, 1956–64, and so on) and not party-specific. The second part is organised in topics, not unlike Blackmer and Tarrow's book, but Lazar's chapters are not specific to one party as they are in the former. These constant parallels between the two parties provide a genuine comparison of these two parties, which results in a clear highlighting of their similarities but also of their differences.[26]

All the difficulties identified earlier (specific versus general, disparity of data sources, lack of cultural equivalence, disparity of the objects compared), as well as the solutions adopted in the truly comparative studies mentioned above, will have to be borne in mind at the design stage of the comparative framework of this study (see below). The next section reviews the shortfalls inherent in the case study, as well as the potential benefits of this approach when carefully constructed.

THE CASE-STUDY METHOD: PITFALLS AND ADVANTAGES

The case-study approach tends to be very detailed, specific and monographic in nature. Although this approach enjoyed a fair deal of success until the 1960s, it has since become the object of strident criticisms by a number of political scientists. In the words of Elliot Feldman:

> Roy Macridis and Bernard Brown complained in the 1950s that cases were done singly as descriptive monographs and did not contribute to theory, and according to Alexander George by the end of the 1960s the case study had fallen into disrepute.[27]

Further evidence of this kind of criticism can be found in an article published by Miles in the late 1970s in which he stated that 'qualitative analysis – and its implicit companion, the case study – cannot yet be regarded as a rational, much less scientific venture'.[28]

The main criticism directed at the case study is its inability to provide findings that could be generalised to other cases. In other words, it is claimed, the specific nature or uniqueness of each case makes it impossible for any researcher to extrapolate any of the findings, or make any valuable contribution to the building of a given theory. Hence, according to this critical view, the case study is merely a means of gathering primary data which can then be included in general, comparative surveys.

On the other hand, some political scientists have given more credit to the case study. For instance, in the early 1970s, Lijphart claimed that carefully chosen and constructed case studies could be 'highly useful instruments in scientific political inquiry'[29] and proposed a typology of six categories of cases, including the 'theory-confirming' and the 'theory-infirming' cases, that is to say cases which could be deemed to be representative enough to confirm or invalidate an existing hypothesis.[30] The usefulness of such test cases was also claimed by Harry Eckstein, who called them 'crucial cases'.[31]

The question which arises with the notion of a 'crucial case', however, is precisely that of representativeness or equivalence. This is a question which is often debated in the social sciences. In fact, as argued by Feldman:

> Regrettably, one can never be certain that a chosen case indeed is crucial or heuristic. There can be no certainty that a particular case is representative of a country or a political system, or even of a category of cases.[32]

There are, however, means to ensure that, through careful design, the cases chosen, even if they may never be equivalent, will be representative if they 'reveal sufficiently similar patterns, or bear sufficiently similar characteristics, to justify systematic comparisons and contrasts'.[33] These means are discussed below.

In an attempt to reconcile historians, adamant that 'each case possesses unique features' and cannot therefore be representative, and political scientists prone to treat each case as a member of a class of phenomena, Alexander George proposes an intermediate approach between the traditional comparative approach and the single case study.[34] He calls this method the 'structured, focused comparison' or 'controlled comparison', which in fact involves a small number of parallel, intensive case studies.[35] George goes on to identify the four tasks to be undertaken by the scholar in the process of designing such a 'focused comparison'. These are:

- specification of the research question and of the objectives of the study (what is the object? what existing theory or hypothesis is to be investigated or tested?);
- specification of the elements or variables to be studied in the case;
- selection of the appropriate cases;
- identification of the data requirements.[36]

Although George's study was published some 20 years ago, few examples of such 'focused', case-based comparisons have been carried out in the field of politics. One notable exception was Elliot Feldman's stimulating study of high-technology project failures in Britain and France.[37]

Significantly, another was precisely in the field of the comparative study of the French and Italian Communist Parties. This was Mario Caciagli's preliminary comparative project based on three red municipalities, Prato (Italy), Cordoba (Spain) and Nanterre (France),[38] a project which unfortunately remained at a very tentative stage.

DESIGNING A 'FOCUSED COMPARISON' BASED ON TWO CASE STUDIES: THE CULTURAL POLICIES OF THE PCF AND THE PCI IN IVRY-SUR-SEINE AND REGGIO EMILIA

The first task of the design of the 'focused comparison' of this study was to identify a research question, that is an existing hypothesis, to be put to the test. The hypothesis to be tested here is that there exists a contrast between the PCF and the PCI. Although commonly found in a number of macro-political studies (see Chapter 1), this hypothesis still needs to be tested thoroughly in the field.

This leads to the second design task, that of the specification of elements or variables. It is claimed here that, in order to control the number of dependent variables, one needs to select a level of study which provides a clear focus. This need is met by restricting the field of study to the micro-political level – the municipal level.

First, the municipal level provides the researcher with primary, qualitative data, such as interviews and the local press, through the observation and study of policy decision-making and implementation. Second, in the case of the PCF and PCI it is at the municipal level that broad statements of policy are most obviously realised – or not – in concrete terms, e.g. in the field of cultural policies or housing. Thus, the municipal level appears to be the most appropriate governmental level for the analysis and comparison of concrete policies implemented by communist parties.

Concentration on policy-making outcomes also enables the researcher to overcome some of the pitfalls posed by the exclusive reliance on discourse analysis of congress speeches, party manifestos, and so on, that is often found in macro-political studies. What can be observed in communist municipalities is a mixture of ideological statements, expressed in the local press and often reflecting the Party's national line, and concrete achievements such as a theatre, a public library, an efficient bus service, etc.

However, a series of problems with this approach might be posed by the interaction between the various tiers of government in France and

Italy in some fields of policy-making and other independent external parameters. For instance, the study of such aspects as the social and/or housing policies of two communist municipalities could have proven highly problematic, since it would have entailed the inclusion of a number of independent external variables: the level of unemployment in the country or in the region concerned; the sometimes conflicting remit of other local authorities (in France, for instance, the department is a major actor in social welfare provision) and of the state; the process of socio-economic change, etc.

To avoid these pitfalls, this study focuses on one aspect of policy-making at the municipal level, that is cultural policy, which is probably the field of policy-making in which municipalities in France and Italy enjoy the greatest margin of independence from central government (see Chapter 3).

This leads to the third task of the design of the study, that of the selection of two representative cases. Given the problems associated with the concept of representativeness (see above), extreme care was required in the identification of two red municipalities, one in France and one in Italy, which offered 'sufficiently similar characteristics'[39] to be considered representative. It is contended here that this is true of the two municipalities chosen, Ivry-sur-Seine and Reggio Emilia, for a number of reasons.

First, both towns are communist strongholds. Each is located in the typical 'red area' of their respective countries: the 'red belt' around Paris, which includes departments traditionally controlled by the communists such as Seine-Saint-Denis, Val-de-Marne and Hauts-de-Seine (see Figure 1 at the beginning of Chapter 5), and the central 'red belt' of Italy which includes the regions of Emilia-Romagna, the Marches, Tuscany and Umbria (see Figure 2 at the beginning of Chapter 6). Each town has had an absolute majority of communists on the local council and a communist mayor for a considerable length of time: since 1925 in the case of Ivry, and 1945 in the case of Reggio.

Second, both municipalities enjoyed the electoral support of social categories typically associated with the PCF and of the PCI, namely skilled industrial workers in the case of the former, small sharecroppers and employees and/or owners of small firms in the case of the latter. Third, Ivry and Reggio are both medium-sized towns (Ivry: *c.* 60,000 inhabitants; Reggio: *c.* 130,000 inhabitants) and, in cultural and intellectual terms, they are both in the shadow of prestigious centres, Paris and Bologna respectively.

The fourth task of the design of this study was the identification of the sources to be used and the disparity of sources available for each case. As already noted, Lazar has identified potential problems here, which were confirmed to some extent. For instance, in the case of Ivry, a useful source of information was the monthly newsletter *Ivry-ma-Ville* published by the municipality and listing, among many other things, the cultural events of the month. Such a monthly newsletter does not exist in Reggio, and other sources had to be consulted (local newspapers, brochures published by the various cultural institutions, etc). Nonetheless, similar qualitative as well as quantitative sources were gathered during research trips to Ivry and Reggio (see Further Reading).

CONCLUSION

This chapter has reviewed the advantages and shortcomings of the comparative approach and of the case study, in an attempt to propose a combination of both methods in the form of a carefully constructed 'focused comparison' (George) based on two red municipalities, Ivry and Reggio. The comparative study of two municipalities is aimed at testing a well-established hypothesis, that is that there exists a contrast between the PCF and the PCI, at a micro-political level, namely the municipal level. It was constructed to ensure that the two municipalities are seen as comparable cases by virtue of the fact that they are representative of French and Italian communism respectively. Some independent variables, such as the socio-economic context and the level of autonomy granted to municipal authorities by the centralised state, are, as it were, neutralised to an extent in the next chapter through the selection of the cultural facet of the policies implemented by the two municipalities, a domain of policy which is to a large extent autonomous.

NOTES

[1] B. Badie and G. Hermet, *Politique comparée* (Paris: Presses Universitaires de France (PUF), 1990).
[2] G. Almond and S. Verba, *The Civic Culture: Political Attitudes and Democracy in Five Nations* (Princeton, NJ: Princeton University Press, 1963), p. 12.
[3] Badie and Hermet, *Politique comparée*, pp. 9–11.
[4] A. Lijphart, 'The Structure of Inference', in G. Almond and S. Verba (eds), *The Civic Culture Revisited* (Boston, MA: Little, Brown and Company, 1980), p. 54.
[5] See S. Verba, N. Nie and J. Kim, *Participation and Political Equality: A Seven-Nation Comparison* (Cambridge: Cambridge University Press, 1978).
[6] See R. Putnam, *The Beliefs of Politicians: Ideology, Conflict and Democracy in Britain and Italy* (New Haven, CT: Yale University Press, 1973) and S. Tarrow, *Between Centre and Periphery: Grassroots Politicians in Italy and France* (New Haven, CT: Yale University Press, 1977).

[7] R. Putnam, *Making Democracy Work: Civic Traditions in Modern Italy* (Princeton, NJ: Princeton University Press, 1993), pp. 13–14.

[8] Ibid., p. 14.

[9] J.F. Soulet, *Histoire comparée des Etats communistes de 1945 à nos jours* (Paris: Armand Colin, 1996), pp. 6–7.

[10] G. Lavau, 'Les partis communistes en France et en Italie', *Etudes*, June (1982), p. 757.

[11] See Soulet, *Histoire comparée des Etats communistes*, pp. 6–7, and Lazar, *Maisons rouges*, pp. 14–16.

[12] See, for instance, E. Page and M. Goldsmith (eds), *Central and Local Government Relations: A Comparative Analysis of West European Unitary States* (London: Sage, 1987).

[13] N. Copsey, 'A Comparison between the Extreme Right in Contemporary France and Britain', *Contemporary European History*, 1, 6 (1997), p. 101.

[14] M. Waller and M. Fennema (eds), *Communist Parties in Western Europe: Decline or Adaptation?* (Oxford: Basil Blackwell, 1988), p. viii.

[15] See S. Courtois and D. Peschanski, 'From Decline to Marginalization: The PCF Breaks with French Society', in Waller and Fennema, *Communist Parties in Western Europe*, pp. 47–68.

[16] See G. Pasquino, 'Mid-Stream and under Stress: The Italian Communist Party', in Waller and Fennema, *Communist Parties in Western Europe*, pp. 26–46.

[17] For a very useful discussion of these issues, see A. Przeworski and H. Teune, *The Logic of Comparative Social Inquiry* (New York: Wiley, 1970).

[18] Soulet, *Histoire comparée des Etats communistes*, p. 6.

[19] Amongst the substantial body of literature devoted to the issues of translation and cultural equivalence, see in particular B. Hatim and I. Mason, *The Translator as Communicator* (London: Routledge, 1997).

[20] Lazar, *Maisons rouges*, pp. 21–2.

[21] E. Feldman, *Concorde and Dissent: Explaining High Technology Project Failures in Britain and France* (Cambridge: Cambridge University Press, 1985), p. 166.

[22] S. Verba, 'Some Dilemmas in Comparative Research', *World Politics*, 20, Oct. (1967), p. 113. See also L. Mayer, *Redefining Comparative Politics: Promise versus Performance* (London: Sage, 1989).

[23] See T. Greene, 'The Communist Parties of Italy and France: A Study in Comparative Communism', *World Politics*, 21 (Oct. 1968 – July 1969), pp. 2–25.

[24] Lazar, *Maisons rouges*, p. 15.

[25] See Blackmer and Tarrow (eds), *Communism in Italy and France*.

[26] Lazar, *Maisons rouges*.

[27] Feldman, *Concorde and Dissent*, p. 166.

[28] M. Miles, 'Qualitative Data as an Attractive Nuisance: The Problem of Analysis', *Administrative Science Quarterly*, 24 (1979), pp. 590–601, quoted in R. Yin, 'The Case Study Crisis: Some Answers', *Administrative Science Quarterly*, 26 (1981), p. 58.

[29] A. Lijphart, 'Comparative Politics and the Comparative Method', *American Political Science Review*, 65, 3 (1971), p. 693.

[30] Ibid., pp. 689–93.

[31] H. Eckstein, 'Case Study and Theory in Political Science', in F. Greenstein and N. Polsby (eds), *Handbook of Political Science*, Vol. 7 (Reading, MA: Addison-Wesley, 1975), pp. 113–23.

[32] Feldman, *Concorde and Dissent*, p. 168.

[33] Ibid., p. 168.

[34] A. George, 'Case Studies and Theory Development: The Method of Structured, Focused Comparison', in P.G. Lauren (ed.), *Diplomacy: New Approaches in History, Theory and Policy* (New York: Free Press, 1979), pp. 43–68.

[35] Ibid., p. 49.

[36] Ibid., pp. 54–6.

[37] See Feldman, *Concorde and Dissent*.

[38] See M. Caciagli, 'Une analyse comparative de trois municipalités communistes en Italie, France et Espagne', *Communisme*, 22–3 (1989), pp. 73–93.

[39] Feldman, *Concorde and Dissent*, p. 168.

3

Cultural Policy-Making in French and Italian Municipalities (*c.* 1960–*c.* 1980)

As stated in Chapter 2, this work is based on two municipal case studies, Ivry-sur-Seine and Reggio Emilia, where communist municipalities have been in power for decades. However, one of the major constraints often associated with the study of policies implemented at the local level is the strong intervention of central government in decision-making at the local level. Thus, both France and Italy are often depicted as very centralised states where there is little room for manoeuvre for local authorities. This is, however, a legalistic interpretation of the local government statutes of both countries.

In view of this, the validity of the crucial, comparative assessment of cultural policy-making in Ivry and Reggio, which is at the core of this study, rests on the assumption that both politico-administrative systems are, all things being equal, quite similar and that municipalities enjoyed a much greater autonomy than is often acknowledged in policy-making at the local level, especially where it matters for this research, namely in the field of cultural policy-making.

Accordingly, the argument made in this chapter is that both France and Italy derive from historically similar legal frameworks and that, in spite of the frequently encountered claim that these frameworks mean very little leeway for municipalities, there is ample evidence, backed up by abundant research in the field, that municipalities in both France and Italy enjoyed a similar degree of independence in policy-making, especially in the field of cultural affairs. A comparison of the cultural policies of the towns of Ivry-sur-Seine and Reggio Emilia is therefore legitimate.

FRANCE AND ITALY: TWO HIGHLY CENTRALISED STATES?

From the point of view of administrative organisation, France and Italy have a number of similarities. These include, for instance, the territorial divisions into comparable tiers of local government, with communes, departments (France) and provinces (Italy), and the more recent regions whose statutes were granted in both countries in the 1970s. At the level of the commune, the key political protagonists are the mayor, assisted by his/her assistant mayors (*adjoints au maire* in France, *assessori* in Italy), and the municipal council, the Italian commune having also a *giunta* or executive committee which shares the executive power with the mayor. Similarly, French departments and Italian provinces each have an elected council, as do the regions in both countries.

These similarities are largely due to the fact that both countries share a common historical legacy, the so-called 'Napoleonic' centralisation process. In France, this process took place in the years 1800–14, when Napoleon Bonaparte continued and completed the centralisation process which had started under the *Ancien Régime*. In Italy, the process of centralisation was much more recent and followed two steps. First, there was the conquest and occupation of a number of states such as Piedmont and Lombardy by the French Napoleonic Empire in the early nineteenth century, which resulted in an administrative reorganisation similar to the one that was taking place in France. Second, there was the process of Italian unification (1860s–1870s), which was led by Piedmont and resulted in the adoption of 'the centralised French-style prefectoral system introduced into Piedmont by Napoleon'.[1]

One key aspect of these two administrative systems was the legal tutelage (*tutelle*, in French) exerted by central government over local authorities through the appointment of the prefect, a high-ranking civil servant nominated by the Ministry of the Interior and sent to a given department or province with very extensive powers of control over local authorities.

In the case of France, this meant that, in theory, every proposed decision or act emanating from even a remote, rural commune had to be submitted to and approved by the prefect, who was sometimes described as the 'king in his department'.[2] In the case of Italy, the administrative tutelage of the state over the communes varied slightly from that of the French state, insofar as the Italian prefect interfered less in the life of Italian communes than the French counterpart.[3]

There was also in both France and Italy a fiscal supervision of local government. In the case of France, according to Yves Mény, the fiscal tutelage was 'a source of profound irritation to elected politicians who protested against the – in their eyes excessive – intervention by the Ministry of Finance and occasionally the prefect'.[4]

Indeed, municipal councils had no fiscal autonomy and relied on the state which decided centrally upon local taxes: 'national supervision of communal and departmental taxation means that local government cannot select the taxes they collect nor the rates of taxation they may impose'.[5] This lack of fiscal and financial autonomy contributed to a restriction of the political choices of municipal councils, and was often perceived as a major obstacle by mayors.

The financial supervision of Italian communes was at least as strict as the French one. Thus, the 1934 law on local government funding, which was passed by the fascist regime (1922–43) and remained in place until the 1970s, conferred on the communes an instrumental role in delivering services on behalf of the state by enforcing a list of expenditure which was compulsory for communes.[6] Thus, any line of expenditure not stipulated by the so-called 'list of communal duties' was deemed optional, and not budgeted for. What this meant in practice was that municipal spending on cultural amenities fell into the so-called 'optional category' and could only be undertaken once the budget had accounted for all the compulsory expenditure. The law of 1977 on decentralisation imposed further limitations on the financial autonomy of communes. While it guaranteed the writing-off of the debts incurred to this date by all local authorities, it abolished their power to resort to borrowings for current expenditure, set strict limitations for spending increases and maintained the requirement to balance the annual budgets of local authorities.[7] In other words, according to Sydney Tarrow, writing in 1977: 'control of public expenditures is seldom located in the commune itself in either country'.[8]

It therefore seems that, in spite of a number of significant differences between the two countries highlighted by Tarrow,[9] France and Italy have formally comparable administrative systems. From a legal and financial point of view, the constraints faced by French and Italian municipalities appear to have been substantial, and the decentralisation processes in the 1970s in Italy and in the early 1980s in France meant tighter budgetary limitations for municipalities in both countries.

However, it could be argued that, in both France and Italy, policy-making at the local level was much more autonomous than is suggested by restricting the examination to institutional and legal constraints. The next section of this chapter examines the real powers of municipalities at the micro-level, in order to establish that, especially in the field of cultural policy-making, French and Italian municipalities enjoyed a similar degree of autonomy from central government.

POLICY-MAKING IN FRENCH AND ITALIAN
MUNICIPALITIES (*c.* 1960–*c.* 1980)

Mayors as 'policy brokers'

In the 1960s and 1970s, a number of scholars challenged the traditional approach to local government, which was based on a static examination of legal and institutional factors, through a more dynamic, interactive approach which looked at the strategies developed by local government protagonists such as mayors to overcome institutional constraints by developing an 'interpersonal complicity' with prefects to the mutual advantage of both parties.[10] Mark Kesselman, in a stimulating study of French mayors, insists on their autonomy and describes them as active policy-makers at the local level.[11] Building on these works and especially on what he calls the 'Bureaucratic-Integration Model' developed in particular by Crozier, Thoenig and Worms, Sydney Tarrow, in his comparative study of French and Italian mayors, develops the concept of the mayor as 'policy broker':

> The notion of policy brokerage departs from older views of local politics which stress personalistic or 'civic' incentives in the strategies of local elites. While the mayor as notable moulds his role to the personal networks around him in the community and the mayor as administrator shapes his actions around the need for 'good government', the mayor as policy broker shapes his adaptive energy to the constraints of the political system. For such a mayor, bringing policy benefits into the community from the state is the single most important incentive that guides his actions.[12]

The notion of 'adaptive' strategy is central to Tarrow's argument: French and Italian mayors, despite the differences between the systemic constraints of the administrative systems of France and Italy, have developed strategies enabling them to make the most of their respective politico-administrative environments.

Thus, the French mayor is described as an 'administrative activist', fully conversant with and integrated into the French *dirigiste* system in which the state and the administrative/technocratic elite are all-powerful, and political partisanship is only a secondary aspect of their strategy of administrative integration.[13] This means that French mayors are successful in attracting benefits and funds irrespective of their political partisanship, as illustrated by the success of communist municipalities in this field. This success, which invalidates the claim often made by communist mayors that their municipalities are discriminated against for

49

political reasons (see, for instance, Chapter 5 on Ivry), is acknowledged by Tarrow and others.[14] Thus, Schain's claim that, 'in general, there is little evidence that communist-governed cities receive less in state aid than those cities governed by other parties' echoes Kesselman's less specific argument that 'political favoritism [in France] is extremely rare and that most grants are given without regard to partisan considerations'.[15]

The success of Italian mayors, on the other hand, is due to their 'adaptive strategy' of actively using the party channels and networks which permeate the Italian administrative system, and they are described as 'political entrepreneurs'.[16] This sort of policy brokerage also applies to PCI mayors: 'Thus the communists, who are most divorced from the individualistic goods and conservative ends of a clientelistic system, have nevertheless been forced to adapt to the techniques of political entrepreneurship.'[17]

Following on this discussion of Tarrow's central argument that, in spite of the differences between the administrative and political systems of their respective countries, both French and Italian mayors have equally managed to adapt to the systemic constraints which surround them, the next section of this study makes the case that, in cultural policy-making, which is the field with which this study is concerned, French and Italian municipalities enjoyed a significant degree of independence from the central state.

The autonomy of cultural policy-makers at the local level in France and Italy

In France, local policy-makers seem to have enjoyed a significant degree of political/administrative independence in the field of cultural affairs. In a study on the cultural policies of French municipalities published in 1983, shortly after the decentralisation laws of 1982, the authors write that: '[more] than ever, the commune is the master of its own cultural policy',[18] which strongly implies that municipalities already enjoyed a high level of autonomy in the field of culture before decentralisation. This argument is given greater emphasis a few pages later: 'culture has always been decentralised in France: the commune is the basic cell of cultural action and cultural life'.[19]

Moreover, this emphasis on the autonomy of local policy-making at the cultural level is part of a wider budgetary autonomy. Thus, Kesselman claims that French municipalities are free to make political choices regarding the allocation of the financial resources of the commune:

> Local governments are legally free to undertake an enormous number of activities. The most usual local responsibilities include

> the routine upkeep of roads, schools, and other public buildings ...
> They may also ... build public baths, parks, monuments, housing,
> sporting fields, nurseries, libraries and industrial parks ... In effect,
> all French communes – from the smallest to the largest – are
> automatically granted the American equivalent of home rule.[20]

A number of concrete examples of such autonomy in the field of
culture can be found. Thus, many French municipalities were able to
finance and build very ambitious amenities in an independent fashion.
The communist municipality of Le Havre decided in the late 1970s to
spend millions of francs on a new building for its *Maison de la Culture*
(1978–82), whose architect was no other than the eminent Oscar
Niemeyer, the man who in the early 1970s had designed, at lavish
expense, numerous buildings in Brasilia as well as the new headquarters
of the PCF (in Place du Colonel Fabien, Paris).

Whether such a project was far too ambitious and expensive for a
municipality the size of Le Havre is a moot point, but the fact of the
matter is that the municipality acted in an entirely autonomous way in
this instance, even managing to obtain substantial financial aid from
central government. Similarly, as Chapter 5 of this study on the cultural
policy of Ivry-sur-Seine will show, the new theatre building, built in the
second half of the 1970s, attracted substantial funding from the state,
which indicates that French municipalities were not only autonomous in
their choice of projects, but also managed to win state subsidies. Thus, in
spite of a strong tradition of centralisation, French municipalities enjoyed
a high level of political and financial autonomy in the field of cultural
policy projects.

The same argument can be made in the case of Italian municipalities.
In areas such as Emilia-Romagna where the PCI held a firm position of
political and social hegemony, communist municipalities were to a very
large extent autonomous from central government and made full use of
their budget, unlike local authorities governed by other political parties.[21]

As in the case of French municipalities, there are numerous instances
of Italian municipalities embarking on fairly ambitious social-welfare
projects without any veto from Rome. The most striking example is
probably that of Bologna, where extensive housing and welfare projects
were undertaken in the late 1940s:

> Bologna, the largest city in the region, became the showpiece of
> communist local government. Under the amiable and reassuring
> leadership of its mayor, Giuseppe Dozza, the city council embarked
> on an ambitious social-welfare programme. The council had limited
> powers or funds at its disposal and matters were not helped by the

fact that for a time the city's prefect was a general, Carlo De Simone. None the less, the council managed to build nine schools, 896 flats, and 31 nursery schools in the decade 1946–1956. Eight thousand children received subsidised school meals; new drains, municipal launderettes, and street lighting were installed; public transport and health care improved significantly.[22]

This study indicates that, as early as in the late 1940s, Italian communist municipalities were managing to have their way in a number of areas of policy-making. Further evidence suggests that this autonomy was also a main feature of policy-making at the local level in the 1960s and 1970s. In a book on Bologna published in the late 1970s, three German researchers give a detailed account of a number of initiatives launched by the municipality in order to promote, for instance, a comprehensive, free public transport system, to preserve and enhance the town's old historic centre, and to develop pre-schooling provision.[23] While these authors do not devote a specific chapter to cultural policy-making in Bologna, the range and extent of the policies undertaken by the municipality suggest that the PCI mayor of Bologna in the 1970s, Zangheri, had a degree of autonomy that also included cultural matters.

By the same token, while the law of 1934 on local government, which remained in force until the 1970s, can be seen as a financial straitjacket for municipalities, the provision for optional expenditure meant that, outside the compulsory policy domains (road maintenance, maintenance of school buildings, etc.), there was complete freedom as to what a municipality wanted to undertake, whatever the field: '[The] provisions for optional expenditure, and the fact that the local authorities are allowed to provide public services at their discretion, means that they are effectively omnicompetent.'[24]

This has crucial implications: since cultural policies fell into the category of optional expenditure, it was left to each municipality to decide which cultural amenities to build and fund, if any, independently from the state administration, the only constraint being that communes had to stick to their annual budget. The argument is that this was manageable, if difficult, especially in the case of communist municipalities with ambitious programmes such as Bologna or Reggio with their comprehensive cultural programmes. Thus, Reggio Emilia launched in the late 1950s a major cultural programme with the takeover of the municipal theatre, in which a variety of expensive cultural activities such as drama, opera and ballet were staged (see Chapter 6 on the cultural policy of Reggio).

Further evidence of the autonomy of Italian municipalities in the field of cultural policy can be found in the 1960s when a number of municipalities in the red regions of Italy decided to deliberately overspend their annual budgets in order to embark on extensive welfare policies. For example, in the case of Bologna, the municipality voted in 1963 to overspend its budget by three billion lire, which marked the 'definitive scrapping of the policy of budgetary balance', in order to fund ambitious welfare and cultural projects.[25] The very fact that communist municipalities were able to breach the long-established legal constraint of balancing their budget in order to promote welfare and cultural activities could be seen as an indicator of the level of autonomy reached by these red municipalities.

CONCLUSION

In this chapter, it has been argued that, in spite of the existence of the widespread idea that French and Italian municipalities were submitted to a very strict administrative and financial tutelage exerted by the central bureaucracies of Paris and Rome respectively, there exists evidence of a long tradition of substantial autonomy in the field of cultural policy-making at the local level.

Thus, a number of examples taken from the field of municipal policy-making suggest that, despite numerous protests by mayors against the so-called straitjacket of central government interference, French and Italian communist municipalities have for a long time been able to make the best of their respective political and administrative environments. This process of taking control of most local affairs, based on a strategy of network-building at the local and national level, enabled mayors and their teams of councillors to push many of their projects through with little resistance from the central administrations of France and Italy. This appears to be the case especially in the field of cultural affairs, which were in both cases left largely to the discretion of municipalities.

In conclusion, the underlying assumption of this study seems to be valid, and the external variable that is central government interference is in this case neutralised. In other words, by undertaking an assessment of the cultural policies of Ivry-sur-Seine and Reggio Emilia, this study amounts in fact to an assessment of deliberate, autonomous political choices made at the local level by the PCF and the PCI according to the strategies of these respective parties.

NOTES

[1] P. Allum, *Politics and Society in Post-War Naples* (Cambridge: Cambridge University Press, 1973), p. 64.

[2] Tarrow, *Between Centre and Periphery*, p. 62.

[3] Ibid., p. 62.

[4] Y. Mény, 'France', in Page and Goldsmith (eds), *Central and Local Government Relations*, p. 68.

[5] Y. Mény, 'Financial Transfers and Local Government in France: National Policy Despite 36,000 Communes', in D. Ashford (ed.), *Financing Urban Government in the Welfare State* (London: Croom Helm, 1980), p. 147.

[6] E. Sanantonio, 'Italy', in Page and Goldsmith (eds), *Central and Local Government Relations*, p. 110.

[7] Ibid., p. 122.

[8] Tarrow, *Between Centre and Periphery*, p. 94.

[9] Ibid., pp. 59–63.

[10] See, for instance, the landmark article by J.C. Thoenig and J.P. Worms, 'Le préfet et ses notables', *Sociologie du travail*, 3 (July–Sept. 1966), quoted in Tarrow, *Between Centre and Periphery*, p. 28.

[11] See M. Kesselman, *The Ambiguous Consensus: A Study of Local Government in France* (New York: Knopf, 1967).

[12] Tarrow, *Between Centre and Periphery*, pp. 111–12.

[13] Ibid., pp. 142–73.

[14] Ibid., pp. 167–71.

[15] See Schain, *French Communism and Local Power*, p. 89; see also Kesselman, *The Ambiguous Consensus*, p. 89.

[16] Tarrow, *Between Centre and Periphery*, pp. 173–202.

[17] Ibid., p. 199.

[18] P. Estèbe and E. Remond, *Les Communes au rendez-vous de la culture: Pour des politiques culturelles municipales* (Paris: Syros, 1983), p. 53.

[19] Ibid., p. 65.

[20] Kesselman, *The Ambiguous Consensus*, pp. 177–8.

[21] F. Spotts and T. Wieser, *Italy, a Difficult Democracy* (Cambridge: Cambridge University Press, 1986), pp. 226–7.

[22] P. Ginsborg, *A History of Contemporary Italy: Society and Politics, 1943–1988* (Harmondsworth: Penguin, 1990), p. 203.

[23] M. Jäggi, R. Müller and S. Schmid, *Red Bologna* (London: Writers and Readers, 1977).

[24] E. Sanantonio, 'Italy', in Page and Goldsmith (eds), *Central and Local Government Relations*, p. 115.

[25] S. Porcu, 'Le PCI et l'administration locale à Bologne (1945–1977)', *Revue française de science politique*, 29, 1 (1979), p. 44.

4

The Cultural Policies of the French and Italian Communist Parties: A Comparative, Strategic Framework

While the study of the concept of culture in general has generated a substantial and controversial body of literature, the study of cultural policies is a relatively new field of political science and history which originated in France. Pascal Ory, a leading French historian of culture, argues that it only emerged as a discipline in the mid-1970s and that France has gained a leading status in this field:

> [It] can be claimed that there now exists a French school specialising in the history of cultural policies, which is at the forefront of research in this field, precisely because France is in a predominant position when it comes to cultural policies.[1]

This situation is attributable to the fact that the very concept of a cultural policy, that is of public intervention and funding in the field of arts and leisure, has a long history in France. As another French specialist of culture argues, 'cultural policy is a French invention'.[2] This specificity, also acknowledged in David Looseley's study of the cultural policies of the Mitterrand era (1981–95),[3] could explain in part why only a limited number of studies on the cultural policies of French political parties have been undertaken.

Similarly, it could be argued that specialists of Italian politics and history have, with a few notable and recent exceptions, neglected the study of the cultural policies of Italian parties. One such exception is Stephen Gundle, although it could be contended that the fact that his study of the PCI and culture was first published in Italian indicates that there is a lack of interest for this topic in the English-speaking world, or at least that there is a much stronger interest in it in Italy.[4]

Accordingly, the first aim of this chapter is to put cultural policies at the core of the study of the French and Italian Communist Parties, and to show that these cultural policies, which embraced numerous aspects, were a central instrument, and not just a mere offshoot, of the conduct and implementation of the overall political strategies of these parties. As Gundle, writing about the cultural policy of the PCI, claims: 'For the PCI cultural struggle always had a special significance. This sphere was not treated as secondary, good only for reinforcing loyalties or forging useful alliances.'[5] His introductory remark could equally be applied to the PCF.

The assumption which lies behind this chapter is that every facet of a cultural policy, be it a commemorative event, the staging of a play, the commissioning of a monumental sculpture or the opening of an historical institute by a communist municipality, can be studied as a political act. Thus, it is argued here that cultural policies always played a particular role in the wider political strategies of these parties.

The first section of this chapter establishes the working definitions of the concepts of culture and cultural policy as they are used in this study, and emphasises the fact that the very notion of culture was highly instrumental in the strategy of the French and Italian Communist Parties. The second section presents a framework based on four concepts embracing the multiple aspects of cultural policy-making (clientelism, 'image-making', hegemony and 'symbol production'), and discusses other concepts which will be used in the two case studies on Ivry-sur-Seine and Reggio Emilia.

BRIEF DEFINITIONS OF THE CONCEPTS OF CULTURE AND CULTURAL POLICY

The concept of culture: a working definition

The concept of culture has long been at the heart of numerous debates among intellectuals in general and in the social sciences in particular, and it could be argued that there are as many definitions of this term as there are schools of thought.[6] It is therefore not within the scope of this study to provide a thorough discussion of the concept of culture *per se*. However, a working definition of this concept which is useful to this study can be found which identifies three main meanings of the term.[7]

The first meaning of the term culture is the traditional, humanistic one according to which culture refers to general knowledge of literary and artistic works. Thus, the accumulation of all the creations of a country forms its culture and part of its history. In brief, this is the 'high' or 'noble' sense of the word culture.

The second meaning of the word is much wider – it is also referred to as civilisation – and encompasses the social values of a society such as religion, as well as other beliefs. As such, culture embraces many forms of artistic and social expression, such as leisure activities, folklore, crafts, popular music, and so on. In this sense, culture is a mirror of a given society in its totality, and access to and mastery of culture is what enables an individual or a group to know themselves and to evolve in their social environment. In other words, this is the liberating aspect of culture, which becomes a synonym for civic and political awareness.

This leads to the third dimension of the concept of culture, the ideological one, which is central to this study. In this sense, the concept of culture becomes instrumental and is placed at the core of ideologies aimed at socio-economic change, such as socialism and, of course, communism. Culture, according to many left-wing theorists, becomes a prerequisite for emancipation and social change. Accordingly, this ideological, instru-mentalist dimension is found in every definition of the concept of culture put forward by communist parties, for which cultural policies become an essential political tool.

The concept of cultural policy

The above, global definition of culture implies that a broad definition of the notion of cultural policy be adopted in this study. In fact, one could follow Pascal Ory, whose approach to the cultural policies of the Popular Front in France (1936–38) is expressed as follows:

> A cultural policy obviously embraces artistic creation, but also scientific creation; creation, but also mediation and leisure activities; the state, but also political parties and associations. Sensitive readers must therefore be warned: the following pages will naturally discuss music and cinema, but also ethnology, propaganda and physical education.[8]

Accordingly, while it is not within the scope of this study to provide a comprehensive treatment of all aspects of the cultural policies of the French and Italian Communist Parties, the examples chosen in this and the following chapters will relate to traditional areas such as drama or sculpture, but also to more ethnological areas such as commemorations, propaganda and the making of symbols.

The French and Italian Communist Parties and the concepts of culture and cultural policy: an historical overview

Both communist parties have developed and amended their own ideological definition of the concepts of culture and cultural policies over several decades, and these present a number of similarities as well as contrasts.

In their early days, the French and Italian Communist Parties, faithfully following the directives of the Comintern in applying the hard, conflictual 'class against class' line (1928–34), were advocates of the theory of the two cultures imposed by Stalin. They claimed that there existed a bourgeois, decadent culture whose aim was to maintain and justify the existing socio-economic order. An example of this can be found in a review of the book *Mort de la morale bourgeoise* (The Demise of Bourgeois Values) (Emmanuel Berl) in a 1930 article written by Paul Nizan, a young French communist intellectual, who wrote: '[B]etween culture ... and the proletariat ..., there cannot be any reconciliation. This is because culture is a system of values erected against the proletariat ... One must have the courage to say: bourgeois culture is a barrier.'[9]

Instead, what was needed according to French communists was a new, 'proletarian culture' to serve the purpose of the revolution. This was mostly to take the form of a proletarian literature produced following the Russian model of *rabcors*, that is to say workers writing about workers and for workers about life in factories, and so on. As a result, according to French historian Jean-Pierre Bernard, a main cultural objective of the PCF in those years was to create a 'proletarian literature' in France, and a second, related objective was to recruit established, bourgeois writers such as Romain Rolland or Henri Barbusse to wage the war against conservative writers.[10]

The apogee of this Comintern line was reached at the Kharkov Congress of Writers held in 1930: 'the literature of the proletariat is nothing other than a weapon in the class struggle'.[11]

For the PCI view on culture in the 1920s and 1930s, although little can be said because Party leaders were in prison or in exile and obviously had higher priorities than to debate the virtues of 'proletarian literature', it could be argued that this cultural line was of lesser importance. Gramsci had already expressed the view, in the late 1910s, that the distinction between bourgeois and proletarian cultures was an arbitrary and fallacious one and that there was only one culture. This attitude could be seen as an early indication that the stance taken by Italian communists on cultural issues was to be more flexible, less sectarian and dogmatic than that of their French counterparts.

A major change in the Comintern line occurred in 1934, when the 'class against class' strategy was jettisoned and replaced by a strategy of broad, anti-fascist alliance which was to lead to the Popular Front coalition in France (1935–38). As a result, the distinction between the two cultures was abolished, and the PCF became an advocate of a single national culture, even if there was still in its eyes a list of 'good' writers or 'progressive' writers whose works could be used and harnessed in a political way, such as Gide, Malraux or Rolland for the contemporary writers, Zola and Hugo for the classics, and of bourgeois, decadent ones. This 'one culture' line was advocated and defended until the Cold War period. As late as 1947, in a pamphlet entitled *La Culture et les hommes* (Culture and Mankind), Aragon strongly challenged the concept of a 'culture of the masses' opposed to a bourgeois culture, and stated that 'culture [was] one and indivisible'.[12]

Thus, in the years 1944–47, the cultural line of the PCF was one of relative tolerance which matched its global strategy of political alliance with other parties, and the Party encouraged open dialogue and debate between its intellectuals and non-PCF ones. The best exemplars of this cultural line are *Action* and *Les Lettres françaises*. The monthly *Action* was a pluralist journal which had been created by Resistance writers during the occupation of France, and its editorial board included a variety of progressive intellectuals and writers who were not *stricto sensu* subjected to the Party's control until the adoption of Zhdanov's cultural line in 1947 (see below). *Les Lettres françaises* was a communist monthly which also remained relatively pluralist until 1947.[13]

Similarly, in Italy, the cultural line of the PCI which prevailed between the Liberation of the Peninsula and 1947 was embodied in Mario Alicata's speech to the Fifth Congress of the PCI (December 1945), in which he officially rejected the dichotomy between the two cultures.[14] Th characterised in editorial terms by a relatively high level of to for instance, found in pluralist, left-wing journals s *Politecnico*, or in the very symbolic publication unde Togliatti's translation of Voltaire's *Treaty on Tolerance*.[15]

The cultural line of the PCF and PCI was drastically altered in 1947 following the creation of the Cominform which in the field of culture resulted in the implementation of Zhdanov's ideas. Zhdanov was a Soviet leader who in 1945 had become the 'number three' in Soviet politics (after Stalin and Malenkov) and was therefore seen as one of Stalin's potential heirs apparent. In fact, he owed his rapid rise within the Soviet hierarchy to Stalin and was devoted to him. In June 1947, Zhdanov became the head of agitprop, that is to say Soviet propaganda.[16] Thus, his role was twofold: he organised the repression of intellectuals in the Soviet bloc, and he became the theoretician of the ideological and cultural dimension of the Cold War, a sort of 'cultural commissar' responsible for the imposition of the new Soviet line to the international communist movement. For example, it was Zhdanov who orchestrated the staunch criticism of the PCI and PCF for their post-war strategy of parliamentarism at the founding meeting of the Cominform in September 1947.[17]

Zhdanov's artistic dogma was known as 'socialist realism', a concept he had coined as early as 1934. It advocated a very strict cultural line for communist artists, writers and intellectuals, namely that artistic and literary creation had to depict the life and working conditions of workers, project the image of 'positive heroes' and, as a result, appeal to workers who would find it easily comprehensible. However, with the Comintern change of strategy in the 1930s (anti-fascist alliances), this line had been applied in a very flexible manner by communist parties, and their intellectuals were not strictly speaking subjected to it.

With the deepening of the Cold War, however, communist intellectuals no longer enjoyed relative freedom, and became subjected to the prescriptive aesthetic of socialist realism. The Zhdanovist cultural line led to the resurrection of the old distinction between proletarian and bourgeois cultures and sciences, and was to affect the French and Italian Communist Parties until the mid-1950s. It also meant that intellectuals had to accept to serve their Party and the working class, to be *au service du Parti* (Verdès-Leroux).[18]

In France, the imposition of the Soviet line in 1947 met with some resistance from a number of PCF intellectuals, and a fierce debate took place. In fact, this debate had already started in November 1946 after the publication, by Roger Garaudy, of an article called 'Il n'y a pas d'esthétique communiste' ('There is no communist aesthetic') in *Les Lettres françaises*. Garaudy, who was at the time in charge of PCF intellectuals, reasserted the pre-Cold War cultural line that communist artists should be given a certain level of artistic freedom and that the Party should not impose socialist realism as the only model or credo to be followed.

This position was fiercely challenged by a group of more orthodox communist intellectuals led by Louis Aragon, who stated that the only acceptable form of aesthetics for a communist artist was Zhdanovism. The outcome of this debate was a clear victory for Aragon, and the socialist realist dogma became the official cultural line of the PCF at its Eleventh Congress held in June 1947. Laurent Casanova became the PCF leader in charge of intellectuals and culture, embodied the Zhdanovist line until the mid-1950s, and summarised the role of communist intellectuals in the following way:

> To espouse all the ideological and political positions of the working class, to defend in all circumstances, and with the utmost determination, all the positions of the Party ... , to cultivate in ourselves the love of the Party and the spirit of the Party in its most conscious form, to give the proletariat any additional arguments and justifications that you can.[19]

As a result, all communist intellectuals, from painters to scientists, were subjected to very strict supervision in the years 1947–54.

The implementation of Zhdanovism was to take a similar form in the PCI. First of all, the debate between Garaudy and Aragon was echoed in the PCI monthly *Rinascita*, which published Garaudy's article and Aragon's reply, and then in the controversy surrounding *Il Politecnico*. *Il Politecnico* was a monthly created at the Liberation, and was edited by Elio Vittorini, a famous novelist who was also a PCI member. For two years, between 1945 and 1947, Vittorini and *Il Politecnico* had enjoyed substantial editorial freedom and published a number of articles and short stories by communist writers as well as non-PCI ones, and the magazine had become, in Gundle's words, 'one of the most lively and original reference points [in Italian culture] in the immediate post-war years'.[20]

However, in 1947, Vittorini was ordered to adopt the socialist realist line and to stop publishing bourgeois writers. A political and editorial battle ensued between Vittorini, who refused to discriminate against bourgeois writers, and Togliatti. A few months later, Vittorini still refused to be subjected to any Party line on culture, and *Il Politecnico* folded when the PCI withdrew all financial support. A few years later, in 1951, Vittorini was expelled from the PCI.[21]

There is therefore evidence that, as in the case of the PCF, the PCI tightened its grip on communist intellectuals. Moreover, it too promoted socialist realism as its artistic dogma. It officially adopted Zhdanovism as its cultural line at its Sixth Congress in January 1948[22] and created a cultural commission which was headed by Emilio Sereni, a staunch advocate of Zhdanovism, who was Casanova's Italian counterpart.[23]

However, with the deaths of Zhdanov (1948) and Stalin (1953) and the thaw which followed Khrushchev's coming to power in the Soviet Union (1956), the cultural line of communist parties was once again altered, and their conception of culture and cultural policy, which remained nonetheless highly instrumental, started to include a number of features which remained prevalent from the late 1950s to the 1970s.

In France and in Italy, as Lazar claims, the relaxation of Zhdanovist policy started in the early 1950s, and both communist parties began to emphasise the national (i.e. anti-American) dimension of culture rather than its socialist realist one.[24] This change was made notwithstanding repeated assertions by communist leaders that the parties had a right to interfere in artistic creation. Thus, in France, Aragon made a speech entitled 'L'Art de Parti' to the Thirteenth Congress of the PCF (June 1954) which was in some ways reminiscent of Zhdanovism, and, in Italy, Togliatti himself played a similar role of intellectual watchdog by reprimanding in writing and under his pseudonym of Rodrigo di Castiglia a number of PCI intellectuals who advocated more artistic freedom.[25]

However, in both cases, it could be argued that, by the early 1960s, Zhdanovism had become obsolete, and both parties appeared to advocate a much more flexible approach to the issues of artistic creation and freedom.

In Italy, the issue of socialist realism was the object of a conference organised by the Gramsci Institute in 1959 and entitled 'Problems of Realism in Italy', during which some of the ideological extremes of Cold War Zhdanovism were discussed.[26] At the Tenth Congress of the Party (1962), the cultural commission, created in 1948 to impose Zhdanovism and responsible for monitoring intellectuals, was scrapped, and PCI intellectuals were encouraged to use the Gramsci Institutes as a place for debate and research.[27] Two years later, in his political testimonial published after his death, Togliatti wrote: 'We must become the champions of freedom in intellectual life, of free artistic expression, and of scientific progress',[28] and this was to become the official cultural line of the PCI.

Similarly, in France, a much more flexible, official cultural strategy was implemented in March 1966 when the Central Committee of the PCF met in Argenteuil to discuss the issue of artistic creation. Much has been written on the Argenteuil Central Committee meeting,[29] but in terms of artistic creation it signalled the official abandonment of Zhdanovism by the PCF. Aragon, who was one of the leading forces behind the meeting and its concluding resolution, wrote:

> One cannot restrict at any time the right of creators to research. This is why the experimental requirements inherent to literature and the arts cannot be denied or impeded, for such interference would seriously hinder the development of culture and of the human spirit itself.[30]

It therefore seems that by the mid-1960s the PCF had adopted a much more flexible cultural policy and attitude on communist intellectuals, which was reflected in the relatively high level of intellectual freedom found in PCF journals in the 1960s.[31]

French historian Jeannine Verdès-Leroux argues that the new, Argenteuil line simply meant that the PCF and its intellectuals had agreed a compromise by which the Party would not interfere in matters of artistic/literary creation on the one hand, but communist intellectuals would not contest the design or discussion of the strategy and policies of the Party on the other hand.[32] In other words, it meant that novelists and painters were free to experiment as they wished as long as they did not criticise or discuss Party policies. This had once been expressed in a somewhat ironic form by Picasso who, talking about Thorez, had said, 'every time I try to talk politics with him, he looks at me in a way which basically means "go and play in the garden"'.[33]

Moreover, Argenteuil's compromise meant that communist social scientists had to be aware that any findings which went against the Party ideological orthodoxy would be severely criticised. In other words, they were free to undertake research, provided that they would not use their findings to contest (even by implication) the Party's strategy.

As a result of these changes, which took place in the late 1950s and early 1960s, the definitions of culture adopted by the PCF and the PCI became much more comprehensive than they had previously been.

In the PCF, several definitions of the notion of culture can be found in a series of texts published after the Argenteuil Central Committee. Thus, in *La Culture au présent* (Culture Today), Roland Leroy, the French communist leader responsible for intellectuals, writes:

> [The] culture of a given society, of an individual, are the result of all their activities. Scientific research and knowledge, their technical implementation, productive labour, information and practice – be they literary, artistic or political – physical education all contribute to the making of culture.[34]

What emerges in this example is that culture is seen as a global entity, that it is not only the traditional arts and humanities but also science, sports, and so on. Thus, culture had become a legacy that belonged to everybody in society, and the main task of the cultural policy of the PCF was to enable workers to master and overcome this legacy in order to free themselves from their socio-economic environment. This new approach saw the end of the old dichotomy of the two cultures and of the challenge to the country's cultural legacy:

> [All] the scientific discoveries and the works of art bequeathed by the past constitute our cultural legacy. A cultural legacy which also includes the tradition and experience of political and social struggles transmitted by those who preceded us ... We reject the nihilist argument that there ought to be a new culture, a *tabula rasa*.[35]

This global, instrumentalist view of culture meant that the new, essential concept at the core of the cultural action of the PCF was to be access of the masses to their own culture, an access which was denied them on account of many factors, from the schooling system to their socio-economic alienation. This access to culture had clear political implications, in the eyes of communists. 'Cultured' workers, argued the PCF, would realise that they were being exploited and would join the struggle for social and political change leading to a revolution. A very similar outlook on culture and cultural policies was found in texts published by the PCI in the 1960s:

> [We] intend to emphasise the liberating aspect of knowledge, the utmost importance of the acquisition by the masses of the instruments which enable the maturation of a critical and rational conception of our present, linked to a deep and thorough knowledge of our past, and [which results in] the visibility of the processes which are at the core of our social and individual lives.[36]

The conclusion must be that the very notions of culture and cultural policy were highly instrumental and political for both communist parties, and that they clearly linked the mass acquisition of culture to their political strategies.

THE CULTURAL POLICIES OF THE PCF AND OF THE PCI: A COMPARATIVE FRAMEWORK

This section aims to establish a comparative, strategic framework of concepts that will be used in the two case studies in the discussion of the various aspects of cultural policy-making. It is based on the assumption that all the aspects of the cultural policies of the French and Italian Communist Parties were instruments in their wider political strategy and can be subsumed under four main concepts: clientelism, image-making, hegemony and symbol production.

Cultural policy as a clientelistic tool

In her study of modern clientelism as a form of government in post-war southern Italy, Judith Chubb refers to the definition of traditional clientelism by anthropologist James Scott:

> [it is] a special case of dyadic [two-person] ties involving a largely instrumental friendship in which an individual of higher socio-economic status [patron] uses his own influence and resources to provide protection or benefits, or both, for a person of a lower status [client] who, for his part, reciprocates by offering general support and assistance, including personal services, to the patron.[37]

This traditional definition implied that a patron–client relationship was based on reciprocity of services, and inequality of status between the patron and the client, and that it was of a personal nature.

However, Chubb argues that with the emergence of mass politics and organisations in the twentieth century, the concept of clientelism could be extended to describe situations where one of the parties – often the patron – is no longer an individual but a collective organisation, such as a political party: 'at this point, the party organisation itself assumes the role of a patron'.[38]

For instance, the DCI (Democrazia Cristiana Italiana, or the Italian Christian Democrat Party), in national government between 1946 and 1994, relied heavily on clientelism to secure their governmental monopoly, especially in the south of the Peninsula. This monopoly was a result of the fact that the DCI controlled access to employment in the area. In his study of post-war politics in Naples, Percy Allum writes: 'In Naples, patronage appointment has been extended to all levels of society. The reasons are simple: Naples is a society of limited resources and unemployment is still rife. In these circumstances, the State provides the chief source of employment.'[39]

Another example of the use of the concept of clientelism to describe the operations of a political party can be found in the field of communist parties. In an article published in 1982, French political scientists Donneur and Padioleau claim that the French Communist Party, in the municipalities it controlled, had generalised the use of clientelism to secure the political allegiance of significant segments of the local population.[40]

In the field of the study of the cultural policies of the French and Italian Communist Parties, the concept of clientelism can usefully be applied to the analysis of the relationship between these parties and a number of communist intellectuals both at the national and at the local levels.

It should be noted that, among the many senses of the term 'intellectual', the definition which is used in this study is not restricted to the traditional meaning (academics, writers), but is extended to include artists (painters, sculptors, film-makers, drama creators, and so on) and journalists, in other words, all those 'intellectuals who have left [written] traces of an intellectual activity',[41] if 'written traces' is also understood here to include works of art.

This working definition excludes a number of what communist parties referred to as 'intellectual categories' (as opposed to workers) such as white-collar workers, technicians and engineers, civil servants and teachers. In other words, a secondary school teacher belonging to the PCF and publishing articles in communist journals (or elsewhere) will fall into the 'intellectual' category, whereas another communist teacher restricting his/her activity to an involvement in a PCF-controlled teaching union will not.[42] A similar definition of the concept of the intellectual which includes artists and journalists but excludes white-collar workers can be found in Nello Ajello's study of PCI intellectuals.[43]

In her *Au service du Parti: Le Parti communiste, les intellectuels et la culture (1944–1956)* (Serving the Party: The Communist Party, Intellectuals and Culture (1944–1956)), the first volume of her thorough study of communist intellectuals, Verdès-Leroux sets out a useful distinction between two categories of communist intellectuals, *intellectuels autonomes* and *intellectuels de Parti*. Autonomous intellectuals were intellectuals who enjoyed an autonomous status and position in French society, that is to say that they were recognised as intellectuals by society in general. This was because they had been trained by the French university system and were established scholars, writers or artists who were often working for and recognised by bourgeois institutions such as universities or *grandes écoles* and were published by bourgeois publishers such as Gallimard. This institutional position meant that these intellectuals did not rely on the PCF cultural and publishing empire for their fame or for their livelihood, and that many of them were able to quit the Party whenever they wished to, as many did in 1956, for they knew they would still enjoy their social status and source of income outside the PCF.[44]

There are many examples of famous autonomous intellectuals and writers who left the Party in the 1940s or 1950s, such as Marcel Prenant, a leading biologist, who left the Party in 1958.[45] The relationship that the Party had with these intellectuals was therefore not truly clientelistic in nature, and it used them as image-making agents (see below).

On the other hand, a true clientelistic relationship existed between the PCF and Party intellectuals, that is to say journalists, writers or artists who owed their fame and their social and financial status to the Party and to the Party only. These intellectuals had to remain faithful to the Party line at all times, since any criticism would have meant the loss of their social and financial status. A few famous examples can be studied to illustrate the clientelistic nature of this relationship.

André Fougeron (1913–98) was from a Parisian, working-class background. He started his artistic career in 1935, under the auspices of Louis Aragon, and some of his works were exhibited in 1937 as part of an exhibition called 'L'Art cruel' organised by Jean Cassou, a writer and fellow-traveller of the PCF. Until then, his work was relatively unknown and it was only after joining the PCF in 1939 and being awarded the Prix National de Peinture (National Prize for Painting) in 1946 that he became relatively known in artistic circles. His major breakthrough, however, occurred in 1948 when the PCF turned him into its fiercest advocate of socialist realism, with a painting called *Les Parisiennes au marché*, which was promoted by the PCF leadership as a sort of manifesto of Zhdanovist art.[46]

At the peak of the Cold War years, during the Korean War (1950–53), and in the absence of Maurice Thorez, who was convalescent in Russia, Fougeron became entangled in the Party's internal rivalries. These opposed Louis Aragon, the protégé of Maurice Thorez, who supported Picasso, and Auguste Lecoeur, the Party 'number two' until his dismissal in 1954. In January 1951, Lecoeur was behind the organisation of a Fougeron exhibition called 'Le Pays des mines', which was to be the painter's claim to fame and the apogee of new realism. In 1953, Lecoeur wrote of Fougeron that he was the 'Aragon of painting', that is to say the best painter in a Party that had in its ranks artists such as Pablo Picasso or the lesser-known Edouard Pignon.[47]

Louis Aragon, who had probably taken this as an offence, wrote a long article on Fougeron's painting *Civilisation atlantique*, exhibited in October 1953. Clearly wanting to settle old scores, Aragon wrote a fierce criticism of Fougeron, who was accused of being 'mediocre and pretentious'. Coinciding with the return of Thorez from Russia and the beginning of Lecoeur's demise, Aragon's article looked like a personal vendetta against Fougeron, Lecoeur's protégé, who had himself attacked Picasso (Aragon's friend) when he had published in *L'Humanité* his (in)famous *Portrait of Stalin* after the death of the Soviet dictator in March 1953, a drawing for which both Picasso and Aragon had been strongly criticised by the Soviets, Lecoeur and the PCF leadership. The ire of the Soviets had come from the fact that Picasso had depicted Stalin as a young man, which was deemed irreverent. By the same token, Aragon was blamed by the Soviets and by Lecoeur for having authorised, as the director of *Les Lettres françaises*, the publication of this 'offensive' portrait.[48]

In any case, the conclusion of Aragon's article on Fougeron's *Civilisation atlantique*, which was 'Il faut dire "Halte-là" à André Fougeron' ('One must say "Stop here" to André Fougeron'), also marked the end of Fougeron's prestige as a painter.

In spite of his demise as the official Party painter, Fougeron remained a communist until his death in 1998 and, as a result, was commissioned by communist municipalities on regular occasions to decorate schools in Ivry-sur-Seine and Pantin.[49] Some of his paintings were also purchased by socialist countries.[50]

The case of André Fougeron illustrates the concept of clientelism at work inside the PCF: it could be argued that, without the support of the PCF and of some of its leaders, Fougeron would perhaps never have enjoyed the fame – and possibly the financial rewards that go with it – that he did. The price to pay for Fougeron was undoubtedly that he had to adjust his art to the Party line: Fougeron was not a realist painter before 1948, and moved away from strict realism after 1953.

This example shows two aspects of the function of clientelism. First, Party intellectuals were part of the political struggle against the bourgeoisie or indeed of internal struggles within the Party. Second, as long as they remained faithful to the Party and even when they were not at the forefront of the ideological war, their allegiance was rewarded in financial and social terms through orders placed by municipalities, municipal libraries or even the people's democracies.

A second example of clientelism can be taken in the field of writing. André Stil, who became in the 1970s a recognised writer in France, made his literary debut with a socialist realist novel entitled *Le Premier Choc* (The First Shock), which depicted the struggle of dockers in Marseilles. In spite of, or perhaps because of, its dubious literary qualities ('They say Coca-Cola smells like piss'; 'A mind as clear as white wine, a blood as hot as red wine'),[51] this overtly simple novel was awarded the Stalin Prize in 1952, and Stil, another Aragon protégé, went on to make a comfortable living as a communist writer, and has remained a faithful member of the Party since then.

A more complex case of clientelism can be found in Louis Aragon (1897–1982), the most famous Party intellectual in France. Having started his literary career in the 1920s with Breton's Surrealists, he joined the PCF in 1927 and, after attending the Kharkov Congress of Writers in 1930, decided to put his literary art to the service of the communist cause, which, unlike many contemporary French writers, he did until his death in the early 1980s. He was a very prolific writer – his complete works filled many French communists' bookshelves – and became in the late 1940s the head of the PCF publishing empire, directing such periodicals as *Ce Soir* and *Les Lettres françaises*, and the Editeurs Français Réunis (one of the Party's publishing houses). He was involved in every aspect of the Party's cultural and literary life.[52]

He was himself the biggest client of the Party, which spared no expense to keep him and his wife Elsa Triolet happy: in 1960, the Aragon couple moved to an eighteenth-century mansion in rue de Varenne, a chic district in Paris,[53] and a few years later the Party bought and renovated for them a former mill in Saint-Arnoult. But the financial gains were only one aspect of Aragon's rewards. He was also the main patron, distributing jobs and promoting younger writers, painters or artists. Many personal accounts have described him as a sort of socialite or Parisian emperor who, with his wife, organised literary events and decided which writer had to be published by the Party, who was – after him, no need to say – the best poet, and so on.

The best critical testimony of the Aragons' cultural empire is probably that of Louis de Villefosse, a former navy officer and fellow-traveller, who depicted in his memoirs the quasi-royal character of the Aragon couple:

> Aragon's taste for all that shines and all that flatters was only too visible, as was his wife's appetite for fame and honours, her immoderate glee in belonging to the *Tout-Paris* ... and how she was attached to the external signs of success and fortune.[54]

A list of all Aragon's literary and artistic protégés would obviously have to start with his own wife Elsa Triolet, whose literary career was, to say the least, boosted by Aragon. In 1944, she was awarded the Prix Goncourt, the highest literary prize in France, for her collection of short stories *Le Premier Accroc coûte cent francs* (The First Tear Costs a Hundred Francs). It is obviously not within the scope of this study to assess the literary quality of Triolet's writings or indeed of Aragon's. Nonetheless, it is interesting to note that her prize came at a time when the CNE (Comité National des Ecrivains, or National Committee of Writers) was all-powerful and that this institution, which was set up at the Liberation of France and gathered writers who had taken part in the Resistance, including many communists and fellow-travellers, was becoming part of Aragon's empire – he became the official head of the CNE in 1946. It could even be argued that the CNE was entirely 'constructed and manipulated' by the PCF.[55]

From then on, Aragon was to attack any critic of Triolet in the fiercest terms. A good example of Aragon's megalomaniac influence can be found in 1946, in the 'Pierre Hervé affair'. Pierre Hervé was a communist writer and journalist who regularly wrote articles for *Action*, a communist journal. Hervé had not only opposed Aragon's stance in favour of socialist realism, but he had also dared to write that, in some respects, some of Triolet's novels and short stories had 'the same troubled atmosphere that was found in some of Sartre's novels' (Sartre and the existentialists were then seen as 'bourgeois, decadent writers'). This sacrilege provoked a furious reaction from Aragon, who wrote a vehement letter to *Action*.[56] Maybe it was a pure coincidence, but Pierre Hervé was then to spend a number of years as the *Humanité* correspondent in the people's democracies, and *Action* was to stop its publication a few years later, in 1952, certainly because it was deemed too 'eclectic'.[57] It would be possible to argue that Aragon, who was then in charge of communist publications, was behind the demise of *Action*.

Other famous protégés of Aragon included Pierre Daix, who was for 20 years chief editor of Aragon's *Lettres françaises* and left the Party after the demise of this journal (1972–73). Another one was Antoine Vitez, a drama director who became famous in the 1970s (see Chapter 5).

However, Aragon was always careful to promote writers who would not tarnish his own prestige, to the extent that, according to Renaud de Jouvenel, once a fellow-traveller, he only promoted poets who were so mediocre that they would remain in their benefactor's shadow.[58]

Thus, it appears that a number of communist poets – many of them now forgotten – artists and Party intellectuals owed their fame and financial rewards to Aragon, who himself owed his to the patronage of Maurice Thorez. Whether or not these intellectuals would have come out of obscurity without Aragon, or indeed whether Aragon himself would have become the name that he now is in contemporary French literature without the Party, remains to be seen. It can safely be argued, however, that their clientelistic relationship to the PCF boosted their fame and their fortune.

There was, however, a price to pay for all the clients, especially in the early stages of their artistic careers. Aragon proved his commitment to communism and 'really existing socialism' on numerous occasions, and he did so with extreme dedication, before he gained enough influence inside and outside the Party to be able to express critical views as he did after the repression of the Prague Spring in 1968. In the early 1930s, the young Aragon, who was a very ambitious poet, went to great extremes to satisfy the PCF that he had renounced his bourgeois origins and embraced the cause of the revolution. Thus, in his early writings, one could find an *Ode to the OGPU*, Stalin's secret political police responsible for all the purges and executions of the regime's political opponents, in which Aragon praised Soviet methods and called for the creation of a French equivalent to the OGPU in order to punish all the 'enemies of the proletariat'.[59] It is revealing to note that, because of the contrived myth that now surrounds Aragon in France, few people know that he wrote such 'poems' as the *Ode to the OGPU* and *Red Front* (1931) or *Il revient*, dedicated to the return of Maurice Thorez to France in 1953.

After the war, in his ambition to become the head of the Party's publishing empire,[60] Aragon indulged in a defamatory campaign against his former friend and rival Paul Nizan – a communist writer and literary critic who was deemed to have betrayed the Party because he had disapproved, in early September 1939, of the Pact signed between Germany and the Soviet Union on 31 August of that year, and had left the Party the following day. The fact that Nizan had been killed while fighting for his country in 1940 and that the PCF had abruptly changed its line in 1941, after Hitler's attack on Russia, meant that the accusation had to take a new form, and the late Nizan, who had devoted most of his adult life to the Party, was then defamed as a *policier* (a police spy), one of the worst insults in PCF jargon. Aragon even went as far as to settle old scores with Nizan in his literary production, portraying him as a traitor and a crook in his novel *Les Communistes*.[61]

Thus, the price to pay for Aragon was total political allegiance. If he became less active in the Party's ideological warfare after the late 1940s, once he had secured his empire, he never publicly criticised the Soviet Union until 1968, when he called the 'normalisation' process that took place after the repression of the Prague Spring a 'Biafra of the mind'. He nonetheless remained a faithful communist until his death, approving of the Soviet invasion of Afghanistan in 1979.[62] He also went to Moscow to receive the Order of the October Revolution in 1972, on the occasion of his 75th birthday, exactly at the time when his journal, *Les Lettres françaises*, folded because of the Soviet-imposed cancellation of all Eastern bloc subscriptions to it.[63]

This clientelism at work in the PCF went beyond writers and artists. It also meant a livelihood for a huge number of journalists working for the numerous communist publications. In fact, the PCF had become a master in creating a clientele of faithful journalists. In his memoirs, Pierre Daix describes the technique used by the Party. It consisted of paying its journalists very meagre salaries, in order to create 'dependence links': 'The journalist who cannot make ends meet will strive to merit fringe benefits that the Party may grant them, benefits that, for some, are sometimes much higher than the salary actually received.'[64]

In order to sustain its clientelistic links with its journalists and intellectuals, the PCF had built a huge publishing empire which comprised newspapers, such as *L'Humanité*, *Ce Soir* and a number of regional papers, periodicals such as *France Nouvelle* or *La Terre* (aimed at farmers), journals such as *La Nouvelle Critique*, *Les Lettres françaises*, *la Pensée* or *Europe*. The PCF also had its own publishing houses, such as the Editions Sociales (for political pamphlets), the Editeurs Français Réunis (for fiction), the Club Diderot du Livre Progressiste, and so on. Moreover, the PCF controlled a vast, captive market to ensure the sale of huge numbers of books through its *Batailles du Livre*, its book stands at the *Fête de l'Humanité*, the numerous municipal libraries of communist towns and the thousands of small libraries run by Party-controlled *Comités d'Entreprise* (Workers Councils) which were obligatory customers of the Party's publications. Added to this was the fact that the PCF was able to attract a huge pool of buyers among Party activists and office-holders.

The most famous communist writers and artists also enjoyed a steady income from the sale of their translated works in socialist countries. To give an indication of the scale of the Soviet publishing machine, David Caute, in his study of fellow-travellers, mentions that, for instance, novels by Romain Rolland (a famous French fellow-traveller) enjoyed a total printing of 1.7 million copies in the 1930s, a considerable amount by any Western publishing standards.[65]

More important, according to Caute, was the issue of recognition of these writers: 'what these figures represent is not so much money as recognition; and the writer's life, after all, is a constant striving after recognition'.[66]

Together, the publishing empire controlled by the PCF and the enormous potential sales outlet of the socialist countries constituted manna for a number of journalists and writers, to the extent that any withdrawal of support for a given journal led to its collapse. Thus, Pierre Daix described the technique used by the Soviet Union and the PCF to put pressure on *Les Lettres françaises* after 1968, at a time when this journal was adopting a critical stance towards the process of 'normalisation' (in fact political and cultural repression) that was taking place in Czechoslovakia. Instead of resorting to blatant censorship, which would have generated an open conflict with the all-powerful Aragon who directed the journal, the Soviet Union, the people's democracies and a number of communist parties cancelled over 6,000 yearly subscriptions to the journal, thus generating financial difficulties. Had the PCF wanted to contain this danger, it could easily have ensured an increase in the number of subscriptions by municipalities, but it did not.[67]

Thus, it could be argued that the PCF, with its vast cultural empire, was able to maintain a strong, clientelistic relationship with thousands of writers, journalists, painters, sculptors and drama professionals. The purpose of this relationship was twofold: first of all, it was to ensure that there was always an army of intellectuals and artists eager to promote the ideas of the PCF through various channels. In a few words, with its 'counter-society' (Annie Kriegel) of intellectuals, the PCF was paving the way for its strategy of implementing a Soviet-style entity in France, or at least was able to defend and justify the foreign policy of the Soviet Union at all times, which in return earned it considerable resources from the Russians. The second objective of this clientelistic relationship was to create the all-powerful myth that the PCF was the *Parti de l'intelligence française*, that is to say the political force which attracted the most influential French intellectuals and artists of their generation. This myth is strongly challenged by Verdès-Leroux:

> For ten years, I worked on this question: [I came to the conclusion that] the PCF was a cultural desert – no famous names, no real works. On the other hand, the great intellectuals of our time, Claude Lévi-Strauss or Fernand Braudel, for instance, had nothing to do with the Party.[68]

Thus, the clientelistic relationship between the PCF and its intellectuals also had an image-making purpose (see below) which was efficient for a long time, for this myth of the *Parti de l'intelligence* was widespread until the 1980s.

The relationship between the PCI and intellectuals appears to be more complex than in the case of the PCF, even if it can be argued that there were similarities between the two parties. Thus, a striking similarity could be found in the fact that the PCI also had its own publishing empire, which was comparable to the PCF one in a number of ways. It first of all included a number of publishing houses, of which the most influential was Editori Riuniti, equivalent to the French Editions Sociales, and a vast number of publications, such as *L'Unità* (daily organ), *Rinascita* (a monthly until 1962, when it became a weekly), *Politica ed Economia*, *Studi Storici*, *Il Contemporaneo*, *Nuova Rivista Internazionale*, and so on.[69] Moreover, the PCI was also able to rely on a huge market made of numerous municipal libraries, hundreds of thousands of Party members and millions of backers, and the lucrative market of the socialist countries, so that its publications were assured healthy sales figures until the 1980s.

The existence of a publishing empire and of a myriad of Party intellectuals in the PCI (Verdès-Leroux's distinction between Party intellectuals and autonomous ones can equally be applied to the PCI) seems to indicate that the PCI controlled vast financial and publishing resources which enabled it to develop a clientelistic relationship with a number of intellectuals, as in the case of the PCF. Moreover, there is evidence to suggest that, at least in the 1940s and 1950s, any strong dissent on behalf of the 'client' led to a rift in the clientelistic relationship, as can be illustrated by the case of the post-war communist monthly *Il Politecnico* (see above).

However, a number of contrasts between the two parties would suggest that there was a difference in the scale of the clientelistic relationships fostered by both parties.

First of all, it seems that there was no equivalent to Aragon's empire in the Italian case: there were, of course, a number of communist writers in Italy, but none reached the mythical dimension of the poet laureate of the PCF. As Nello Ajello argues in his study of Italian communist intellectuals, despite the onerous constraints imposed on intellectuals during the years of Zhdanovism (1947 to the early 1950s) in Italy as well as in France, no Italian poet was inclined or forced to emulate Aragon's various Odes to his Party or to Maurice Thorez. In fact, Ajello suggests that a telling contrast between the two parties could be found in an issue of the PCI monthly *Rinascita* dated January 1945. It had published a translation of Aragon's *Ode to My Party*, most typical of the French poet's commitment to lauding his Party ('My Party, My Party, I thank you for your lessons'), and, on the next page, a poem by communist poet Umberto Saba on the Liberation of Florence. While both pieces were obviously politically committed, Ajello makes a clear distinction between the two poets – Aragon was content to flatter his Party in a simplistic style, while Saba was lauding the courage of Italian partisans in a moving poem – and argues explicitly that an Italian equivalent to Aragon would have been very hard to find.[70]

Secondly, the contribution of socialist realist painters and sculptors to the decorating of public buildings in communist towns, which became all too evident in any French communist municipality in the 1940s and 1950s, can scarcely be found in towns such as Reggio, Bologna or Modena, where artistic creation seemed to follow much more classical inspiration.

Thirdly, when it comes to the role of intellectuals, there is no PCI equivalent to the PCF so-called 'watershed of Argenteuil' (see above). The very fact that the PCI leadership did not feel the need to officialise the creative autonomy of artists and intellectuals in their own fields can be interpreted as a sign that such autonomy had *de facto* been granted at a much earlier stage, possibly as early as at the Ninth Congress of the PCI (1960). These elements combine to suggest that PCI intellectuals were much more autonomous than their French counterparts, or, at the very least, that they were not submitted to the same level of suspicion and were not always on probation.

It therefore seems that the policies of the PCF and PCI towards their intellectuals diverged to a certain extent, especially after the beginning of the 1950s, when the PCI started to use its intellectuals to harness Gramsci's work in order to legitimise the new course of action taken by the Party (the *via nazionale*), whereas the French communists remained faithful to orthodox, Soviet-style Marxism–Leninism.

Cultural policy and 'image-making'

The second concept which can be used in the study of cultural policies is the concept of 'image-making', or 'shop window effect'. This was used by both parties and aimed at creating a positive image outside the Party, and various means were used to this effect.

First of all, the two parties had among their ranks a number of intellectuals who performed a significant political role. Writing about the PCI, Gundle argues that communist intellectuals 'identified the party with high culture, won it prestige, gave it a high profile, and assisted the conquest of a substantial measure of influence among intellectuals and in the arts', thus performing a function of political legitimation of the PCI in

Italian cultural circles.[71] A similar image-making factor was the way in which both parties constantly sought recognition from bourgeois institutions, through the award of literary prizes, and so on. In a pamphlet published in the late 1970s, Hélène Parmelin, a journalist and cultural critic at *L'Humanité*, wrote:

> We [communists] adore official awards, medals, we praise all that is praised. A crown on a communist, and we go into a trance. Especially when it is not us who do the praising, but the *Figaro*. Which proves – or seems to prove – that this is not just a Party view, or a view harnessed by the Party, but that it is the truth.[72]

This example shows that the PCF was keen to see its intellectuals and artists recognised by the bourgeois world (the *Figaro* is, to the PCF, the archetype of bourgeois and conservative press), for it contributed to the making of a positive image outside the ranks of the Party. This also explains why, with communist artists such as Picasso or Aragon, the PCF was ready to accept a few infringements of its dogmatic line, insofar as these artists did not go beyond certain limits.

Secondly, both parties strove to attract fellow-travellers who would temporarily and/or occasionally support some of their views through the signing of a petition, a manifesto or an appeal, or through the publication of works conciliatory towards communism. These fellow-travellers were a great asset to the two parties because of the fact that they were not party members. This meant that they could not stand accused of being Moscow agents or court scribes in the bourgeois press, and it could be argued that fellow-travellers, because of their independence, were in fact much more useful to communist propaganda than Party intellectuals – a point argued by several scholars.[73]

Many examples of fellow-travellers can be found in France, from André Gide in the 1930s to Jean-Paul Sartre in the 1950s and 1960s. The latter was particularly useful in the struggle against anti-communism in 1950s France ('Je dis qu'un anticommuniste est un chien', 'To me, an anti-communist is a dog'). He also helped the PCF conceal the dark realities of 'really existing socialism'. When asked about human rights violations in the socialist bloc, Sartre once replied: 'il ne faut pas désespérer Billancourt', by which he meant that one did not want to reveal the true nature of these regimes in order not to disillusion the working class (Billancourt, the famous Renault factory, was for decades a stronghold of communism in France). Party propagandists could not have done a better job.

The PCI also enjoyed the company of a number of fellow-travellers such as writer and film-maker Pasolini, or film-maker Zavattini, who contributed to enhancing the prestige of the Party in Italian society.

The concept of image-making was also present in the cultural policies of communist municipalities in both countries, as is discussed in Chapters 5 and 6.

Cultural policy and hegemony

The third main concept used in this comparative study of the cultural policies of the PCF and the PCI is the concept of hegemony, developed by Italian philosopher and PCI founder Antonio Gramsci.

While there is no scope here to provide the reader with yet another attempt to interpret or reinterpret Gramsci's concept of hegemony, which is – like Gramsci's political thought in general – the object of numerous scholarly studies,[74] this section gives a working definition of this concept which will be used in the two case studies, and examines the harnessing of Gramsci's legacy by PCI leaders since the late 1940s.

A good starting point for the definition of the concept of hegemony can be found in Gramsci's *Prison Notebooks*, in which he wrote: '[an] analysis of the balance of forces – at all levels – can only culminate in the sphere of hegemony and ethico-political relations'.[75]

With this concept, Gramsci thought he would be able to understand why, in a given society, the ruling class was accepted as such by the other social strata, why a sufficient level of consent had been achieved by the elite to maintain its position of power. He then came to the conclusion that, before any major process of socio-political change could take place, it was necessary for a social group, or an alliance of groups, to achieve a sufficient level of ideological hegemony in society. It could be argued that, to Gramsci, the notion of class struggle was not primarily of an economic nature, but was in essence rooted in political and ideological fields.

Thus, whereas for Lenin and his followers the revolutionary process was to precede and impose the hegemony of the ruling party in the cultural/ideological field, Gramsci expressed the idea that, because the situation was not ripe for a revolution in Italy at the end of the First World War and in the early 1920s, the PCI had to adopt a strategy different to that of the Bolshevik Party in Russia. In this analysis, Gramsci had clearly drawn the lessons of the patent failure of the revolutionary factory councils movement in Turin, which had taken place in the late 1910s and in which he had played a significant role.[76] This failure was to prove highly influential on Gramsci's political strategy. He therefore advocated, in a famous military metaphor, a long-term strategy of 'war of position', as opposed to a violent 'war of movement', that is to say a frontal assault on the political institutions. The war of position meant that the PCI had to progressively disseminate communist ideas among the population in order to pave the way for a large, popular consensus around its ideas, at which stage the Party would become an acceptable ruling force. Thus, the aim of the war of position was to gain hegemony in the cultural and intellectual spheres.

What remains highly controversial, of course, is the issue of the Party's strategy once this status of hegemony was achieved. Thus, some scholars argue that Gramsci envisaged a revolutionary process (war of movement) aimed at creating a Bolshevik-style society, while others emphasise the democratic nature of Gramsci's political thought.[77]

In fact, leaving aside the substantial debate around the interpretation of Gramsci's ideas, there is ample evidence that the PCI, in the late 1940s, embarked on a process of harnessing Gramsci's legacy for reasons of political expediency.[78] This is acknowledged by virtually every specialist of Gramsci and/or Italian politics. British journalist Matt Frei, for instance, summarises this process as follows:

> Some chose to see the *Notebooks* as a celebration of Stalinism, others as an affirmation of a watered-down socialism. In any case, Gramsci was dissected and borrowed to underpin whichever line the Party's leadership chose to paper over the cracks.[79]

The same point is made, albeit in more academic style, by Benedetto Fontana: 'Gramsci's writing became the source through which the postwar politics of the Italian communists could be theoretically justified and ideologically legitimated.'[80]

Moreover, in ideological terms, Stephen Gundle writes that Gramsci played a symbolic role by 'deflecting attention away from Marxism–Leninism and the cultural models of the Soviet Union under Stalin', an argument also put forward by Albertina Vittoria who points out that the main objective of the cultural policy of Togliatti in the late 1950s, when the Gramsci Institutes were created, was to assert the specific nature of Italian Marxism against the Marxist–Leninist orthodoxy embodied by the USSR.[81]

In fact, it can be argued that the PCI used the concept of hegemony to enhance its national credentials by playing Gramsci against Lenin. Thus, by claiming that, according to Gramsci, hegemony and consent had to precede the transition to a communist society, the PCI was able to assert, even if only by implication, that it did not have to follow Lenin's revolutionary model, in which the hegemony of the Party followed the revolution. The PCI leadership, from Togliatti to Berlinguer, played the card of the specific, Italian nature of Gramsci's thought in order to distance their party from Soviet dogma. Togliatti, as already noted, resorted to the writings of his late comrade to substantiate his strategy of *via italiana*. Approximately 20 years later, when faced with the arduous task of justifying his strategy of 'historic compromise', Berlinguer also borrowed from Gramsci's legacy, especially the concept of the 'historical bloc'.

In France and in Italy, various means were used to attempt to establish the hegemony of the communist parties in civil society. One of these was the organisation of numerous conferences and events involving non-communist intellectuals.

In France, a good example of such a policy was the *Semaines de la pensée marxiste*, created in the early 1960s under the auspices of the Centre d'Etudes et de Recherches Marxistes (the CERM, created by the Fifteenth Congress in 1959), which became the Institut Maurice Thorez after the death of the PCF Secretary-General in 1964. The debates of the *Semaines de la pensée marxiste* were organised by Roger Garaudy, who was then the official Party philosopher (he was in 1966 replaced by Lucien Sève and was eventually expelled in 1970) and an exponent of dialogue and exchanges between Marxists and Christians.

The *Semaines* were 'big shows in which the Communist Party tried to demonstrate its power, its influence, by inviting famous intellectuals, of all opinions, with the exception of intellectuals who were self-proclaimed Marxists'.[82] Thus, famous guests at the *Semaines* included Jean Fourastié in 1961 (Fourastié was a leading economist expert on socio-economic change in post-war France; his most famous book remains *Les Trente Glorieuses* (The Thirty Glorious Years)), Alfred Grosser in 1963 (a Germanist and political scientist) and René Rémond in 1974 (a famous French historian and political scientist, of Christian democratic convictions, author of *Les Droites en France* (The Right Wing in France)). What the PCF tried to achieve through such events was certainly hegemony, by demonstrating its will to confront other ideologies and at the same time accepting – or pretending to accept – the fact that there could be a dialogue between these and Marxism–Leninism. It can be argued that this strategy of cultural/intellectual hegemony was successful to a large extent until the mid-1970s, and can be illustrated by two examples.

First, at the time of the fierce public controversy which followed the publication in France of the *Gulag Archipelago*, in 1973–74, a number of progressive Christians joined the PCF in its attacks against Solzhenitsyn, who was portrayed in *La Lettre* (a left-wing Christian periodical) as a 'pure product of czarism', 'a petty bourgeois who reacts like a petty bourgeois',[83] echoing the *ad hominem* nature of PCF diatribes against the Soviet dissident. This strongly suggests that the PCF had managed to instil 'Sovietophilia' in broad circles of the French intelligentsia, or at least that criticism of the Soviet Union as a socio-political system was a sort of taboo in France until the mid-1970s. Similarly, the French daily *Le Monde*, originally known for its political independence inherited from its founder Hubert Beuve-Méry, was seen, under its chief editor Jacques Fauvet, to be quite sympathetic to French communists, to the extent that some suggested that Fauvet was in the 1970s a 'neo-fellow-traveller'.[84]

The PCI also engaged in such activities in the same period, though it could be argued that the dialogue with other ideologies – especially the Christian one – was much more constructive and genuine than in the French case. In fact, similar activities to the *Semaines de la pensée marxiste* were organised by the various Gramsci Institutes created in a number of Italian towns in the early 1960s, and even smaller municipalities such as Reggio Emilia, which never had a Gramsci Institute, created a philosophy centre in the second half of the 1960s (see Chapter 6).

As a result of this strategy of 'hegemony-seeking', the PCI held until the early 1990s a position of hegemony in academic circles with regard to, for instance, the interpretation of the history of the Resistance and the War of Liberation (1943–45), as noted in Chapter 1.

Communist parties as producers of symbols

The fourth concept used in this study is the concept of 'identity-making' through the use of symbols and symbol-producing institutions. In his *Politics and Symbols*, David Kertzer, drawing inspiration from the works of Pierre Bourdieu and Michel Foucault on the complex nature of power, argues that the creation and use of symbols are at the core of politics: '[At] its roots, politics is symbolic, because both the formation of human groupings and the hierarchy that spring from them depend on symbolic activity.'[85]

Even if Kertzer's overall assumption that politics is all about symbols is questionable, several of the issues he discusses are worth exploring in this study of the cultural policies of the PCF and PCI. First of all, Kertzer examines the question of the creation of political symbols: why and how does a political party create symbols? He then examines the role of the (re)writing of history by a party such as the PCI, and argues that history is used by the Party to legitimate its political strategy at any given time. Second, Kertzer argues that these symbols are used by the Party to create a strong sense of identity, of belonging together against other political groupings: 'us versus them',[86] 'fascists versus anti-fascists', 'communists versus Catholics',[87] and so on. Kertzer then proceeds to examine the process of the dissemination of symbols and myths in the collective memory of the communist rank and file, and identifies various means and rituals used to this effect. These include the discourse and language of the Party, its festivals, the anniversaries it chooses to commemorate (1917, 1945), the social gatherings (sporting events, Gramsci clubs in Italy, where people meet to talk, play cards and drink wine and coffee), lay rites such as communist funerals, and of course the cultural policies of the Party.

This analysis can usefully be complemented by the framework designed by Marie-Claire Lavabre in her study of the collective memory of the French communists. In this work, Lavabre discusses the concept of memory as a main constituent of any collective identity. She first discerns three concepts, three different memories. First of all, she identifies the notion of 'living memory' (*mémoire vive*), that is to say the memory of individual communists, embracing 'real' memories (e.g. the memories of an older communist who took part in the Resistance), 'transmitted' memories (e.g. memories passed on from one generation to the other) and 'learnt' memories (e.g. the knowledge of history acquired through various media, such as the school, the Party historiography, etc.).[88] The author then proceeds to identify the existence of an 'historical' or 'official memory' (*mémoire historique* or *officielle*), which is presented as the memory produced by the Party through its historians, its publications, its mass-celebrations, such as the *Fête de l'Humanité* and its mythology.[89] In other words, the historical memory embraces symbols and a manner of interpreting history generated by the Party and is the outcome of a dedicated enterprise to rewrite the past, the history of the Party, in order to legitimate its present path or strategy.

Last, Lavabre introduces the notion of 'collective memory' which according to her is the mental sphere where the two previous memories can meet and correlate to compound a shared intellectual and emotional field, where there is a sense of community, where the socialisation of communists operates. In other words, a group of individuals share a sense of identity ('I am a French communist') thanks to the permanence of a collective memory composed both of individual memories and of fragments of official memory interiorised by the individuals forming the group.[90]

The thesis which is central to the book, however, is that the collective memory of PCF members cannot be strictly equated to the official memory produced by the Party. In other words, the author argues that the collective memory of PCF members is not restricted to the official history of the PCF, that the latter cannot be imposed on individuals and that this identity-strengthening collective memory can only exist when and where the official memory interacts with the living memories of the French communists.

In other words, Lavabre argues that the Party is not the one and only producer of memory and that the activists will necessarily have fragments of their living memories induced by non-Party sources. This is the case, for instance, with the way French communists 'recollect' the French Revolution of 1789: Lavabre shows that French communists were not always inclined to espouse or retain the official Party interpretation, focused on the concept of a bourgeois revolution, and that they tend to prefer the national, republican rendition of 1789 learnt at school.[91]

In fact, Lavabre's work seems to suggest that, in order to forge a strong, collective identity within a group, a political party needs to produce an official history which will overlap with the living memories of the individuals of this group.

The main appeal of Lavabre's model is that it can be applied to some aspects of the cultural policies of communist parties. It is therefore stimulating to try to apply these notions to answer the following questions: what specific means did the PCF and PCI use in their attempt to create a strong collective memory? To what extent do these parties' official histories and favourite symbols differ from one another? A detailed examination of the cultural policies of the PCF and PCI in Ivry and Reggio will provide tentative answers to these crucial questions.

CONCLUSION

The first aim of this chapter was to outline the highly political, instrumentalist nature of the cultural policies of the French and Italian Communist Parties. Both parties always saw culture and cultural activities as an integral part of their overall political strategy, and their respective cultural policies evolved with their strategies. Similarly, they were subjected to the onerous constraints of the Zhdanovist credo of socialist realism in the late 1940s and early 1950s. This substantiates the argument made in Chapter 1 that, despite a series of contrasts (e.g. the PCF maintained a higher degree of political control over its intellectuals than the PCI), these parties have to be studied as phenomena situated at the junction between a national, societal dimension and an international, teleological one.

The second aim of this chapter was to provide a comparative, strategic framework based on a number of key concepts, such as clientelism, image-making, hegemony and identity/symbol production. These concepts can usefully be applied to the study of the cultural policies of the PCF and the PCI at the local, micro-political level.

NOTES

1 P. Ory, *La Belle Illusion: Culture et politique sous le signe du Front populaire, 1935–1938* (Paris: Plon, 1994), p. 12.

2 J.M. Djian, *La Politique culturelle* (Paris: Le Monde-Editions, 1997), p. 11.

3 D. Looseley, *The Politics of Fun: Cultural Policy and Debate in Contemporary France* (Oxford: Berg, 1995).

4 Gundle's seminal study was first published in Italian: S. Gundle, *I comunisti italiani tra Hollywood e Mosca: la sfida della cultura di massa (1943–1991)* (Florence: Giunti, 1995). It was then published in 2000 in English: Gundle, *Between Hollywood and Moscow*.

5 Gundle, *Between Hollywood and Moscow*, p. 6.

6 For a recent synthesis of the debate on the concept of culture in the social sciences, see for instance A. Kuper, *Culture: The Anthropologists' Account* (Cambridge, MA: Harvard University Press, 1999).

7 Djian, *La Politique culturelle*, pp. 17–18.

8 Ory, *La Belle Illusion*, p. 12.

9 P. Nizan, *Pour une nouvelle culture* (Paris: Grasset, 1971), pp. 26–7.

10 J.P. Bernard, *Le PCF et la question littéraire, 1921–1939* (Grenoble: Presses Universitaires de Grenoble, 1972), p. 10.

11 Ibid., p. 64.

12 L. Aragon, *La Culture et les hommes* (Paris: Editions Sociales, 1947), p. 8.

13 J. Verdès-Leroux, *Au service du Parti: Le Parti communiste, les intellectuels et la culture (1944–1956)* (Paris: Fayard/Minuit, 1983), pp. 198–208.

14 N. Ajello, *Intelletuali e PCI, 1944–1958* (Bari: Laterza, 1979), pp. 34–5.

15 Ibid., p. 35.

16 N. Werth, *Histoire de l'Union Soviétique* (Paris: Presses Universitaires de France, 1999), p. 383.

17 For a detailed, eyewitness account of the staunch criticism faced by both parties at this meeting, see E. Reale, *Avec Jacques Duclos au banc des accusés à la réunion constitutive du Cominform à Szklarska Poreba* (Paris: Plon, 1958).

18 Verdès-Leroux, *Au service du Parti*.

19 L. Casanova, 'Responsabilités de l'intellectuel', in 'Rapport aux intellectuels communistes, salle Wagram, 28 February 1949', *La Nouvelle Critique*, March (1949), p. 31, quoted in Lazar, *Maisons rouges*, p. 70.

20 Gundle, *Between Hollywood and Moscow*, p. 25.

21 For a detailed account of the Vittorini/*Politecnico* case, see Ajello, *Intelletuali e PCI*, pp. 113–37. For a shorter account in English, see Gundle, *Between Hollywood and Moscow*, pp. 28–30.

22 Ajello, *Intelletuali e PCI*, p. 143. See also Gundle, *Between Hollywood and Moscow*, p. 48.

23 For a portrait of Sereni, see Ajello, *Intelletuali e PCI*, pp. 147–51. See also Gundle, *Between Hollywood and Moscow*, p. 49.

24 Lazar, *Maisons rouges*, p. 73.

25 On the role of Togliatti's *alter ego* in the early 1950s, see Ajello, *Intelletuali e PCI*, pp. 257–9, and Gundle, *Between Hollywood and Moscow*, p. 50.

26 Gundle, *I comunisti italiani tra Hollywood e Mosca*, p. 213.

27 Gundle, *Between Hollywood and Moscow*, p. 119.

28 Togliatti is quoted in Gundle, *Between Hollywood and Moscow*, p. 119.

29 For an excellent summary of this debate, see J. Verdès-Leroux, *Le Réveil des somnambules: Le Parti communiste, les intellectuels et la culture (1956–1985)* (Paris: Fayard/Minuit, 1987), pp. 113–27.

30 Ibid., p. 119.

31 Lazar, *Maisons rouges*, p. 126.

32 Verdès-Leroux, *Le Réveil des somnambules*, pp. 112–27.

33 H. Parmelin, *Libérez les communistes* (Paris: Stock, 1979), p. 249.

34 R. Leroy, *La Culture au présent* (Paris: Editions Sociales, 1972), p. 32.

35 Ibid., p. 98.

36 P.P. D'Attorre (ed.), *I comunisti in Emilia-Romagna: Documenti e materiali* (Bologna: Gramsci Institute, 1981), p. 286.

37 Scott is quoted in J. Chubb, *Patronage, Power and Poverty in Southern Italy: A Tale of Two Cities* (Cambridge: Cambridge University Press, 1982), p. 4.

38 Ibid., p. 4.

39 Allum, *Politics and Society in Post-War Naples*, p. 160.

40 A. Donneur and J. Padioleau, 'Local Clientelism in Post-Industrial Society: The Example of the French Communist Party', *European Journal of Political Research*, 10, 1 (1982), pp. 71–82.

41 Verdès-Leroux, *Au service du Parti*, p. 21.

42 Ibid., p. 21.

43 Ajello, *Intelletuali e PCI*, p. vi.

44 See Verdès-Leroux, *Au service du Parti*, pp. 19–21.

45 For a detailed account of Prenant's relationship with the PCF, see his memoirs: M. Prenant, *Toute une vie à gauche* (Paris: Encre Editions, 1980).

46 For a detailed account of the rise and fall of Fougeron, see M. Lazar, 'Le réalisme socialiste aux couleurs de la France', in M. Winock (ed.), *Le Temps de la guerre froide* (Paris: Le Seuil, 1994), pp. 191–210. See also D. Berthet, *Le PCF, la culture et l'art (1947–1954)* (Paris: La Table Ronde, 1990), pp. 162–73.

47 Lazar, 'Le réalisme socialiste aux couleurs de la France', pp. 201–3.

48 For a detailed account of the 'Portrait of Stalin affair', see, for instance, Desanti, *Les Staliniens*, p. 376, or Verdès-Leroux, *Au service du Parti*, pp. 305–8.

49 *L'Humanité*, 15 September 1998.

50 Interview with André Fougeron, in Winock (ed.), *Le Temps de la guerre froide*, p. 140.

51 For a critique of Stil's *Premier Choc*, see Verdès-Leroux, *Au service du Parti*, p. 273.

52 For an insightful, if at times complacent, biography of Aragon, see P. Daix, *Aragon, une vie à changer* (Paris: Le Seuil, 1975). For a short, critical account of Aragon's work and political life, see Verdès-Leroux, *Le Réveil des somnambules*, pp. 356–64.

53 J.P. Bernard, *Paris rouge, 1944–1964: Les communistes français dans la capitale* (Seyssel: Champ Vallon, 1991), p. 182.

54 L. de Villefosse, *L'Oeuf de Wyasma* (Paris: Julliard, 1962), pp. 207–8.

55 J. Verdès-Leroux, *Refus et violences: Politique et littérature à l'extrême droite des années 1930 aux retombées de la Libération* (Paris: Gallimard, 1996), p. 7.

56 Desanti, *Les Staliniens*, pp. 109–11.

57 Verdès-Leroux, *Au service du Parti*, pp. 198–200.

58 R. de Jouvenel, *Confidences d'un ancien sous-marin du PCF* (Paris: Julliard, 1980), p. 60.

59 The full text of Aragon's *Ode au Guépéou* can be found in Courtois (ed.), *Le Livre noir du communisme*, pp. 356–7.

[60] D. Desanti, *Les Aragonautes: Les cercles du poète disparu* (Paris: Calmann-Lévy, 1997), p. 239.

[61] Verdès-Leroux, *Le Réveil des somnambules*, p. 285.

[62] Ibid., p. 363.

[63] Ibid., p. 358.

[64] P. Daix, *J'ai cru au matin* (Paris: Laffont, 1976), p. 201.

[65] D. Caute, *The Fellow-Travellers: A Postscript to Enlightenment* (London: Weidenfeld & Nicolson, 1973), p. 12.

[66] Ibid., p. 13.

[67] Daix, *J'ai cru au matin*, p. 423.

[68] J. Verdès-Leroux, 'Qui a signé l'Appel de Stockholm?', in Winock (ed.), *Le Temps de la guerre froide*, p. 114.

[69] Shore, *Italian Communism: The Escape from Leninism*, p. 12.

[70] Ajello, *Intelletuali e PCI*, pp. 52–3.

[71] Gundle, *Between Hollywood and Moscow*, p. 21.

[72] Parmelin, *Libérez les communistes*, p. 162.

[73] See, for instance, Caute, *The Fellow-Travellers*.

[74] For a very comprehensive study of this concept, see, for instance, J. Martin, 'Gramsci and Political Analysis: Hegemony and Legitimacy' (PhD dissertation, Bristol University, 1993).

[75] D. Forgacs, *A Gramsci Reader: Selected Writings, 1916–1935* (London: Lawrence & Wishart, 1988), p. 217.

[76] On the Turin factory councils and their failure, see M. Clarke, *Antonio Gramsci and the Revolution that Failed* (New Haven, CT: Yale University Press, 1977).

[77] For a useful summary of this controversy, see B. Fontana, *Hegemony and Power: On the Relation between Gramsci and Machiavelli* (Minneapolis, MN: University of Minnesota Press, 1993), pp. 3–6.

[78] The best synthesis on the harnessing of Gramsci's legacy by Togliatti in the 1940s and 1950s is probably S. Gundle, 'The Legacy of the Prison Notebooks: Gramsci, the PCI and Italian Culture in the Cold War Period', in C. Duggan and C. Wagstaff (eds), *Italy in the Cold War: Politics, Culture and Society, 1948–1958* (Oxford: Berg, 1995), pp. 131–47.

[79] M. Frei, *Italy: The Unfinished Revolution* (London: Mandarin, 1997), p. 54.

[80] Fontana, *Hegemony and Power*, p. 3.

[81] Gundle, *Between Hollywood and Moscow*, p. 19. A. Vittoria, *Togliatti e gli intelletuali: Storia dell'Istituto Gramsci negli anni cinquanta e sessanta* (Rome: Editori Riuniti, 1992), pp. xxii–xxvii.

[82] Verdès-Leroux, *Le Réveil des somnambules*, p. 113.

[83] M. Winock, *Le Siècle des intellectuels* (Paris: Le Seuil, 1999), p. 745.

[84] Ibid., p. 749. Also, as already noted in Chapter 1, Fauvet had in the 1960s written a fairly complacent history of the PCF.

[85] Kertzer, *Politics and Symbols*, p. 4.

[86] On the issue of 'us' versus 'them', see also Shore, 'Ethnicity as Revolutionary Strategy', pp. 27–53.

[87] On this issue, see also Kertzer, *Comrades and Christians*.

[88] Lavabre, *Le Fil rouge*, pp. 12–20.

[89] On the *Fête de l'Humanité* and its mythology, see N. Gérôme and D. Tartakowsky, *La Fête de l'Humanité: Culture communiste, culture populaire* (Paris: Messidor/Editions Sociales, 1988).

[90] Lavabre, *Le Fil rouge*, pp. 12–20.

[91] Ibid., pp. 68–88.

5

Ideology and Clientelism in the Cultural Policy of the PCF in Ivry-sur-Seine (*c*. 1965–*c*. 1985)

Following the comparative discussion of the cultural policies of the French and Italian Communist Parties and of a number of related concepts, this chapter presents the first of the two case studies which form the core survey of this study. Accordingly, attention will turn now to the efforts and resources deployed by the PCF in Ivry-sur-Seine between the mid-1960s and the mid-1980s in the field of culture.

A brief presentation of Ivry as a typical stronghold of French communism and of the main institutional protagonists at the local level is followed by a detailed discussion of various cultural amenities and activities implemented by the PCF in this red municipality.

IVRY-SUR-SEINE: A TYPICAL STRONGHOLD OF FRENCH COMMUNISM

Ivry-sur-Seine: historical and socio-economic background

Ivry-sur-Seine is a medium-sized town situated on the banks of the Seine river in the southern suburbs of Paris, in the French department of Val-de-Marne (see Figure 5.1).

Its population, of 60,000 or so inhabitants in the early 1980s, has remained generally stable in the past 30 years.

The town has a long history of industrialisation which started in the 1880s when a number of firms established themselves near its fluvial harbour, Ivry-Port, and by the 1930s it was the town with the highest number of industrial firms in the whole suburban area around Paris. In 1954, there were in Ivry seven firms employing at least 500 workers each. While there was no high degree of industrial specialisation as there was in neighbouring Vitry, where Rhône-Poulenc had a major chemical plant,

Figure 5.1   Map of the Paris 'red belt'

the main industries found in Ivry were metallurgical plants, foodstuffs and chemical plants.[1]

As a result of this high degree of industrialisation, Ivry's population was predominantly a working-class one. The 1931 national census found that 66 per cent of all the Ivryens were industrial workers, a percentage which was still over 50 per cent in the early 1960s.[2] From an architectural and housing point of view, Ivry is characterised by a number of tower blocks, which were built between the 1930s and the mid-1970s, and are typical of the French communists' predilection for modernist or postmodernist architecture. This emphasis on concentrated housing was by no means devoid of any political connotation, as it was to make it easier for the PCF to control the local population and to ensure that Ivry remained one of its chief bastions.[3]

'Ivry-la-Rouge' (Red Ivry): the showcase of French municipal communism

According to many observers, Ivry-sur-Seine is one of the most typical French communist municipalities: 'Held by the Party for more than 60 years without any interruption other than the Second World War, the town quickly became one of the shop windows of municipal communism.'[4]

This view is echoed by Paul Thorez, son of Maurice Thorez, in his somewhat cynical recollections of his youth: 'Our good town [was] a true state within the state, a sort of people's democracy in the French Republic, the prefiguration of a socialist regime French-style, as claimed on every street corner by the street name plaques.'[5]

As in the case of Reggio Emilia (see Chapter 6), Ivry had elected socialist mayors at the end of the nineteenth century (Ferdinand Roussel, elected in 1896, was the first-ever left-wing mayor of Ivry) and in the early years of the twentieth century (Jules Coutant, another socialist, who was elected in 1908, was nicknamed the 'Emperor of Ivry').[6]

A few years after the split which divided the French left at the Tours Congress of December 1920 and led to the creation of the PCF, Ivry was one of the first French municipalities to be won by the communists in 1925. The new mayor, Georges Marrane (1888–1976), was to remain in charge of the municipality until 1965, when he retired from politics, with the interruption of the Second World War (1939–44) during which all communist mayors were removed from office. In 1965, Jacques Laloë (b.1930), a younger PCF activist, replaced Marrane as mayor of Ivry. He was 'close to Georges Marchais',[7] the then rising star of the PCF who was to become the PCF leader in 1972 and whose constituency was in the Val-de-Marne department, in what appears to have been a wider strategy of retiring older mayors in this area in order to make way for a new generation of office-holders who owed their promotion to Marchais. For instance, Marcel Trigon, who became the communist mayor of Arcueil (a town also situated in Val-de-Marne) in 1964, was chosen by Marchais to succeed Marius Sidobre, an older communist who belonged to the same generation as Marrane.[8] Jacques Laloë was to remain the mayor of Ivry until December 1998, when he was replaced by Pierre Gosnat, a member of a well-known PCF dynasty.[9]

Electoral results at municipal elections, held every six years on a two-ballot majority system, confirm the notion of 'Ivry-la-Rouge' as a bastion of French communism. Thus, the PCF-led list usually attracted an impressive absolute majority of the votes at the first ballot, with scores of 79 per cent in 1965, 77 per cent in 1971, 85 per cent in 1977, 77 per cent in 1983 and 79 per cent in 1989. It was only in 1995, after a 30-year period of deindustrialisation and for the first time in 70 years, that the PCF did not obtain an absolute majority at the first ballot and had to go to the second ballot to secure election.[10] Notwithstanding some rather strange electoral practices in the case of communist municipalities in general and in the case of Ivry in particular,[11] these results indicate that Ivry was a PCF bastion for over 70 years.

Moreover, Ivry was – and still is – a model of PCF orthodoxy. Marrane, who ruled over Ivry for 40 years, was an orthodox communist who was described as the 'reference office-holder for communist municipalities'.[12] Indeed, Ivry never experienced any local dissidence from elected office-holders, unlike other municipalities such as Saint-Denis, whose mayor Jacques Doriot was excluded from the PCF in 1934 for breaching the Comintern line of 'class against class' and proposing an alliance with other left-wing parties. Indeed, Ivry was symbolically chosen as the municipality in which the national PCF conference of June 1934 condemning Doriot's 'deviance' was held. Other examples of dissidence from PCF mayors can be found in Gennevilliers under the mayorship of Lucien Lanternier[13] or in a number of other towns.[14]

The persistent orthodoxy of Ivry is undoubtedly the result of the strict political tutelage of the PCF national leadership. In fact, Ivry became in the 1930s the electoral fiefdom of PCF Secretary-General Maurice Thorez, who remained the MP for this constituency until his death in 1964. In an anecdotal, yet telling account of his years as a PCF activist, Gérard Belloin writes that Thorez's involvement in the running of Ivry went as far as the regular monitoring of the menu of the local school canteens.[15] The late Thorez was then replaced by Georges Gosnat (1914–1982), another PCF leader who as national treasurer of the Party had a key influence in national as well as local PCF politics.[16] He was the son of Venise Gosnat (1894–1972), another French communist who had already been active in securing the PCF hold on Ivry in the late 1920s and early 1930s.[17] It is also worth pointing out that Pierre Gosnat (b.1948), the son of Georges and grandson of Venise, replaced Jacques Laloë as mayor in December 1998.

It can therefore be argued that Ivry mayors have constantly been under the tight supervision of the PCF national leadership, a control summarised by Pronier in his study of French communist municipalities:

> The preposterous example of a mayor under supervision [*tutelle*, in the French text] is undoubtedly that of Jacques Laloë in Ivry. All the close observers of the political life in Ivry agree in recognising the crucial role played for a very long time by Georges Gosnat in municipal affairs. Treasurer of the PCF and MP for the constituency of Ivry, he was in fact the real mayor of this town.[18]

This obvious involvement of highly influential members of the central apparatus of the Party and of the Val-de-Marne federation – itself one of the most powerful departmental federations of the PCF – in the local affairs of Ivry-sur-Seine makes this town a particularly relevant basis for a case study of the implementation at the local level of the policies of the PCF. Therefore, the assumption on which this case study operates is that the municipal teams of Ivry have constantly tried to implement in their town the policies decided by the PCF for its municipalities. This means that assessing the policies implemented by the municipality of Ivry in a particular field amounts to assessing the policies elaborated by the highest decision-making level of the PCF.

CULTURAL POLICY-MAKING, CONTROL AND POLITICAL ORTHODOXY IN IVRY

In order to outline and understand the developments of the cultural policy of Ivry between 1965 and 1985, a brief presentation of the decision-making actors and institutions behind this policy is useful. At the highest level of the decision-making process at municipal level was the communist mayor, Jacques Laloë, who was subjected to the Party's close supervision. Just below him was the assistant mayor in charge of cultural affairs who was, in the case of Ivry, a very influential politician. In this municipality, there were between 10 and 12 assistant mayors (*adjoints au maire*), and there appeared to be a sort of hierarchy amongst them (similar to the hierarchy existing amongst the ministers of a given cabinet) – a hierarchy quite noticeable in the local press. In fact, assistant mayors were often referred to as the 'first assistant mayor' or the 'third assistant mayor'. In the Ivryen hierarchy, the assistant mayor in charge of cultural activities was usually in third or fourth position in this hierarchy, but it should be noted that the same assistant mayor was in charge of both education and cultural activities.

The assistant mayor for cultural affairs headed the Service Municipal des Affaires Culturelles (Municipal Department for Cultural Affairs), which was created in 1966 and whose task was to co-ordinate the planning of all municipal cultural activities in Ivry and to liaise with all the local voluntary associations (*Associations loi 1901* or non-profit-making associations) such as the *ciné-club*, the *photo-club*, the philatelic association, etc. Most of these non-profit-making associations were gathered in the Centre Culturel Ivryen, created in 1962, when a large group of communist municipalities met to create the Fédération Nationale des Centres Culturels. From 1965, the honorary president of the Centre Culturel Ivryen was Laloë and the Centre was exclusively funded by the municipality, so the question of its independence appeared to be a problematic one, as was the question of the relationship between the municipality and the local voluntary associations.

It seems that some of these associations (for instance, the *ciné-club*, the philatelic association, the *photo-club*, the Union des Artistes d'Ivry, the geology club) received in 1980 financial contributions from the municipality, but that some others did not. What were the criteria used by the communists to decide whom to subsidise or whom not to subsidise? Did the municipality tolerate non-communist associations?

The official Party line on this question was that all local associations contributed to the local life of the community and, according to Marcel Rosette, the PCF leader in charge of local government issues in the 1970s, communist municipalities had to 'respect their autonomy and seek their participation in the thinking of the elaboration of municipal policies'.[19] In fact, the apparent political dependence of the Centre Culturel Ivryen casts a doubt on the political autonomy of these associations in Ivry. According to Jean Montaldo, communist municipalities always discriminated against associations which were not run or controlled by the Party.[20]

Thus, it looks as if the decision-making processes in Ivry were very centralised – with institutions such as the Service Municipal des Affaires Culturelles and the Centre Culturel Ivryen controlled by the local communists – and followed a sort of top-down model, thus reproducing the working of the PCF itself.

The next level to consider, however, is the local population: were the Ivryens at all involved or at least consulted in the process of decision-making leading to the implementation of the cultural policy? The official line of the Party kept reasserting the so-called 'democratic nature' of communist municipalities and insisting on the participation of the citizens in the implementation of policies designed for them: 'We cannot envisage a society truly democratic ... without an unequalled participation of the citizens in the running of local affairs.'[21]

In January 1978, Francine Ecosse, then working with André Minc at the head of the Service Municipal des Affaires Culturelles, was asked by a journalist of *Ivry-ma-Ville*, the local communist newsletter, the following question: 'Who makes the cultural calendar of events for the next year?' She replied:

> a commission composed of elected office-holders, managers of the *Service des Cours Municipaux* [Municipal Department for Classes], cultural councillors; in this commission also take part, from time to time, representatives of the local community, in particular representatives ... of local trade unions, of the local schools (parents and teachers) ... and of the *Centre Culturel Ivryen*.[22]

This answer put – deliberately or not – the emphasis on local communist leaders and on representatives coming from PCF-controlled institutions, such as the Centre Culturel Ivryen or the local teaching union, as well as on people appointed by the municipality (e.g. music teachers in charge of municipal classes) whose open opposition to any development could have cost them their job.

However, a new development occurred in December 1980 when the Service Municipal des Affaires Culturelles decided to organise an open debate to discuss cultural events for the 1981 season. A public meeting was held in January 1981 where all the citizens interested in the cultural life of their town were invited to submit their views to a panel of the people in charge of the cultural life of Ivry. The rationale behind this initiative was outlined by Francine Ecosse:

> [The public meeting will be] the starting point of an informative and permanent dialogue with, for instance, an annual presentation [of the calendar of events to come] followed by an assessment meeting at the end of each season ... This should enable us to rethink our actions with regard to the needs of the local population and, as a result, to attempt to adjust our cultural calendar to these needs.[23]

The extent to which this initiative, which has been repeated twice a year since January 1981, actually enabled Ivryens to contribute actively to the making of the cultural calendar has yet to be established. In fact, one could be tempted to argue that, in spite of the official credo of local democracy and citizens' participation, the average Ivryen was not really involved in the choice of events for the forthcoming cultural season, and to conclude that the French Communist Party and its organisations seemed to control the cultural life of Ivry to a very large extent.

In terms of the design of its cultural policy, the Ivryen PCF again appears to have been orthodox, in that most local pamphlets and statements related to culture in Ivry faithfully echoed the PCF views in this field (discussed in Chapter 4). Thus, for Ivryen administrators, culture was a highly political field and the conservative governments of the Fifth Republic prior to 1981 were strongly criticised for their elitist approach which kept the working class excluded from culture and cultural activities:

> The current [1976] government, that of the 25 big families which plunder our Nation, does its best to circumscribe the popular will to attend cultural activities. Schools as well as universities are selective and segregational, and subjected to profit-making objectives.[24]

In fact, the Ivryen communists usually argued that the exclusion of the majority of the French people from cultural activities was the result of the government's use of several levers, the most obvious one being the budget. It was indeed constantly repeated, in the local communist literature of the 1970s, that the government was not spending enough public money on cultural facilities and activities, therefore forcing the artists and companies of the cultural sphere to break even financially through high prices and thus reinforcing the cultural exclusion of the working class: 'This year, the budget of the Ministry for Cultural Affairs amounts to a pathetic 0.37 per cent of the national budget.'[25]

This criticism was quite useful to the local communists, for it enabled the municipality to take pride in their policies in this field by stating that, unlike the government, they devoted a significant part of their budget to cultural amenities:

> Contrary to the current government which thinks that culture is superfluous ... , we insist on the social dimension of culture, on the fact that culture is indispensable to the full development of the human being. These different ways of viewing culture are reflected in budget choices: the government spends 0.5 per cent of its resources on culture, whereas the municipality of Ivry devotes 4 per cent of its annual budget to culture, that is to say eight times more.[26]

These figures seem to have been consistent and it appears indeed that, during all the period studied, the municipality of Ivry always spent close to 4 per cent of its annual resources on cultural infrastructures and activities.[27]

Accordingly, every local achievement in the field of culture was presented to the population of Ivry as a victory over the passivity – if not at times the resistance – of the government and always described local policy-making in terms of a struggle against a hostile government.

This highly political view of cultural policy-making as something vindictive was the cornerstone of the guidelines on communist municipal policy in this field issued by the PCF in 1977 in Marcel Rosette's *La Gestion municipale dans l'action* (Policy-Making at the Municipal Level), which were followed to the letter in Ivry. This pamphlet, written by an influential PCF leader (Rosette was in charge of local government matters and of the central schools of the PCF in the 1970s; he was also the mayor of Vitry-sur-Seine, a town adjacent to Ivry), was the first comprehensive attempt by the PCF to issue clear guidelines in all fields of policy-making at the municipal level. At the beginning of his chapter on cultural policy, Rosette strongly emphasised the integrated nature of any communist cultural policy, thus echoing what could be found in the local communist literature prior to 1977: 'The municipal cultural policy should under no circumstances constitute a separated area [of policy-making]. It is, on the contrary, a significant sector to develop in the general framework of the struggle for a democratic change.'[28]

Rosette's guidelines on cultural policy were organised under three main headings which distinguished between three areas of cultural action. The first of these sectors was the field of information and cultural education. It included the promotion of activities such as art and drawing classes, music classes, evening classes for adults, literacy classes, mother-tongue classes for immigrants and their children, conferences and seminars on various topics and/or countries (in particular socialist countries), exhibitions and workshops on science and technology.

The second sector of action to be promoted, according to Rosette, was that of the dissemination of culture, in other words the development and funding of cultural events accessible to everybody, such as plays, shows, concerts, exhibitions, as well as the investment in subsidised cultural infrastructure such as public libraries and cinemas.

The third sector identified by Rosette was that of the development of aid to artistic creation and material support to artists, a sector described as a 'fundamental requirement of our cultural policy'.[29] This support for artists had to be applied to all the arts – theatre, plastic arts, sculpture, dance, music – and could take several forms: subsidies to a drama company, grants to individual artists, open competitions and prizes aimed at rewarding new talent, and the involvement of some of these artists – sculptors in particular – in the decorating of the town.

As regards the question of artistic creation, Rosette's pamphlet faithfully echoed the Argenteuil line adopted by the PCF in 1966 (see Chapter 4): '[The cultural policies of communist municipalities should] respect the freedom of research of the artist ... and recognise the right to be wrong as well as the right not to be understood by the main part of the population.'[30]

Thus, it appears that there was indeed an orthodox approach to cultural policy-making in French communist municipalities, and that individual mayors such as Laloë in Ivry faithfully followed national guidelines. The next sections of this chapter examine this cultural policy-making on the ground by means of concrete examples of cultural amenities and programmes.

THE LOCAL COMMUNIST NEWSLETTER, *IVRY-MA-VILLE*

One of the key vehicles for the promotion of the cultural life of Ivry and for the dissemination of political symbols constitutive of the PCF identity

– and indeed a very useful basis for research – is the free local newsletter entitled *Ivry-ma-Ville* (IMV), written, published and distributed to all Ivryen households by the municipality. This periodical was launched in 1971 and was representative of the desire of the communist municipality to inform its citizens of what was happening in Ivry.

This emphasis on 'information' – some might say indoctrination or propaganda – is very typical of French communist municipalities where newsletters have always been taken very seriously. Thus, there was already a newsletter in the 1930s called *Le Travailleur d'Ivry*,[31] and many other communist municipalities had their own newsletter equivalent to IMV in the 1970s, which suggests that the Ivry newsletter was part of a nationwide initiative by the PCF. As a result of this policy, the municipality of Ivry invested substantial amounts of public money on information and public relations, and was often criticised for this.

An example of such a controversy occurred in 1991, and while it took place after the period which is examined in this study (1965–85), it is worth quoting for it substantiates the propaganda argument. In an article on the meeting of the municipal council which had discussed and approved the municipal budget for 1991, various political groups were quoted as expressing their concerns with and/or their opposition to the municipal budgetary allocations for public relations matters. Thus, the socialist group, which voted in favour of the proposed budget, nonetheless expressed its reservations:

> As regards the operating budget, we have noticed that priority has been given to subsidies to associations, but we are unclear as to what the underlying policy is. Thus, an amount in excess of five million francs is allocated (to *Ivry-ma-ville*, *Radio-Ivry* [a local FM station funded by the town] and *Allez-Ivry* [a public relations campaign to promote the town]), which could be better spent elsewhere.[32]

In a far less implicit statement, the right-wing councillors (who form a very small minority on Ivry's municipal council) declared:

> We notice, as always, the hegemony of the communist majority. You, ladies and gentlemen [the communist councillors], prefer to invest in propaganda (FF 800,000 in total), to the detriment of social and welfare expenditure (FF 541,000), in spite of what you always profess.[33]

The priority given to information matters meant that an orthodox communist was chosen to be the 'Mr/Mrs Information' in the municipality. In Ivry, the activist in charge of such matters in the 1970s and early 1980s was Antoine Castro, who became more and more influential over the years and was promoted to the prestigious position of first assistant mayor in May 1980, thus becoming the most powerful person in town after the mayor himself. According to Pronier, this emphasis on information also concealed a highly political reality, namely that the PCF intended to make sure its line was adhered to at the local level by promoting an orthodox communist in a key position and giving him the title of *adjoint à l'information* (assistant mayor in charge of information). Furthermore, Pronier claims that this key position made the information person the likely successor of the mayor in charge.[34]

This emphasis on information at the municipal level was further found in the late 1970s with a new initiative launched by the municipality, an information van, whose official task was, according to Antoine Castro: 'to strengthen the links between the local population and the communal administration, between the citizens and their elected office-holders and to develop local democracy'.[35] When asked if the information van would not disseminate 'one-way propaganda', Antoine Castro, quite naturally, strongly denied that this was the objective of this new service.[36]

In fact, in spite of the municipality's claim that all these efforts in the information area were only aimed at informing and consulting the local population for the sake of local democracy, other evidence suggests that a lot of the articles published in IMV amounted to more-or-less subtle PCF propaganda.

Most of the topics covered fell under one of the following categories: criticism of the right-wing government of France under the presidencies of Pompidou and Giscard (1969–81), denunciation of capitalism and its effects, self-glorification of the action of Ivry in order to protect and defend its citizens, mythologisation of the countries of 'really existing socialism' until 1989–90 (see below), to the extent that most feature articles faithfully echoed what could be found in the national PCF pamphlets of the time, such as Marchais' *Défi démocratique* (The Democratic Challenge),[37] and the tone of the newsletter was very similar to that of *L'Humanité*, the PCF daily newspaper.

While it is not the object of this study to analyse in a detailed fashion the content of this local press which does not fall in the field of cultural policy *stricto sensu*, it is worth pointing out that it was certainly a very powerful vehicle for the creation and consolidation of political symbols which were at the heart of PCF identity, especially since information was according to Rosette and other communists one of the facets of the cultural policy of the PCF in its municipalities. Among these symbols was first of all the notion of combat or struggle, so central to the identity of French communism:

The main component of the French communist identity is the cult of the 'struggle' [*lutte*]. A *faux naïf* asked Georges Marchais: 'What is a communist?' He replied: 'A man who struggles' ... Who it is who struggles and what it is that they struggle for are only secondary aspects of the *struggle* in general ... Thus, the *struggle against* being easier to generate than the positive struggle, the history of the Party is filled with 'No to ...' slogans, while 'For ...' slogans are scarce.[38]

The best examples of this in IMV were the active campaigns launched by the municipality in order to save local factories from closure, as best illustrated by the staunch struggle orchestrated by the Ivryen communists in a bid to save the local SKF plant, a wheel-bearing factory based in Ivry. Other components of PCF identity found in IMV were the central role of the working class, the defence of the 'oppressed' peoples of the world (always in right-wing, conservative dictatorships such as Pinochet's Chile) and the superiority of the Soviet Union and other socialist countries.

The combination of all these symbols which have shaped IMV since 1971 amounts to what Pronier called a *culture de bastion* (stronghold culture) in which the PCF ('us') were portrayed as the *forteresse assiégée* (besieged fortress) fighting against 'them', the surrounding capitalist society, and paving the way for a better world embodied by the Soviet Union.

With regard to the superiority of Soviet-style models, a few significant articles can be mentioned, with a view to contrasting the PCF and the PCI. In January 1981, after a decade when the Soviet myth had been faltering after it had suffered a number of setbacks at the international level (the dissidence of Solzhenitsyn and others, the invasion of Afghanistan in December 1979) and in France (see the Kehayans' critical account of the Soviet Union which resulted in their exclusion from the PCF[39]), IMV published an article depicting the Soviet Union as heaven on earth.

This article, entitled 'Sur le chemin du bien-être: Voyage en Union Soviétique' (The Road to Well-Being: A Soviet Journey) was so flattering to the Soviet regime that it was reminiscent of some of the most biased pro-Soviet panegyrics published in France in the 1930s, during the dissemination of the Soviet myth.[40] The article, written after a trip to Krasnaya-Presnia, the Moscow district twinned with Ivry, was written in such an emphatic style that it is revealing to quote significant extracts from it:

In factories, where socialist democracy is at work, nothing can be decided upon or implemented without the consent and initiative of the workers ... The October Revolution is alive in every discussion ... Our purpose is not to elevate the Soviet Union to the status of a model, or to conceal some aspects which we find difficult to understand or which are negative to us. But it is crucial to fight the mendacious and hateful campaign [*campagne mensongère et haineuse*, in the French text] which is being orchestrated about this country and its people. Every testimony, every discussion is evidence that popular well-being and the desire to achieve peace [in the world] are their crucial aims.[41]

By contrast, this sort of apology of the Soviet Union, which was to be found in IMV throughout the 1980s, was becoming scarcer and scarcer in the PCI publications of the time. In fact, Berlinguer's Party had strongly opposed the Soviet invasion of Afghanistan in 1979 and, as a result, the PCI was moving further away from Soviet apology. The PCF, on the other hand, had publicly approved the Red Army intervention on French TV and was in a phase of clear realignment towards Moscow.

Another illustration of the teleological dimension of communism in Ivry can be found at the very end of the 1980s, albeit in a subtler form. In November 1989, IMV devoted its front cover to a Soviet handball player who had moved to Ivry to play for the local team and was portrayed as the 'red star of handball'. In the article about this player, which duly mentioned his sporting achievements, the Soviet Union was mentioned in passing, in subtle fashion, in the words of the sportsman: 'of course, this move [from the Ukraine to Ivry] worries us. This is only human. Sometimes, we feel nostalgic about the USSR. It is normal for a family who love their country.'[42]

Another feature of IMV which falls directly in the field of cultural policy-making was the regular articles on historical events, which contributed to the dissemination of orthodox PCF official historiography. Among the themes covered were the Resistance and the Liberation, which offer great comparative merits since these were topics at the core of the local historiography produced in Reggio Emilia (see Chapter 6). In an article published in April 1975 to commemorate the 30th anniversary of the defeat of Nazi Germany (8 May 1945), the local communist journalist placed great emphasis on the decisive role of the Red Army and on the sacrifices made by the Soviets:

A cruel and bloody war brought devastation to all the countries in which it took place. Amongst all these, one cannot deny that it is the Soviet Union which suffered the greatest losses in human lives and in material goods ... Alongside the regular armies sent by the governments of the anti-Hitlerian coalition – the USSR, the United

States, Britain – considerable armed forces made up of partisans deployed a strategy of 'guerrilla' warfare against the political and military power of Nazism. These forces struck terrible blows at the enemy.[43]

In this article, the emphasis was clearly placed on the crucial role of the Soviet Union (which was named first in the list of Allied countries) and of the partisans who, in France, were mostly communists (or at least this was the implication of this reference to partisans). Thus, the municipality of Ivry was echoing the all-powerful, orthodox 'Stalingrad effect' to preserve the image of the Soviet Union as the main contributor to the crushing of Nazism. This effect is summarised by Nicolas Werth in the following terms:

> [The] fact that the USSR had paid the highest price in human terms in order to achieve victory over Nazism concealed the very nature of Stalin's dictatorship and exempted the regime of the suspicions which had appeared years earlier – and it seemed many years earlier – at the time of the Moscow trials and of the Germano-Soviet Pact.[44]

In any case, the point here is that this version of the Liberation contrasted clearly with the pamphlet published by a PCI historian in Reggio at the same time (1975) in which much less emphasis was placed on the role of the USSR (see Chapter 6).

Another prominent theme of the local literature was the dialogue with Christians in Ivry, reflecting at the local level a key aspect of the strategy of the communist parties of western Europe (see Chapter 4) also very noticeable in Italy (see Chapter 6). The relationship between communists and Christians had been very tense prior to the 1930s. In fact, there was a tradition of fierce anticlericalism in Ivry, illustrated, for instance, by a 1900 municipal decree issued by Ferdinand Roussel, a socialist mayor, which banned the wearing in public of any ecclesiastic dress, or by the imposition of *parrainages civils* (non-religious patronage) in order to compete with the widespread tradition of church christenings, which were still organised in the late 1920s.[45] This was still the climate in Ivry in 1933, when a devout Catholic, Madeleine Delbrêl, wrote: 'Pray for Ivry where the official sin of red secularism is displayed in atrocious fashion. Satan reigns. Only the Cross will defeat it.'[46]

This conflictual relationship was to change in 1936, when Maurice Thorez launched his famous appeal to Christians: 'Catholiques, je vous tends la main' ('Catholics, I stretch out my hand to you'), which has remained the official PCF line since. As a result, a more harmonious relationship slowly emerged between the municipality and local Catholics, illustrated by the inclusion in Delbrêl's book about her experience as a Christian missionary in Ivry in the years 1930–57 of a letter sent to her by Venise Gosnat in which he reiterated his 'deep, brotherly friendship', in spite of a number of political disagreements.[47]

In the early 1980s, the politics of dialogue between Catholics and communists were relayed repeatedly in IMV in various forms. Thus, a long article was published in September 1980 under the title 'Communistes et Chrétiens' (Communists and Christians), which summarised the relationship:

> During the Second World War, communists, Christians, patriots joined forces once more to fight the Hitlerian invaders and fascism. Since then, numerous talks, contacts and exchanges of ideas have taken place between communists and Christians, about topics such as civil rights, the sovereignty of France and the development ... of the individual.[48]

By the same token but in a more subtle form, the contribution of the Church to the history of Ivry was noted in several issues of IMV. For example, in an article on Ivry in the early Middle Ages, the author, Pierre Forni, a local historian who wrote numerous articles for IMV, insisted on the positive role played by monks and local saints in the fifth and sixth centuries.[49]

Three tentative remarks can be drawn from this study of the Ivryen newsletter as a vehicle for cultural dissemination and symbol production. First, despite the genuine informative nature and usefulness of a number of sections of IMV, most articles with a so-called cultural/historical vocation often amounted to more-or-less blatant communist propaganda aimed at disseminating the orthodox PCF views on topics such as French society, international affairs or historical events. For instance, the ideological framework of historical writings, also found in a book on Ivry commissioned by the municipality and written by local PCF historians Fernand Leriche and Jacques Varin, was a faithful reflection of official PCF historiography. This contrasts quite clearly with the work of communist historians in Reggio (see Chapter 6) and confirms the more general contrast existing between the historiographies produced by the PCF and the PCI identified by authors such as Lazar.[50]

Second, IMV was used as a vehicle for promoting the Soviet Union and other socialist countries as models, especially at a time when the Soviet myths were being challenged (1970s to early 1980s), and the emphatic tone of the articles on these countries reflected the unflagging fealty of the PCF to Moscow. Again, this contrasts clearly with the symbols produced by the PCI in Reggio in the 1970s, which were mostly national and Republican (see Chapter 6).

Third, it could be argued that most articles devoted to French society tended to portray Ivry as a 'counter-society' and contributed to the strengthening of the teleological dimension of French communism discussed in Chapter 1. The high ideological content displayed in the newsletter was also to be found in the public library, as illustrated by the next section of this chapter.

THE PUBLIC LIBRARY IN IVRY-SUR-SEINE

In Ivry, the municipal library was created in the mid-1920s and grew steadily in the 1960s and 1970s. According to statistics provided by the municipality, the number of books held by the library increased from 4,000 in 1925 to 100,000 in 1976, the number of book loans increased from 20,000 in 1925 to 200,000 in 1976, and the total readership reached 12,000 in 1976 for a town of 60,000 inhabitants.[51]

Despite the facts that there are no alternative statistical sources available and that the notion of readership is often vague and ill-defined (see our discussion of the library readership in Reggio, Chapter 6), this membership rate of about 20 per cent of the local population seems to have put Ivry well above the French average rate (4.5 per cent) and enabled the municipality to claim that its public library was 'one of the most substantial libraries in France'.[52]

This development reflected the increasing significance of the diffusion of public reading for communist municipalities, a significance which was both political and educational in nature:

> [On] the one hand, the scientific and technological revolution has given birth to huge human training needs. It is necessary for the workers as well as for the whole country to devote more time and more means to education ... At the same time, democratic changes are required. Millions of men and women have questions about the crisis our society is facing at the moment and about how to overcome this crisis. They want to understand and act, to think by themselves and to take charge of their own future.[53]

The local emphasis on public reading was in fact a faithful reflection of the PCF line of the 1970s, found in its *Manifeste pour le livre* (Manifesto for Public Reading) (1975) which was widely published in a revised form in paperback under the title *La Bataille du livre* (The Book Struggle) in 1976.[54] In this pamphlet, the authors blamed the French government for neglecting public reading ('in terms of public reading, France is a cultural desert'[55]) and contrasted this so-called cultural underdevelopment with the situation in socialist countries:

> The example of the Soviet Union is particularly significant. In 1917, 71.6 per cent of the population were illiterate ... This rate was still at 43.4 per cent in 1926. However, in less than 60 years, illiteracy has disappeared in the USSR, and 50 million Soviets were taught to read and write, including in regions and linguistic areas where there was no tradition of writing prior to 1917. The Soviet Union is today the first country in the world in terms of public library attendance ... This shows that, having started from a much lower point, socialism achieved more and quicker results in this field than capitalism ... To give these examples does not imply at all that we seek to emulate such or such a 'model'. But the experience of other countries shows that, in order to overcome the current crisis and open new prospects in terms of reading, a complete process of political change is needed.[56]

This long quotation clearly illustrates that, to the PCF leadership and administrators, public reading was first and foremost a political and ideological field. This high ideological bias prompts the question of whether the books on offer at the municipal library were just a collection of Marxist–Leninist classics and PCF pamphlets, or whether there was genuine diversity in the range of works available. On this matter, the municipality played the official card of political pluralism. In an interview given to IMV in 1972, Henri Deluy, director of the municipal library, declared: 'there is no censorship in the choice of books purchased by the library', and gave two examples of the diversity of the library's collections, General de Gaulle's *Mémoires de guerre* (War Memoires) and a book by former Gaullist minister Maurice Couve de Murville.[57]

While it is very difficult to assess this self-proclaimed diversity on the basis of the constantly updated library catalogues, some evidence suggests that in fact censorship did take place in communist-run libraries and that they were used to a large extent as tools of political indoctrination.

First, Pierre Daix, a French communist intellectual who had been the chief editor of the *Lettres françaises*, claimed that his books were removed from PCF-controlled libraries after his disgrace from the Party in 1973–74 and that all these libraries cancelled their subscription to his journal: 'my name was scored out from all the lists and my books were removed from PCF-controlled libraries'.[58] This would tend to confirm the fact that censorship did take place. Second, an examination of the new acquisitions of the municipal library recommended to the Ivryen population in IMV shows that, for a great majority of them, these were works published by the Editions Sociales, the publishing house of the PCF. In the 1977 summer issue of IMV, the books presented to the public included the following: *Les Truands du patronat* by Marcel Caille, a high-ranking CGT leader who depicted French employers as ruthless gangsters, *Paris, déclin ou renaissance: Les communistes et l'avenir de la capitale* by Henri Fiszbin, leader of the Paris federation of the PCF, which was in fact a Party manifesto, *Survivre à New York* by Maurice Goldring (a university professor who had spent a year as a visiting scholar in the United States) and in which the author strongly criticised the American model, a book edited by Alain Duny on the crisis of the school system in France, and *Voyage avec les cadres* by René Le Guen, another PCF/trade union leader, which specialised in issues concerning middle-management employees.[59] Even the presentation of a book for 6-year-old children, *Nicole et Djamila*, contained a noticeable PCF bias: 'Nicole's father gives a lift home to Djamila whose father was injured working in the factory. Life in HLM blocks [French high-rise housing estates] and workers' solidarity combine to make this book heart-warming reading.'[60]

This kind of propaganda would confirm that the PCF administrators in Ivry used every book as a political tool, and suggests that, even if the municipal library was quite well stocked, it was merely seen by the municipality as a vehicle for the dissemination of PCF orthodoxy.

ARTISTIC EDUCATION IN IVRY: THE EXAMPLES OF MUSIC AND DRAMA

In the late 1960s and early 1970s, the municipality of Ivry identified the local schools as one of the key areas for their cultural policy-making: 'Our first priority must be the development of our cultural action in schools, with the indispensable co-operation of the teaching profession.'[61] In fact, for the year 1970, no less than 40 per cent of the municipal budget for cultural affairs was devoted to cultural activities in local schools, e.g. classes in drawing, music or sport. The priority given to cultural actions in schools continued to prevail throughout the 1970s and, to a lesser extent, in the 1980s. In 1976, for instance, this priority was stated once more, but the emphasis was put on the idea that the municipalities should not try to replace the government in this field, and that they should in fact ask for more governmental funds to run their cultural classes:

> Yes, the schools are the fundamental basis for a true cultural education. The schools will be able to play this indispensable role only if they are given the necessary means, such as: qualified

teachers trained by the Ministry for National Education and employed by this public service; more material means provided exclusively by the state.[62]

In other words, the French communists realised that their cultural action in schools had maybe been too ambitious – and probably too expensive – and concentrated on other institutions, such as extra-curricular classes open to all, children and adults. The main development in this field was probably the *Cours et Ateliers Artistiques Municipaux* (municipal artistic classes and workshops) funded exclusively by the municipality and using a system of fees calculated on the basis of the income of the family of the child registered for these activities, thus implementing the idea of social justice: the poorer you are, the less you have to pay to attend music classes. For the year 1977, for instance, the fees ranged from FF 35 to FF 400 for a year of tuition, whilst the municipality claimed to spend an average of FF 1,000 per pupil.[63]

The activities offered in this framework included dance and music tuition at the Conservatoire, which had been created in 1958 and was attended by over 500 pupils in 1976, classes in harmonic gymnastics, launched in 1946 and welcoming over 800 pupils in 1976, with a decentralised structure, the classes being held in five different *quartiers* (districts) of Ivry, and visual arts classes offered by L'Atelier des Arts Plastiques, created in 1959.

The Conservatoire was perhaps the most significant example among these facilities, because it was aimed at promoting classical musical education, a kind of education usually unaffordable for working-class families. The Conservatoire was still in operation in 1994, and in 1988, for instance, the fees it charged were still based on family income and ranged from FF 140 to FF 758 per year, which looked very affordable for this kind of tuition, especially if compared with similar institutions in other suburban towns or in Paris. The Conservatoire offered tuition in a wide range of musical instruments, and the number of students attending classes remained stable throughout the period, between 500 and 600, although it should be mentioned that increasing demand for these services led the Conservatoire to reject 200 new applications every year in the 1980s, due to the lack of financial and material resources. In 1988, the municipality invested FF 500,000 in new equipment and facilities for the Conservatoire.[64]

The development of this institution seems to have given a number of Ivryen youngsters – or adults – the opportunity to learn and develop musical skills such as playing the piano or the violin which are traditionally restricted to the bourgeois elites, and it can be assumed that, without the significant financial effort of the municipality, a very large majority of the pupils of the Conservatoire would not have been able to afford the usual cost of classical musical tuition.

The cultural education programmes launched by the municipality were by no means restricted to the field of musical education. Another relevant example of cultural activity, aimed this time at adults more than at youngsters, was the creation of the Atelier Théâtral (drama workshop) in January 1972, under the management of Antoine Vitez, the newly appointed director of the professional drama company. The rationale behind the creation of this workshop was to create in Ivry a dual structure for drama, with the Théâtre des Quartiers d'Ivry (TQI), a company of professional actors on the one hand, and the Atelier Théâtral, designed to offer the local population of Ivry the opportunity to attend acting classes on the other hand. Both activities were headed by Vitez, who was also a professor of drama studies in Paris. In a 1976 interview, Vitez said:

> The Workshop of Ivry is not – it is crucial to repeat this here – a traditional drama school. If it were, it would be just another school among the many existing in the Paris area … It is, on the contrary, a workshop whose first aim is the enjoyment of acting in itself and the initiation to this enjoyment of a group of participants preferably coming from Ivry.[65]

This activity, which included at least 12 hours of tuition a week in different areas of Ivry, and which invited a number of directors and/or professional actors to teach the workshops, was entirely funded by the municipality.

The two examples of the Conservatoire and of the Atelier Théâtral suggest that the action of the municipality in the field of cultural education could have been quite positive and attractive to the local population, judging by the ever-increasing demand for various classes and workshops and by the very reasonable fees asked by the municipality for these activities.

However, these efforts could also be interpreted as a shop-window strategy designed to attract non-communist elements of the local population, in particular some of the middle-class families which increasingly started to settle in Ivry in the 1960s, by creating the image of a non-sectarian administration dedicated to the provision of quality services. This shop-window effect was also prominent in the field of avant-garde drama creation.

AVANT-GARDE CREATION IN IVRY: ANTOINE VITEZ AND THE THÉÂTRE DES QUARTIERS D'IVRY

In the field of contemporary drama, the contribution of the municipality of Ivry has been noted by a number of observers of French cultural life.[66] Created in January 1972 and managed by Antoine Vitez (1930–90), the Théâtre des Quartiers d'Ivry had achieved national fame by the end of the 1970s. In recognition of his tremendous achievements, Antoine Vitez was in 1981 offered the direction of the Théâtre de Chaillot, one of the best theatres in France, before being appointed in 1987 to the most prestigious position in the world of French drama, that of administrator of the Comédie-Française.

The creation of the Théâtre des Quartiers d'Ivry in the 1970s: the political and cultural context

Originally, the municipality of Ivry decided to create its own theatre company in order to promote artistic and literary creation as well as the dissemination of drama knowledge. This initiative was far from being an isolated one; in fact, it was a policy the Party had determined at the national level. No fewer than eight other communist towns in the 'red belt' around Paris decided to establish their own theatre companies in the 1960s or early 1970s: Aubervilliers, Aulnay, Bobigny, Chelles, Gennevilliers, Nanterre, Saint-Denis and Vitry.[67] In Aubervilliers, for instance, the Théâtre de la Commune was founded in 1961 by drama director Gabriel Garran, as a result of an initiative launched by his political mentor Jack Ralite, assistant mayor in charge of culture.[68]

It should be noted, however, that this PCF policy was itself part of a general, nationwide trend towards what was described as 'decentralised theatre', as many theatre directors and actors, influenced by the example of Jean Vilar (1912–1971) who had wanted to bring theatre to a wider, popular audience (he had created the Avignon festival in 1947 and was director of Théâtre National Populaire between 1951 and 1963), wanted to 'set up their own theatre company in a deprived urban area or provincial town which had never had a resident theatre company before'.[69]

This enthusiasm for local theatre, promoted by the PCF, followed strong political motivations. The Party saw its municipalities as an ideal terrain from which to counterbalance what it called the cultural, bourgeois hegemony of Paris in the world of drama, and knew that it could count on the fact that a plethora of left-wing actors and directors would seek employment in newly founded theatre companies. Thus, Jack

Ralite recalled Gabriel Garran's appointment as drama director in his municipality:

> When people heard that we were about to launch something in Aubervilliers ... , some drama people came here to offer their services. At this time [1960–61], no town – or at least no communist town – had drama professionals working for them. So, they came to talk, and we listened, and, one day, Garran came to see us. He had come to work with us.[70]

It was in this context that in 1972 the municipality of Ivry appointed Antoine Vitez as director of the new company, the TQI.

The work of Vitez and of the TQI: a success story?

In the 1970s, Ivry did not have any purpose-built theatre, as the new theatre only came to be inaugurated in 1981. Yet these material constraints did not seem to affect Vitez, the newly appointed director of the TQI. On the contrary, he seemed to like the idea of working and staging in non-conventional places: 'I like unusual places; I liked the reception room in the town hall. I also very much liked the Conference Room, now destroyed. I liked the fact that it was not ordinary.'[71] In these odd places, Antoine Vitez staged a total of 33 plays between 1972 and 1981, including *Electra* (Sophocles), *Faust* (Goethe), *Mother Courage* (Brecht), $M = m$ (Pommeret), *Phaedra* (Racine) and *Les Cloches de Bâle* (Aragon).

Some of these performances achieved national fame and recognition, as seen in newspapers of the time, newspapers one cannot accuse of indulging in constant pro-communist propaganda. For instance, in *Le Monde*, Michel Cournot wrote in his review of *Phaedra*: 'An excellent idea[;] one remains breathless until the end [of the play] in front of such science, splendour and mastery',[72] while, in *France-Soir*, the same event was described as 'the height of virtuosity'.[73]

It seems that the work of the TQI had captured the interest of Parisian cultural circles, and Vitez was crowned with success at the national level, for instance in Avignon in 1976 with his Molière tetralogy. It could be argued, however, that Vitez's invitation to stage his plays at the Avignon festival (the most prestigious drama festival in France, it is organised on a yearly basis and is to drama what the Venice festival is to cinema) could be explained by the fact that the administrator of this festival in the 1970s, Paul Puaux, was also a member of the PCF.

Yet, the success of Vitez at the national level prompts the following question: were the same plays which were praised by the drama critics and specialists also seen and enjoyed by the working-class population of Ivry? In other words, the problem is to establish whether the plays of the Théâtre des Quartiers d'Ivry were accessible to the man in the street, or whether they were only appreciated by the well-educated cultural elites of the Paris area.

Vitez himself claimed that his work targeted both audiences. In 1977, he produced a new, obscure concept in the field of drama which he called *le théâtre élitaire pour tous*, *élitaire* being a French neologism generated from the terms *élitiste* (elitist) and *égalitaire* (egalitarian). Vitez's new approach was supposed to combine the two aspects, and was highly ambiguous. On the one hand, he launched many experiments and innovations in staging, which could only have been appreciated by a specialised audience. On the other, he claimed he was seeking to disseminate a political message understandable to a large number of people. This ambiguity was never overcome by Vitez, who stated:

> This formula is obviously a contradiction in itself. Theatre can never be more than *élitaire*, to me, for even when there is a large audience, it still represents only a tiny proportion of the whole population. This fundamental elitism of theatre must be for all, and when I say 'must', it is not only because I wish it.[74]

This obscure concept led Vitez to adapt novels and classical plays in a very intellectual, avant-garde fashion. In his study of contemporary French drama, David Bradby describes *Catherine*, an adaptation by Vitez of Aragon's *Les Cloches de Bâle*, in the following terms:

> *Catherine* consisted of eleven actors sitting down and having dinner around a table, going slowly through each of the courses in French style, from the soup at the beginning to coffee and liqueurs at the end. At the beginning, Vitez seized a copy of Aragon's novel and began to read aloud from it. The reading passed from one actor to another, with occasional movements when the readers took on some characteristics of Aragon's people. But it remained essentially a *reading* of a novel, not a dramatisation in the usual sense. Vitez claimed that to stage a novel means not simply to put it into dialogue but to stage its narrative texture as well.[75]

This suggests that this kind of experimental drama, praised by regular theatregoers and the Parisian intelligentsia, was most unlikely to attract the ordinary Ivryen.

There was in fact a controversy around this issue, which started quite early in the 1970s. Vitez himself, on the one hand, was convinced that he had managed to attract part of the local community. Writing in October 1976 about a project for the conversion of an old building into a new theatre, he attempted to make his point:

> In fact, this will be much more than an ordinary theatre … This is very important for the local life of Ivry and for the diffusion of culture in general. For our audience has changed in the past five years. This audience, today, is not only made up of the Parisian intellectual circles we were criticised for favouring because of the nature and the content of our work. More and more, slowly but surely, the local audience has begun to go to the theatre regularly; everyone acknowledges this.[76]

However, some critics did not share Vitez's confidence. In December 1974, for instance, Matthieu Galey, a famous literary critic, wrote in his review of *Un couple pour l'hiver*: 'Vitez and his disciples often seem to go a long way towards a very abstract art, hard to decipher, for the elitist delight of an audience which come from somewhere other [than Ivry].'[77] Moreover, this criticism also appeared in the words of Philippe Adrien who succeeded Vitez as director of the TQI in 1981 and who claimed to be a great admirer of his predecessor: 'The fame of the Théâtre des Quartiers d'Ivry is unquestioned at the level of the Paris region and at the national level. However, a relatively small proportion of Ivryens go to the theatre in their own town.'[78]

It is instructive to compare the achievements of the TQI to those of other theatre companies also based in communist municipalities. In Aubervilliers, for instance, the issue of the audience was also debated in the early 1970s. Recalling a local PCF meeting held in this town, journalists Harris and de Sédouy noted that one of the participants had expressed the view that the audience was made up of *habitués* (regular theatregoers) and that is was 'stagnant'.[79] This clearly indicated that, in municipalities where experimental, avant-garde drama was performed, it failed to attract a wide local audience.

On the other hand, another company was the Théâtre du Soleil led by Ariane Mnouchkine and established in the town of Gennevilliers, which was to become very successful in attracting a huge audience. Mnouchkine, who was, like Vitez, working for a communist municipality, had a different approach to drama and the audience it should attract. She had acknowledged at the end of the 1960s the failure of the kind of obscure, avant-garde political theatre Vitez and others were still advocating in the 1970s and decided, in agreement with the municipality of Gennevilliers, to try to attract large numbers of people – rather than a small intellectual elite – by staging plays and shows including a political message which was easily understandable. The Théâtre du Soleil therefore staged plays such as *1789* and *1793*, which attracted more than 250,000 spectators each.[80]

This comparison shows that theatre companies based in communist municipalities had different approaches to producing political theatre, and supports the argument that Vitez's style is not likely to have attracted many spectators from the mostly working-class population of Ivry.

So far, we have mainly considered Vitez's input at the head of the TQI, but the contribution of the municipality to the success of this theatre company should by no means be neglected. Indeed, as early as 1972, the municipality was behind the creation of the Théâtre des Quartiers d'Ivry and massively subsidised its actors, even if at the time there were no proper theatre facilities in Ivry. In 1975, the theatre company went through a period of serious financial problems, was declared bankrupt in February 1976 and was required to cease its activities and sell its meagre assets. The municipality then supported Vitez by sending a delegation including Jacques Laloë and Georges Gosnat to the Ministry for Cultural Affairs. It obtained, for the first time since 1972, a financial contribution from the government as well as the right for the TQI to carry on with its activities. This contribution, which became regular from 1976, was aimed at helping the municipality both with the running costs of the theatre company and with the new project for the conversion of an old building in Ivry into a modern, properly equipped theatre for the town. The new, purpose-converted theatre was inaugurated four years later, on 8 March 1980, and the total cost of this amenity was as illustrated below:[81]

Investment by the municipality of Ivry	FF 5,870,000
Governmental grant	FF 980,000
Grant from the PCF-held	
Conseil Général du Val-de-Marne	FF 450,000
Total cost of the new theatre	FF 7,300,000

To put these figures in context, the overall spending of the municipality for the year 1980 amounted to 166 million francs in total, but the investment spending amounted to less than 11 million francs.[82] In other words, the total investment of the municipality in a new theatre, which took place over several years, represented at the time 50 per cent of the total investment spending for one year – a significant effort indeed.

It can therefore be argued that the success at the national level of the TQI can be attributed to two factors: the personality and talent of its founder, Vitez, and the impressive financial support of the municipality of Ivry. The successful development of the TQI should, however, be viewed against the fact that Vitez and his company never managed to attract the population of Ivry and that the objective of 'educating the masses' was therefore not met by the theatre in Ivry.

On the other hand, it can be stated that the successes of Vitez contributed to strengthening the dominant position of the PCF within the world of French drama and to creating a positive image outside Ivry among Parisian cultural circles. What was, however, the relationship between Vitez and the Party? Did the Party ever exercise some sort of ideological control over his work?

Antoine Vitez, the Party and the question of censorship

It is revealing to examine first of all the conditions surrounding Vitez's appointment in 1972. In fact, it appears that Vitez, despite his talent and merit, was also appointed for obvious political reasons. First, he had been a member of the French Communist Party for a number of years – since 1956 in fact – and, like his colleague Gabriel Garran, was seeking to establish himself in a communist municipality. Second, and very importantly, he had worked as Aragon's personal secretary in the early 1960s. In particular, as a translator of Russian, Vitez had helped gather the documentation Aragon needed to write his *History of the Soviet Union* published in 1962. Vitez was still on very good terms with the 'cultural emperor' of the Party in the 1970s and acknowledged the 'explicit and implicit support of Aragon'.[83] These words, coming from Vitez himself, seem to suggest that he got the job in Ivry thanks to Aragon's highly influential patronage.

In fact, Aragon's influence was also found in the case of Aubervilliers, as recalled by Jack Ralite in an interview:

> We launched the theatre, we did a number of things, and I must say, talks with A. – you know A. – well, he took part in the whole design of the structure of the theatre, and he used to say 'it's super'. He never created any problems for me.[84]

This quotation, in which one can only guess that A. stands for Aragon, would strongly confirm the argument that his influence was wide-reaching in the world of communist drama.

Third, Vitez, like many of his colleagues, was committed to promoting what was called 'political theatre'. After the death of the founder of the TQI in 1990, Leonardini, drama critic for *L'Humanité*, recalled one of Vitez's oft-repeated statements that 'theatre is a violently political form of art'.[85]

These three pointers suggest that Vitez was appointed for political reasons as well as for artistic ones. On the other hand, it should not be assumed that Vitez, for his part, accepted the position in Ivry for political reasons only. He also intended to develop his work in his own way, without receiving his orders from any watchdog. In a book published in 1981, he wrote:

> The welcome I got in Ivry was friendly and sensible ... I told them 'you can accept my plans or not, as you wish – but I'm not blackmailing you' ... They told me 'yes'. Without knowing if my work would be accessible to 'the masses'; on the contrary, sure that it would not ... They made me accept only one condition: that I would also take charge of the drama workshop, which I did.[86]

It therefore appears that Vitez was determined to put his work beyond any sort of control from the communist municipality. That his independence was respected during his days in Ivry is demonstrated by the fact that his somewhat esoteric, obscure ideas of *théâtre élitaire* met no open opposition there. Artistic independence from the Party was also found in the case of Gabriel Garran in Aubervilliers, as recalled by his mentor Ralite: 'Right at the beginning, when he [Garran] arrived, we [the communist municipality] told him: "you are free"',[87] which seems to substantiate the argument that drama directors in communist municipalities enjoyed a high degree of artistic latitude.

Yet, can we conclude that Vitez was entirely free to do what he wanted, that no censorship at all was applied to his work? In answering this question, it is helpful to consider the definition of censorship offered by Hungarian intellectual Miklos Haraszti in his book *L'Artiste d'Etat* (Velvet Prison), which examines the question of censorship in socialist countries. In Haraszti's view, censorship in some socialist regimes was very different from the traditional form characterised by the intervention of an external control body after the creative work has been produced. In a regime where ideology was omnipresent and all-important, censorship had become much more subtle and had moved towards self-censorship, that is to say that the artists knew themselves what they could do and what they could not. In other words, the artists knew the limits that their work had to respect and did not need the external intervention of the censor to regulate their work; the artists became their own censors.[88]

More importantly, Haraszti also explains that, in such cases as Hungary, censorship had become much softer in the 1970s than it had been in the Stalinist era. As long as artists remained within the broad realm of official ideology, and most of all that their work did not explicitly challenge the legitimacy of the regime and of 'really existing socialism', it was accepted. Moreover, the artist did not necessarily have to produce widely accessible works of art, as in the Zhdanovist era of socialist realism. As long as the work was translatable and could be harnessed by the dominating organisation (the Party) to enhance its propaganda, there was no need to control or repress the artist, or to impose such or such a type of creation on him/her: 'My work permit includes only one obligation: that my work be usable for state culture.'[89]

The concept of self-censorship, and more importantly the two 'commandments' that artists were not to oppose directly the system or the Party and that they agreed – or did not oppose the fact – that their work would be harnessed by the Party, can usefully be applied to the case of Ivry in order to explore the relationship between Vitez and the PCF.

In fact, the PCF's acceptance of Vitez's elitist avant-garde drama can be explained by the fact that the communist drama critics were able to use the plays in their own local or national propaganda by interpreting (or reinterpreting) Vitez's work in a fashion understandable to the man in the street and compatible with the Party orthodoxy. For instance, in a review of Vitez's adaptation of the previously mentioned novel *Les Cloches de Bâle* (Aragon), a play called *Catherine*, the local communist Fernand Leriche wrote: 'In these years [the early 1910s], workers organised themselves, bloody struggles took place ... , and the long-lasting strike by taxi drivers, in 1911, against the monopolies which were emerging, highlighted the fundamental role of the working class.'[90]

Thus, even if the innovative, experimental staging by Vitez of Aragon's novel probably failed to attract many Ivryens, the fact that the PCF was able to translate the message into a legible text consistent with its own ideology was sufficient for the Party not to interfere with Vitez's creative talent.

Moreover, the circumstances of Vitez's departure from Ivry can also be clarified in the light of Haraszti's analysis. In November 1979, Vitez decided to leave the PCF because of a strong political disagreement with the Party. Two years later, he wrote:

> The rift, in myself, in the fact that I have ceased to be a member of the Communist Party, is not a philosophical one. It was a political decision. A protest ... I do not think that the Communist Party can change. One has to accept it or not, without hoping that it will change.[91]

These comments, taken in conjunction with the foregoing analysis, cast light on the motives behind Vitez's departure from Ivry. Since he had criticised the Party and challenged its legitimacy and ideology, Vitez himself knew that he could no longer keep his post in Ivry. It is probable that the Party never had to make it explicit that he had to resign and that Vitez used the highest form of self-censorship by deciding himself to quit.

Some might argue that, because he was offered the position of director of Chaillot after the election of François Mitterrand in 1981, it is difficult to draw any definite conclusion on the exact circumstances of Vitez's departure. However, the fact that he never gave a detailed account of what really happened in 1979–80 gives added weight to the self-censorship argument.

The study of the cultural policy implemented by the PCF in the field of drama in Ivry in the 1970s suggests that, in spite of the Argenteuil line of 1966, a degree of political control was still exercised by the Party until the early 1980s. The case of Vitez and the TQI reveals that new forms of censorship were at work, which were much softer and more discreet than in the Cold War years. Even so, it can be concluded that the PCF's tendency to reduce every aspect of culture to its ideological and political dimensions was always at the heart of its strategy for cultural action.

CINEMA IN IVRY: FROM INDOCTRINATION TO THE PROMOTION OF FRENCH CULTURE

Another relevant example of the action of the municipality in the field of the dissemination of culture can be found in the development of cinema facilities in Ivry in the 1970s and early 1980s. In fact, this desire to invest in such facilities echoed the traditional communist view, reiterated in 1977 by Rosette, that cinema had to be seen as a 'much preferred tool for mass cultural dissemination'.[92]

The potential of films as vehicles for revolutionary propaganda emerged after the Bolshevik Revolution of 1917, and the commissioning of films by the Soviet authorities led to the creation of numerous, famous works, such as *The Battleship Potemkin* (1925), *October* (1928) or *Old and New* (1929) by director Sergei Eisenstein, which all had a clearly defined agitprop purpose, in these cases the glorification of the 1905 Revolution, of the October Revolution and of Stalin's collectivisation of Russian agriculture respectively. In a similar fashion, French communists used the film industry to commemorate such events as the French partisans' heroic fight against the Germans in 1944–45 (see, for instance, René Clément's *La Bataille du Rail* released in 1945 or his *Paris brûle-t-il?* released in 1966).

During the Cold War, the PCF became a staunch advocate of the defence of the French film industry against what it called the 'imperialist invasion' of France by Hollywood productions. These two notions that, as a key vehicle for mass culture, cinema could be used for propaganda purposes as well as a means to fight so-called 'American imperialism' by promoting French culture were found in Ivry-sur-Seine in the 1970s and the 1980s.

The action of the municipality towards the local distribution of films started in the 1970s with the financial support to the local *ciné-club*, a non-profit-making association which was also a member of the Centre Culturel Ivryen.

This programme was, however, very limited in scope, reaching only a limited number of cinema-goers: indeed, the *ciné-club* only had 174 members for the 1976–77 season, in which it showed only 15 films. These films and documentaries had a clear political message, and dealt with topics such as childhood, Palestine and the nuclear industry.[93]

The action of the municipality in the field of cinema was expanded in the early 1980s. Thus, while films and political documentaries were still shown and discussed during sessions organised by the *ciné-club*, the municipality decided, in a bid to attract a higher number of cinema-goers, to purchase in 1981 a local cinema called the Luxy. This cinema had changed proprietors several times in the 1970s and had even been for a time an adult-only cinema. The main motivation of the communist municipality behind this bid was to protect the film industry against the prevailing profit-making logic of Hollywood, a theme reminiscent of the PCF discourse on the film industry discussed above:

> We have programmed classics as well as new films, operas and intimist works, spectacular films as well as committed ones. We have defended the French film industry by exploiting ... its assets, without neglecting foreign films. We have drawn from many film industries, not just the American one.[94]

By 1987, the Luxy cinema had shown 496 different films, had attracted 165,501 spectators (including children) and was classified as a *cinéma d'art et essai*, a label given in France to cinemas showing a high proportion of quality and/or French films. This enabled the municipality to obtain an annual governmental grant of FF 30,000.[95]

A brief examination of the range of films offered tends to confirm the argument that the Luxy privileged French and European productions to the detriment of Hollywood ones, even if Hollywood hits such as *Indiana Jones* were shown in 1984. Thus, while it could be argued that this emphasis on French and European films was by no means an exception in a country such as France which invests considerable resources in the defence of its *exception culturelle*, the more-or-less subtle anti-American tones of Ivryen administrators tend to confirm the idea that, to them, the cinema was a political tool as well as a cultural amenity.

ARTS SUBSIDIES IN IVRY SINCE 1972:
THE TRIUMPH OF *ART MONUMENTAL*

Like many other French communist municipalities, Ivry has a long tradition of devoting considerable resources to modern artistic creation through the commissioning of sculptors, painters, and so on. While in the 1940s and 1950s this took the form of socialist realist works such as paintings by Fougeron or others (see Chapter 4), after the Argenteuil watershed of 1966, the PCF decided to promote experimental, abstract works of art. A key concept behind the policy of Ivry in this field was the integration of works of art into the architecture of the town. In other words, it meant that the work of art had to be permanently displayed in a public, open-air space where everyone in the community could enjoy it without having to go to the museum. This form of art is commonly called *art monumental* and has been actively supported in Ivry since the 1970s.

In 1979, for example, the municipality launched an initiative almost unique in France at the time and called 'La Bourse d'Art Monumental' (Grant for Monumental Art). The organisation of this competition is as follows: every second year, the municipality of Ivry invites artists from any nationality and any plastic arts discipline (painting and sculpture in particular) to take part in the competition by sending a portfolio of photographs, drawings or plans concerning projects for works of art integrated into an urban environment. The applications are then assessed by a commission including two artists, two art critics, an architect, a museum curator, the assistant mayor for cultural affairs and another elected office-holder, the cultural councillor for plastic arts and the winner of the previous grant.[96]

The commission then selects six candidates who are invited to exhibit their work in Ivry, each receiving a grant of FF 4,000 (1989) to fund a new project. At the end of the joint exhibition, a winner is selected and awarded the first prize (FF 20,000 in 1989). The winner is also invited to organise a personal exhibition of his/her work and, more importantly, to submit a project for the realisation of a work of monumental art which will be purchased by the municipality of Ivry. This initiative, which has been repeated every second year since 1979, has attracted a significant number of applications (over 490 in 1989).[97]

In addition to this competition, the municipality also commissioned several artists, in the 1970s and the 1980s, to contribute to the dissemination of monumental art in Ivry, and spent considerable amounts of public money on these works. By the early 1990s, a total of 33 works of art (including works by the laureates of the Bourse d'Art Monumental) had been commissioned.[98] While these works were produced by different artists following various experimental routes, they tend to have a number

115

of features in common. First, they tend to be more or less abstract in their form, as illustrated by *La Muraille*, a sculpture by Jean Amado. Second, they are usually made of modern building materials, including concrete and metal (see in particular *l'Arête*, by sculptor Bernard Pagès). Third, they are all situated in a busy public place and therefore are part of the daily life of the Ivryens. Thus, *La Muraille*, is situated on a central square (Place de la République), just outside the entrance to the underground station through which thousands of people travel daily, *l'Arête* is on a pedestrian square (Place Voltaire) surrounded by housing blocks and *Pacha Mama*, by Jack Vanarsky, lies on a pedestrian footpath in a public park, so that Ivryens crossing the park actually walk over the work of art. It has been argued that, irrespective of one's aesthetic appreciation of such works, the total cost of these works of art was undoubtedly high for a town the size of Ivry: FF 1.3 million for *la Muraille*, FF 1 million for *Pacha Mama* and FF 800,000 for *l'Arête*.[99] The communist adminis-trators, aware of any potential criticism of their budgetary allocation, justified their action by stressing the fact that art was indispensable to everyone:

> People do not just live on bread. They also need cultural sustenance. The cost of a work of art can be envisaged in the same way as the cost of any other amenity or collective equipment. It is all credit to our town to have had the courage and the desire to promote creation in a social system where money, Americanisation and commercial production are all-powerful ... As a crucial element in the development of any human being, art must be part of our daily life as much as other human activities are. Monumental art is a genuine living museum which benefits the population every day.[100]

Such references to the so-called 'Americanisation' of culture, already found in the case of cinema, reflected the tendency of the PCF in Ivry to use even very abstract works in a clearly understandable fashion. It could also be argued that this policy was clientelistic in nature. In fact, out of the 33 works commissioned by the municipality prior to 1991, five were created by the same artist, Marc Charpin, and three by another artist, Daniel Pontoreau.[101] Another work, a mosaic for a secondary school, was created by Catherine Lurçat, the daughter of André Lurçat, a famous communist architect who had designed the Karl Marx school in Villejuif, a building which had attracted considerable attention in 1930s France.[102] The fact that the same artists were commissioned on several occasions, and that an artist 'with a name' in the French communist world was also commissioned, strongly suggests, irrespective of the artistic merits of these artists, that clientelism was a key aspect of this municipal policy.

With regard to the artistic freedom of these sculptors, this probably meant that, as in the case of Vitez's drama productions, they were free to produce even the most abstract works provided they did not challenge the legitimacy of the Party and local administrators were able to introduce these works to the Ivryen population through their omnipresent political prism.

CONCLUSION

A number of aspects can be concluded from this study of the cultural policy of Ivry in the years 1965–85. First, it seems to have followed the general line of the PCF at the national level, especially the guidelines issued by Rosette in 1977, and was by no means deviant from PCF strategy.

Secondly, this case study has established that the cultural policy of Ivry was pervaded by political and ideological objectives: the municipality always tried to use its cultural policy and amenities to educate the population of Ivry and to disseminate orthodox PCF views and symbols, in a bid to maintain and strengthen the Party's hold on the municipality. This was quite obvious in the case of the public library, or in numerous articles published by IMV.

Thirdly, the municipality of Ivry used some aspects of its cultural policies as a shop-window effect to attract praise from the French cultural elites. This was clearly the case with Vitez's drama company. The aim of this type of policy was to demonstrate to French society that a communist municipality was able to promote avant-garde artistic creation of the highest level in fields such as drama or sculpture.

Fourthly, this case study has suggested that the relationship between the PCF and artists working in its municipalities has changed dramatically since the Zhdanovist era. Thus, most artists working in Ivry in the 1970s and 1980s seem to have been free to engage in the most experimental, avant-garde research, which resulted in the production of abstract works which were diametrically opposed to the socialist realist credo which was imposed on PCF creators in the late 1940s and early 1950s. The fact that these avant-garde works were not easily accessible to the local population did not seem to matter, as long as they were easily translatable by local communist critics into easily understandable political statements. Thus, censorship became much more subtle than in the 1940s and 1950s, and, as long as artists did not challenge the PCF on crucial matters, their work did not encounter any interference from the Party.

Fifthly, it seems that the PCF used its expensive – at times lavish – cultural policy to create jobs and to commission artists, thus contributing to the creation of a *clientèle* of artists, teachers, librarians, and so on. One could easily object that in a medium-sized town such as Ivry, the Party was only able to maintain a fairly small *clientèle* of cultural workers. However, it could be argued that, if the phenomenon is considered on a larger scale, by examining all the municipalities held by the PCF in the 1970s and the 1980s, it becomes obvious that the Party controlled large sectors of French cultural life (see, for instance, the case of French drama).

Overall, the PCF used its cultural policy in Ivry to maintain its hegemony at the local level through the dissemination of orthodox values and the creation of a faithful *clientèle* of cultural workers, to strengthen the stronghold culture typical of French communist municipalities, and to promote socialist countries as models. This confirms the assumption that this party had a very marked teleological dimension.

NOTES

[1] A. Fourcaut (ed.), *Banlieue rouge, 1920–1960, Années Gabin, années Thorez: Archétype du populaire, banc d'essai des modernités* (Paris: Autrement, 1992), pp. 161–2.

[2] Ibid., p. 162.

[3] Ibid., p. 164.

[4] Ibid., p. 163.

[5] P. Thorez, *Une voix, presque mienne* (Paris: Gallimard, 1986), pp. 123–4.

[6] Fourcaut (ed.), *Banlieue rouge*, p. 163.

[7] O. Bertrand, 'Trois vies dédiées à Ivry-la-Rouge', *Libération*, 19–20 December (1998), pp. 10–11.

[8] M. Trigon, *Retour aux sources: Lettres à mon fils* (Paris: Le Temps des Cerises, 1994), pp. 76–9.

[9] On the Gosnat family, spanning three generations of communist leaders, see Bertrand, 'Trois vies dédiées à Ivry-la-Rouge', pp. 10–11.

[10] Ibid., pp. 10–11.

[11] On communist municipalities in general, see S. Ronai, 'Comment conserver une municipalité communiste: observations de terrain', *Communisme*, 22–23 (1989), pp. 93–105. Also extremely useful and specifically devoted to Ivry is H. Lerolle, 'De certaines coutumes électorales du PCF: le cas d'Ivry-sur-Seine', *Communisme*, 18–19 (1988), pp. 19–32.

[12] Fourcaut (ed.), *Banlieue rouge*, p. 190.

[13] R. Pronier, *Les Municipalités communistes* (Paris: Balland, 1983), p. 76.

[14] For other examples of communist dissidence at the local level, see Dreyfus, *PCF, crises et dissidences*, pp. 223–9.

[15] G. Belloin, *Nos rêves, camarades* (Paris: Le Seuil, 1979), pp. 90–1.

[16] For a short biography of Georges Gosnat, see, for instance, P. Robrieux, *Histoire intérieure du Parti communiste: Biographies; Chronologie; Bibliographie*, Vol. 4 (Paris: Fayard, 1984), pp. 276–7.

[17] Ibid., p. 277.

[18] Pronier, *Les Municipalités communistes*, p. 95.

[19] M. Rosette, *La Gestion municipale dans l'action* (Paris: Editions Sociales, 1977), p. 205.

[20] Montaldo, *La France communiste*, p. 162.
[21] J. Laloë, *Ivry-ma-Ville*, 44, October (1976), p. 2.
[22] F. Ecosse, *Ivry-ma-Ville*, 54, January (1978), p. 2.
[23] F. Ecosse, *Ivry-ma-Ville*, 86, January (1981), p. 19.
[24] F. Leriche, 'Le droit à la culture', *Ivry-ma-Ville*, 44, October (1976), p. 2.
[25] Ibid., p. 2.
[26] A. Minc, 'La culture, aussi nécessaire que l'air qu'on respire', *Ivry-ma-Ville*, 49, June–July (1977), p. 7.
[27] See, for instance, *Ivry-ma-Ville*, 77, February (1980), p. 3.
[28] Rosette, *La Gestion municipale dans l'action*, p. 198.
[29] Ibid., p. 204.
[30] Ibid., p. 205.
[31] Fourcaut, *Banlieue rouge*, p. 27.
[32] *Ivry-ma-ville*, 197, January (1991), p. 11.
[33] Ibid., p. 11.
[34] Pronier, *Les Municipalités communistes*, p. 73.
[35] Antoine Castro, *Ivry-ma-Ville*, 57, April (1978), pp. 6–7.
[36] Ibid., p. 7.
[37] See G. Marchais, *Le Défi démocratique* (Paris: Grasset, 1973).
[38] F. Hincker, 'Les hommes contre', in A. Spire and J. Chancel (eds), *La Culture des camarades* (Paris: Autrement, 1992), pp. 25–6.
[39] See N. and J. Kehayan, *Rue du prolétaire rouge: Deux communistes français en URSS* (Paris: Le Seuil, 1978).
[40] On the construction and dissemination of Soviet propaganda in France in the 1920s and 1930s, see S. Coeuré, *La Grande Lueur à l'Est: Les Français et l'Union Soviétique, 1917–1939* (Paris, Le Seuil, 1999).
[41] F. Jouineau, 'Sur le chemin du bien-être: Voyage en Union Soviétique', *Ivry-ma-Ville*, 87, January (1981), pp. 20–3.
[42] 'Zubkov, l'étoile rouge', *Ivry-ma-Ville*, 184, November (1989), pp. 30–1.
[43] 'Le 8 mai', *Ivry-ma-Ville*, 32, April (1975), p. 12.
[44] Courtois (ed.), *Le Livre noir du communisme*, p. 270.
[45] See Fourcaut (ed.), *Banlieue rouge*, pp. 163–70.
[46] Quoted in Fourcaut (ed.), *Banlieue rouge*, p. 160.
[47] M. Delbrêl, *Ville marxiste: Terre de mission* (Paris: Le Cerf, 1970), p. 20.
[48] F. Jouineau, 'Communistes et Chrétiens', *Ivry-ma-Ville*, 83, September (1980), pp. 24–5.
[49] P. Forni, 'Ivry à l'aube du Moyen-Age', *Ivry-ma-Ville*, 98, January (1982), pp. 24–5.
[50] Lazar, *Maisons rouges*, p. 18.
[51] *Ivry-ma-Ville*, 44, October (1976), p. 7.
[52] Ibid., pp. 6–7.
[53] Ibid., p. 7.
[54] A. Spire and J.P. Viala, *La Bataille du livre* (Paris: Editions Sociales, 1976).
[55] Ibid., p. 103.
[56] Ibid., pp. 111–12.
[57] H. Deluy, *Ivry-ma-Ville*, 14, February–March (1972), p. 19.
[58] Daix, *J'ai cru au matin*, p. 421.
[59] *Ivry-ma-Ville*, 49, June–July (1977), pp. 8–9.
[60] Ibid., p. 8.
[61] J. Pourre, *Ivry-ma-Ville*, 8, September (1970), p. 18.
[62] A. Minc, *Ivry-ma-Ville*, 44, October (1976), p. 3.

[63] *Ivry-ma-Ville*, 44, October (1976), p. 12.

[64] Data on the Conservatoire for the year 1988 are extracted from *Ivry-ma-Ville*, 164, January (1988), pp. 27–9.

[65] A. Vitez, 'L'Atelier Théâtral', *Ivry-ma-Ville*, 44, October (1976), p. 14.

[66] See, for instance, the entry on Antoine Vitez in A. Hughes and K. Reader (eds), *Encyclopedia of Contemporary French Culture* (London: Routledge, 1998), pp. 552–3.

[67] *Ivry-ma-Ville*, 193, September (1990), p. 36.

[68] A. de Sédouy and A. Harris, *Voyage à l'intérieur du Parti communiste* (Paris: Le Seuil, 1974), p. 364.

[69] D. Bradby, *Modern French Drama, 1940–1980* (Cambridge: Cambridge University Press, 1984), p. 139.

[70] De Sédouy and Harris, *Voyage à l'intérieur du Parti communiste*, p. 370.

[71] A. Vitez, *De Chaillot à Chaillot* (Paris: Hachette, 1981), p. 22.

[72] *Le Monde*, 15 May 1975.

[73] *France-Soir*, 14 May 1975.

[74] A. Vitez, interview given in 1977, quoted in *Ivry-ma-Ville*, 191, June (1990), p. 39.

[75] Bradby, *Modern French Drama*, p. 222.

[76] A. Vitez, in *Ivry-ma-Ville*, 44, October (1976), p. 9.

[77] M. Galey, in *Le Quotidien de Paris*, 20 December 1974.

[78] P. Adrien, 'Le théâtre, une forme essentielle de communication', in *Ivry-ma-Ville*, 95, October (1981), p. 12.

[79] De Sédouy and Harris, *Voyage à l'intérieur du Parti communiste*, p. 365.

[80] Bradby, *Modern French Drama*, pp. 191–213.

[81] Data extracted from *Ivry-ma-Ville*, 76, January (1980), p. 6.

[82] Ibid., pp. 6–7.

[83] Vitez is quoted in *Ivry-ma-Ville*, 191, June (1990), p. 39.

[84] De Sédouy and Harris, *Voyage à l'intérieur du Parti communiste*, p. 368.

[85] Vitez is quoted in J.P. Leonardini, *Profils perdus d'Antoine Vitez* (Paris: Messidor, 1990), p. 64.

[86] Vitez is quoted in *Ivry-ma-Ville*, 191, June (1990), p. 39.

[87] De Sédouy and Harris, *Voyage à l'intérieur du Parti communiste*, p. 370.

[88] M. Haraszti, *L'Artiste d'Etat: De la censure en pays socialiste* (Paris: Fayard, 1983), pp. 6–12.

[89] Ibid., p. 122.

[90] F. Leriche, *Ivry-ma-Ville*, 39, February (1976), p. 13.

[91] Vitez, *De Chaillot à Chaillot*, pp. 65–6.

[92] Rosette, *La Gestion municipale dans l'action*, p. 203.

[93] *Ivry-ma-Ville*, 49, June–July (1977), p. 9.

[94] *Ivry-ma-Ville*, 158, June (1987), pp. 25–6.

[95] Ibid., pp. 25–6.

[96] *Ivryculture*, December (1988), p. 3.

[97] Ibid., p. 3.

[98] *Ivry-ma-Ville*, 199, March (1991), p. 7.

[99] Ibid., p. 7.

[100] Ibid., p. 10.

[101] Ibid., p. 11.

[102] On the Karl Marx school in Villejuif, see Fourcaut (ed.), *Banlieue rouge*, pp. 197–206.

6

The Cultural Policy of the PCI in Reggio Emilia (*c.* 1960–*c.* 1980): A Pragmatic, Societal Approach to the Provision of Public Amenities and Services

Following the discussion of the cultural policy implemented by the PCF in Ivry-sur-Seine, attention will turn now to the efforts and resources deployed in such policy-making by the PCI in Reggio Emilia with a view to establishing whether a clear contrast between these two communist parties can be identified on the ground. Accordingly, a similar framework to the previous chapter will be used in this second case study in order to facilitate the comparison between the two parties.

However, in order to reflect the disparities in the historical and institutional developments of the two cases studied, some aspects of the cultural policies of the PCI in Reggio will be discussed which do not have a direct equivalent in Ivry. For example, the implementation of 'symbol-producing' or 'memory-making' institutions (such as the Banfi Institute and the Cervi Institute) are the object of detailed analysis in order to emphasise the societal nature of Italian communism as seen at work in Reggio.

A brief presentation of Reggio Emilia as a stronghold of Italian communism and of the main institutional protagonists at the local level is followed by a detailed discussion of various cultural amenities and activities implemented by the PCI in Reggio.

REGGIO EMILIA: A STRONGHOLD OF ITALIAN COMMUNISM

Reggio Emilia: historical and socio-economic background

The town of Reggio Emilia is located about 65 kilometres north-west of Bologna, the administrative capital of Emilia-Romagna, a region which lies in the centre of the northern half of the Italian peninsula (see Figure

6.1). This region is part of the wealthy Padana plain, which stretches from Turin in the West to Ravenna and Rimini on the Adriatic coast. The main urban population centres of Emilia-Romagna, in decreasing order of population, are Bologna (c. 500,000 inhabitants), Modena and Parma (c. 180,000 inhabitants each), and Ravenna and Reggio (c.130,000 inhabitants each).

The region is principally agricultural: Emilia-Romagna is, amongst all 20 Italian administrative regions created in 1971, the one with the highest agricultural income, and can therefore be described as the 'corn loft' of the Peninsula. There are, however, industrialised areas in Emilia-Romagna, mostly based around Parma (food, textile and shoemaking industries), Ravenna (oil and chemical industries), Reggio (food, textile and mechanical industries) and Modena (metal and mechanical industries such as machine-tool manufacturing), while the capital city of the region, Bologna, is also an industrial centre (metallurgical and chemical industries, shoemaking) and has a highly developed tertiary sector. Moreover, the whole region is further characterised by a very dynamic network of small and medium-sized firms which form the backbone of its economy.

This mixture of agriculture, food industry and a network of small and medium-sized industrial companies is in itself a key factor in understanding the success of the Italian economy. This economy, together with the very active role played by the local Resistance in the Liberation of Italy in 1945, has led a number of scholars to describe the region as a major political stronghold of Italian communism. It is a stronghold which extends to what has become known as the central 'red belt' of Italy, a vast area including four regions: Tuscany, the Marches, Umbria and of course Emilia-Romagna. In a comparison of typical red areas in France and Italy, Lazar writes:

> Italy is not devoid of red suburbs. Around its main industrial cities, such as Genoa, Turin or Milan, the PCI has also established its hegemony over working-class communities ... However, this type of communist territory has not reached the scale it has in France ... [This is because] the centre of gravity of the PCI is located in the red areas of central Italy, in particular in Emilia-Romagna.[1]

'Reggio la Rossa' (Red Reggio): key local protagonists between 1960 and 1980

Reggio Emilia, whilst less famous than neighbouring Bologna, the 'showpiece of Italian communism',[2] is nonetheless a bastion of Italian

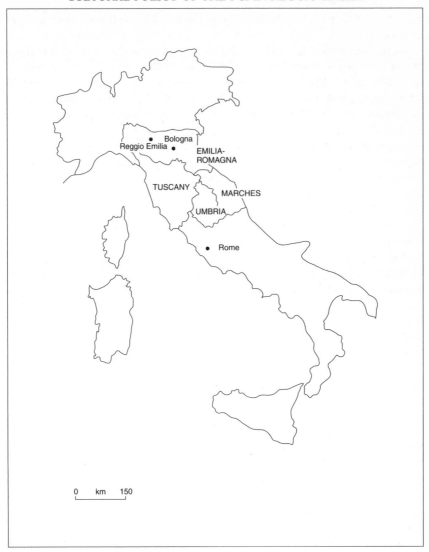

Figure 6.1:   Map of Italy and Emilia-Romagna

communism. At local government level, the PCI has held an absolute majority of seats on the municipal council since the Liberation of Italy in 1945, and all the mayors of Reggio since that date have been communists (PDS members after 1991).

As in the case of French local government, the mayor is a key actor at the local level, and two individuals strongly influenced the policy-making

123

process in Reggio between the 1960s and the 1980s, Renzo Bonazzi and Ugo Benassi.

Renzo Bonazzi, who had been active in the local Resistance, joined the PCI a few years after the Liberation, in 1949, and was the mayor of Reggio between 1962 and 1976. He was elected to the Italian Senate in 1987 and became President of the Reggio Theatre in 1995.[3] As mayor in the 1960s, he was behind a number of fundamental changes in the management of the town in general, and in the *svolta* (turning point or revolution) which characterised service provision, especially in the field of culture. It was indeed in the early 1960s that left-wing municipalities in Emilia-Romagna decided to put culture at the top of their political agenda, even if it meant incurring budget deficits. According to Bonazzi, prior to that time, spending on culture had been, under the laws regulating local finance, optional spending that should only occur if there were available funds (see Chapter 3).[4]

Under Bonazzi's tenures as mayor, and in co-ordination with the other PCI-held municipalities, culture became necessary spending and was put at the core of municipal action. This led to a number of developments, some of which will be discussed below. Thus, it could be argued that Bonazzi was a key player and that he was the driving force, in agreement with regional PCI leadership, behind Reggio's 'cultural revolution' of the 1960s.

The next mayor, Ugo Benassi, belonged to the same political generation and was the mayor between 1976 and 1987, promptly following in Bonazzi's footsteps. He has given a detailed account of his actions as mayor in *Piazza Grande: Il mestiere di sindaco* (Central Square: The Office of Mayor), published in 1989, in which he presented a balance sheet of the council's work under his leadership.[5] After retiring as mayor in 1987, he became President of the Cervi Institute.[6]

As in French local communism, a controversial question arises when discussing politicians at the local level: are the mayor and the councillors autonomous from the local/regional or even national leadership of the Party, or do they strictly follow Party orders?

When asked this question, Bonazzi replied that, while there were never any Party 'directives' to be strictly followed, the PCI provided some 'inspiration' for the policies of local administrators, and suggested a strong interaction between the Party and the municipal council. For instance, issues related to the theatre were discussed both by the local PCI cultural commission and by the municipal council, and the PCI indicated general directions, while the council was in charge of implementing cultural policies.[7]

On the other hand, Benassi strongly denied any PCI interference in municipal policy-making, and argued that the relationship between the

Party and the municipality was one of 'mutual autonomy': 'I have to say that, in my 11 years as mayor, I never received any directive from the Party.'[8] He then proceeded to strengthen his argument by using the legalistic, constitutional distinction between local government, which is accountable to the state and to the local population, and the PCI, which is only one of many political organisations.[9]

There is, however, crucial documentary evidence to suggest that there was strong interaction between the local PCI and the local authorities. Thus, the confidential minutes of a local PCI committee meeting held on 12 November 1979 (during Benassi's first tenure) to discuss the celebration of the tenth anniversary of Alcide Cervi's death by the Cervi Institute – officially an autonomous local association – corroborate the suspicion of interference. In these minutes, there is evidence that the PCI local leadership made decisions on the calendar of events, including a visit by the President of the National Assembly and the President of the Republic, and a possible visit by the PCI Secretary-General, Enrico Berlinguer. The minutes also refer to various sources of funding, including sources controlled by the PCI, such as the Cassa di Risparmio (a co-operative savings bank) and the Federation of Co-operatives, and local government sources such as the province of Reggio and the municipality of Reggio.[10]

Although it could be argued that this example is based on a local, non-profit-making association which was not, therefore, an elected tier of local government, the level of Party interference in this association, both in decision-making and funding, as well as Bonazzi's somewhat ambivalent statement, would suggest that comparable interference took place at municipal level. Elected office-holders, such as the mayor, were also at least to some extent accountable to local PCI leadership. Thus, local Party control over PCI-held local government was probably similar to that encountered in France.

However, control by the Party national leadership over Emilian and/or Reggian communists was more complex than it is in France and in Ivry, where the local Party was always under strict supervision from national leaders such as Thorez, Gosnat and Marchais (see Chapter 5). A number of factors seem to suggest that, notwithstanding the Leninist organisational structure of the PCI, Emilian communists enjoyed a much greater level of autonomy from Rome than their French counterparts did from Paris. Antonio Zambonelli, local historian and PCI member, notes:

The 1950s saw the emergence of 'Emilian communism', and I underline the term 'Emilian', because it was a particular, specific variant ... When I was young [Zambonelli was born in 1937], comrades from the South accused us of reformism, of betraying the cause of the working class ... To us Emilians, the policy of the PDS is not totally new. It is the continuation of our old political line.[11]

Although it would obviously be naïve to take this statement at face value, non-PCI scholarly sources tend to substantiate the argument that Emilian communists enjoyed relative autonomy from Rome. For instance, Maria La Falce argues that, after the first regional conference of the Emilian PCI (1959), which was a turning point for Emilian communism, the regional Party apparatus, led by a new generation of leaders such as Guido Fanti and Renato Zangheri, became relatively autonomous from the national executive of the Party.[12] In Lazar's words:

> [The national executive of the PCI] always had an ambiguous relationship with Emilia-Romagna: in the years of its glory, Emilia-Romagna was [the Party's] laboratory and showpiece, but, with the exception of the 'historic compromise' era, the majority of PCI leaders have always regarded Emilia-Romagna with suspicion because of its reformist leanings.[13]

Similarly, Pridham writes about the 'regionalisation of PCI structures', which started in the 1960s and gained impetus in the 1970s.[14]

It could be argued that, as a result of this suspicion, a sort of compromise was found between Emilian communists and the Via delle Botteghe Oscure (the PCI's headquarters in Rome): the Emilian communists, because of their overwhelming political success in their region, were granted a certain level of autonomy, but, on the other hand, they were prevented from altering the overall course of PCI strategy, which is reflected in the fact that virtually none of the national post-war leaders of the PCI came from Emilia-Romagna.

THE PUBLIC LIBRARY IN REGGIO

In Reggio, the public library, also known as the Biblioteca Panizzi, prides itself on a long history. The idea of the creation of a public library first emerged in the aftermath of the popular, French-inspired Revolution of August 1796 which resulted in the creation of a Reggian Republic. This led in turn to the creation of a 'National Library', a reflection of the Enlightenment philosophy and of the ideas of the French Encyclopaedists in the field of public reading. The new library was installed in the Palazzo San Giorgio, a former Jesuit convent attributed to the municipality after the eviction of the religious congregations from Reggio. In 1814, however, with the Restoration and the end of Italy's revolutionary phase, the National Library of Reggio was closed by Duke Francis IV. In 1865, after the departure of the Duke, it was decided to reopen the library to the population of Reggio.[15]

The next crucial stage in the history and development of the public library came with the election of a socialist municipality in Reggio in 1899. In fact, the socialist philosophy of a library accessible to all members of the population led to the inauguration of a second municipal library in 1910. It was a true reflection of the socialists' commitment to popular education through generalised, public reading, and it was named the Biblioteca Popolare (Popular Library).

This new, highly ideological institution – the idea was to spread socialist ideas in order to increase workers' political awareness and electoral support for the PSI (the Italian Socialist Party) – was, in fact, based upon the notion of the two opposing bourgeois and proletarian cultures discussed in Chapter 4. In early twentieth-century Reggio, this distinction was embodied by the coexistence of two libraries, the Panizzi Library on the one hand, where all the old manuscripts and collections were stored and whose access was mostly restricted to scholars and intellectuals, and the Biblioteca Popolare on the other hand, which was much more geared towards the public. The latter organised a whole series of conferences, exhibitions and debates of a political nature, and widely promoted reading among workers and farmers. However, this distinction between the two cultures was jettisoned in the early 1950s and this in turn led to the creation of a modern library in Reggio in the 1970s.

The setting up of the public library as a truly modern and accessible service took place in the late 1960s and early 1970s. Until that date, the coexistence of two libraries, a so-called 'municipal' one for students and teachers and a 'popular' one inherited from the socialist administration, had remained a constant feature of public reading provision in Reggio. This can be explained by the fact that the fascist regime had abolished the 'popular libraries' in all formerly socialist municipalities and that, after the Liberation, there was a strong political desire to reopen such libraries in left-wing municipalities. Hence, for a period of more than 20 years (from 1945 to the mid-1960s), the two public reading amenities remained in existence in most Emilian towns.

In the 1960s, however, this political distinction was challenged for several reasons by the new philosophy of the PCI regarding public administration. First of all, as discussed earlier, the PCI (re)discovered Gramsci's criticism of the distinction between proletarian and bourgeois cultures and officially abandoned this distinction.

Secondly, it was a period when the PCI redesigned its municipal policies, which became geared towards the provision of quality services accessible to the largest possible numbers. In his detailed historical survey of the cultural policies implemented in Correggio (a small town close to Reggio also held by the PCI since 1945), Viler Masoni discusses how this municipality also merged its two former libraries to create a new, modern one in the 1960s.[16]

This suggests that this new, pragmatic approach to the provision of public services was emerging simultaneously in most Emilian towns in these years, which seems to indicate the existence of a concerted policy on the part of the Emilian leadership of the PCI. Thirdly, the Emilian communist administrators were seeking a greater level of budgetary efficiency and had become all too aware of the fact that the coexistence and overlapping of two libraries was very costly to the town and represented a waste of public resources.

Last but not least, the PCI was very aware of the socio-economic changes which had transformed Emilian society since the end of the 1940s. It acknowledged the fact that the population had reached high levels of education and literacy, and that the need to educate what was a previously semi-literate working class was no longer an imperative. It was argued, instead, that the communist administration had to satisfy the general population's demand in terms of cultural and library facilities. This highly pragmatic approach to managing a changing socio-economic environment led the PCI administrators to merge the two libraries into a modern, well-equipped facility.

However, for technical and financial reasons, this decision took several years to implement, and it was only in 1975 that the new, unified Biblioteca Panizzi opened its doors to the Reggian population.[17] The implication is that, by this date, the PCI had abandoned its traditional ideological tenets on public reading and had adopted a truly pragmatic approach, mainly because it had realised that society had undergone tremendous social changes in the post-war period.

The underlying philosophy of the new library was to provide a modern and efficient service to the entire Reggian population. To this effect, the new director of the library, Maurizio Festanti, partly sought inspiration from the American model of public libraries. He was also inspired by the work of Antonio Panizzi (1797–1879), a Reggian intellectual who had spent most of his life in exile in England, where he had been for a number of years the principal librarian at the British Museum. In recognition for his contribution to the advancement of librarianship, Panizzi was knighted in 1868.

In order to follow in Panizzi's footsteps, Festanti, a graduate in history and library studies, spent several months in the United States in order to study the organisational principles of American libraries. Following this experience, he decided in 1978 to implement in Reggio the concept of open-shelf access to books. This constituted a revolutionary approach in the Italian context, for open-shelf libraries were extremely uncommon in Italy in these years.[18]

In Festanti's words, this change was a complete *svolta*, a 'Copernican revolution' which transformed the library from a kind of 'book museum' to a widely accessible instrument largely open to the public. This complete reorganisation was accompanied by the adoption of the Dewey classification, the most commonly used library classification in American and British libraries. Thus, the public library in Reggio has striven to become one of the most modern and accessible libraries in Italian cities of a comparable size.[19] Did it manage, however, to attract large numbers of Reggian citizens?

When asked about the readership of the new Panizzi, Festanti argues that, following the 'revolution' of 1978, the number of readers grew at a considerable pace.[20] This is confirmed by the Biblioteca Panizzi brochure: in 1977, before the introduction of the open-shelf structure, there were only 6,482 people registered with the library, whereas, by 1988, this number had been multiplied by six to reach 37,349,[21] in a town whose population remained generally stable (*c.* 130,000). These figures would imply that, by the late 1980s, one in 3.5 Reggians used the library.

It should however be noted that in any assessment of library readership, a distinction ought to be made between the total number of registered users, some of whom might only have registered with the library on a specific occasion, and the number of active users or readers. In fact, such a distinction is found in a study on the Panizzi readership published in 1989, which acknowledged the fact that only about 50 per cent of all registered users were regular users or readers (*lettori*) who borrowed on average ten items per calendar year.[22]

In spite of this distinction, it seems that the ratio of active users (one in seven) remained high for a town of the size of Reggio, and that this number or ratio compared very favourably to ratios in other Italian towns[23] – a point reiterated by Festanti in September 1995. The tremendous growth in library use since the end of the 1970s can be further substantiated by the exponential increase in the total annual number of book loans, from 41,188 in 1977 to 119,789 in 1983 and 186,898 in 1988.[24]

It can therefore be argued that the new policies implemented in the 1970s in the field of public reading were very successful in attracting a steadily increasing number of active users in a provincial town like Reggio, which was devoid of any sort of university structure.

However, this success prompts the question of the social composition of this readership. Was it mostly a working-class readership or a more bourgeois, middle-class one? The only data available regarding this issue are for the year 1988 and are reproduced in Figure 6.2.

Library members	% of total membership
School pupils aged 14+	40.1
Employees/technicians	16.3
Children under 14	11.6
Manual workers	7.7
Teachers	6.3
Unemployed	4.7
Housewives	3.7
Retired	3.4
Shopkeepers	2.8
Professionals	2.5
Others	0.9

Source: Data adapted from Panizzi Library (Reggio Emilia),
La Biblioteca Panizzi di Reggio Emilia, p. 9.

Figure 6.2:   Readership of the Panizzi Library

First of all, it appears that the working classes (manual workers) only accounted for less than 8 per cent of the readership, a relatively low percentage. This would imply that the readership of the public library was not a working-class readership. Secondly, it appears that teachers, school pupils and children, with a combined total of 58 per cent, were by far the largest population group represented in the overall readership. This finding confirms Gundle's claim that by the 1970s PCI administrators had scaled down their involvement and belief in class-based cultural politics:[25] the library had in the late 1970s to early 1980s become a true public service aimed at 'the people' in general.

Given this background, it could be argued that, for PCI administrators such as Festanti, the 'revolution' equated to the provision of a good public service, and not to the indoctrination of the masses. The ideological dimension of the Reggio library administrators was very low compared to that of Ivryen ones. Indeed, it could safely be argued that few French communists would openly have sought inspiration from an American model in the 1970s.

THE MUNICIPAL THEATRE IN REGGIO FROM 1957 TO THE LATE 1970S: AVANT-GARDE OR TRADITION?

The municipal theatre (Teatro Municipale, often referred to as *il Municipale* by Reggians) was founded in 1857 and remained privately owned and managed for exactly a hundred years until the town of Reggio decided to take over the building and its administration in early 1957. It is a beautifully decorated, classical theatre building with a capacity of about 1,300/1,500 seats, and resembles many an Italian theatre.[26]

The council's decision to take over *il Municipale* was motivated by several factors. First of all, from a financial point of view, the previous owners had run into difficulties, and the future of the theatre was becoming very uncertain. Indeed, many local theatregoers feared that it would become derelict in a matter of years if no alternative solution to private management was found. More importantly, as mentioned earlier, the late 1950s saw the beginnings of the major *svolta* which was to characterise the cultural policy of Reggio in the early 1960s.

As part of this drive to promote a dynamic cultural life in Reggio, the municipal council saw the theatre as a key institution which could be used in a number of ways to encourage wider sections of the population – school pupils, workers, farmers, pensioners – to attend cultural events which had until then only attracted the bourgeois elites of the area.[27] This concept of easy access to culture through drama and other classical activities such as opera and ballet was the main objective of the new, publicly administered *Municipale*, and its corollary objective was to stage quality events performed by top companies from the world over in what was often described as a grey, provincial town.

Thus, according to Armani, organiser of various cultural events in Reggio and one of the contributors to the book on the Reggio Theatre, the criteria used to select events in Reggio were not political or ideological, but strictly cultural criteria, that is to say that what was sought in an event was quality and innovation irrespective of its content.[28]

Accordingly, the administrators of the theatre were keen to organise programmes of events drawing from a wide variety of works, repertoires and companies, from classical operas such as *The Magic Flute* to avant-garde drama plays staged by the Living Theatre company (see below), from eighteenth-century Italian drama to twentieth-century Russian ballet. Thus, a quick glance at the repertoires represented in the successive programmes of events of the *Municipale* would suggest that diversity was a key concept to its administrators. This self-proclaimed diversity is examined below. Most of the numerous events in this succession of programmes fall into three artistic categories: drama, ballet and opera.

As asserted above by Reggio cultural administrators, the key objectives of the municipal takeover of the *Municipale* was to bring drama to a new audience on the one hand, and to promote experimental creation on the other. These two objectives are not always compatible with each other, as suggested by the case of Ivry-sur-Seine and Vitez's elitist work (see Chapter 5), for experimental drama tends to be quite hard to understand for an audience new to drama. As a result of these objectives, a mixture of avant-garde events and traditional plays was staged, the latter kind of drama being given increasing emphasis towards the end of the 1960s.

An example of avant-garde, experimental drama in Reggio: The Living Theatre

The most significant example of avant-garde, experimental drama staged in Reggio is undoubtedly that of the works of the Living Theatre. This drama company was at the forefront of experimental drama, and its founders, American dramatists Julian Beck and his partner Judith Malena, were closely associated with America's radical left.[29] By the early 1960s, it had become quite famous amongst European dramatists and left-wing cultural administrators, as recalled by Jack Ralite, a French communist specialising in cultural issues and close friend of Antoine Vitez.[30]

According to Bonazzi, then mayor of Reggio, the Living Theatre had been 'constrained to leave the USA' in September 1964, although no reasons are given for this, and arrived in Reggio in the early months of 1966, looking for support in the form of a place to stage their latest creation, *Frankenstein*.[31] The municipality was very keen to provide technical and financial assistance to Beck's company, which staged various scenes and rehearsals of their play in ordinary places such as 'popular circles' (PCI-held cultural/associational buildings) and other public buildings, therefore taking drama to the population of various Reggio districts.[32] After this, the Living Theatre was to stage a number of plays in Reggio (see Figure 6.3).

The Living Theatre company was characterised by the collective nature of its work (all company members took part in the writing and staging of their plays), by its self-proclaimed independence from any institution (hence the need to move from town to town and from country to country) and by its political commitment which was to reveal and

Date	Event/play	Venue in Reggio
21 April 1966	The Brig	Municipal Theatre
May/June 1966	Production/rehearsal of Frankenstein	Verdi Room
10 June 1966	Mysteries and Smaller Pieces	Gramsci Circle
July 1966	Frankenstein (dress rehearsal)	Verdi Room
16 May 1967	Frankenstein	Municipal Theatre
12 November 1969	Antigone	Municipal Theatre
21 December 1975	Sette Meditazioni sul Sadomasochismo Politico (Seven Meditations on Political Sadomasochism)	Sports Complex
January 1976	Oratorio di Appòggio allo Sciopero Confit (Oratorio in Support of the Confit Strike) (4 shows)	Various town squares
June 1980	Antigone	Zucchi Room

Source: Data extracted from Reggio Emilia, Living Theatre in Reggio Emilia (Reggio Emilia: Tecnostampa, 1995), p. 21.

Figure 6.3:   Living Theatre events in Reggio Emilia, 1966–80

condemn any institutionalised form of repression or violence in contemporary societies.

Living Theatre plays were always provocative and disturbing, and relied heavily on visual effects. The company was committed to what is known in drama and literary circles as the 'theatre of cruelty' (théâtre de la cruauté), a theory formulated in the late 1930s by French dramatist and poet Antonin Artaud (1896–1948). According to Artaud, modern drama had to break away from its strong reliance on the spoken word and emphasise instead the power of images. Consequently, drama actors were urged to make full use of their bodies and of visual, violent acting in order to provoke a reaction among the audience, to force them to take part in what was to become a collective event, in order to overcome the traditional gap between the actors and their passive audience.[33]

As disciples of Artaud, Beck and his company performed acts of actual violence, sadomasochism and nudity on stage, and aimed to generate strong reactions among the spectators. Thus, the opening scene of Frankenstein saw a group of actors sitting on stage around a naked man while the audience was still getting seated, with a loudspeaker announcing that in three minutes the central actor would start to levitate as a result of the other actors' collective will. After the three minutes and several such announcements ('he will start to levitate in one minute'), the actor inevitably failed to levitate, the speaker announced this failure, and the other actors, infuriated, ran to him, beat him and chained him on to a metal pole before carrying him among the theatre through rows of seats, to the apparent delight of an equally infuriated audience.[34]

Such spectacularly visual and unusual performances, which were repeated in most of their plays, attracted contrasting reactions from the audience and from the critics, who used adjectives such as 'exceptional', 'most interesting', 'shocking' and 'disconcerting' in their reviews of the play.[35] One critic for the local daily, *Gazzetta di Reggio*, noted with some scepticism that the large audience had been disconcerted, scared and puzzled by the plays,[36] but most were enthusiastic about the Living Theatre's highly innovative and provocative approach.

A few conclusions can be drawn from the involvement of the municipality of Reggio with the Living Theatre. First, the municipality still prides itself on the initial support it gave to Beck's company, as can be seen in the fact that it devoted a special booklet to the Living Theatre as late as in 1995. This would suggest that Reggio was trying to create an image of a municipality at the forefront of cultural innovation at a time when the Living Theatre company were *personae non gratae* in most US and European cities. Indeed, in a review of the stagings of *Frankenstein* abroad, a writer for the local information newsletter could hardly conceal a pride shared by other Reggians: 'The Living's *Frankenstein* has met with success abroad. It was born in Reggio.'[37]

The fact that the local audience was often disconcerted was seen in a positive light by cultural administrators who argued that, beyond the audience's like or dislike of the plays, what had mattered was that large segments of the local population had been exposed to innovative political drama and had reacted – positively or not – to it. Moreover, Reggio was able to associate itself with the national and international fame enjoyed by the Living Theatre through its close, early association with the company, which was also remembered fondly by Beck and Malina who in return were keen to praise the city, as the number of letters and newspaper articles found in the 1995 booklet bear witness.[38]

Thus, the role played by avant-garde drama in Reggio appears to bear some similarities to the role of Vitez's TQI in 1970s Ivry, even if Vitez's approach to drama was very different from Beck's, the former putting a lot of emphasis on obscure dialogues. In both cases, the success of avant-garde drama was used to promote the image of an innovative, modern town dedicated to artistic creation. However, one major difference was that, in the case of Reggio, drama was not restricted to avant-garde creation. Indeed, the bulk of drama activities in Reggio was borrowed from a much more classical, traditional repertoire.

Targeting a wide audience: 'conventional' drama in Reggio

The second dimension of drama provision in Reggio was to bring to a wide, local audience the classics of Italian and worldwide drama, whether traditional or modern. Since the municipality did not have its own drama company, it invited recognised Italian companies to stage their plays in the *Municipale*. Figure 6.4, which lists all the events mentioned in the book edited by the Reggio municipality, gives a reasonable representation of the plays and events which were staged.[39]

The range of plays and authors illustrated in Figure 6.4 prompts the crucial remark that there was a genuine diversity in the repertoire proposed. Indeed, while there were a number of plays by committed Marxist playwrights such as Bertholt Brecht and Vladimir Mayakowsky, the vast majority of plays programmed borrowed from the classical repertoire (Shakespeare, Middleton, Molière for foreign drama, Goldoni for Italian drama) to the modern one, with again a variety of schools being represented: the 'theatre of the absurd' (Ionesco, Pinter), existentialist drama (Sartre), Italian tragicomedies (Pirandello) and modern English-speaking drama (Miller, O'Neill, Osborne). This level of diversity was also found in the directing style: indeed, a fair number of Italian drama companies drawn from the four corners of the Peninsula were invited to play in Reggio, which meant that the audience was exposed not to just one or two directing styles, but to a great variety of actors and dramatists. This variety, clearly a result of the municipality's choice not to have its own, resident drama company would suggest that a genuine effort was made to attempt to attract as wide an audience as possible (see below). This was not the case in Ivry-sur-Seine where the decision to support one company inevitably resulted in a quasi-monopoly on drama exercised by Antoine Vitez for nearly ten years.

This genuine diversity tends to confirm the claim of the cultural authorities of Reggio that they sought to attract a wide audience by staging works of quality and international renown, and by pricing tickets appropriately. There are data which do indeed show that the price of theatre tickets was significantly lower in Reggio than in the rest of Italy. Thus, in 1968, the average price of a drama ticket was 2,154 lire in Reggio, 2,419 lire in Emilia-Romagna and 3,164 lire in Italy, and in 1975 it was 2,485 lire in Reggio, 3,105 lire in Emilia-Romagna and 3,834 lire in Italy.[40]

There is good statistical evidence that a significant proportion of the local population responded positively to this policy by attending the theatre in significant numbers. Thus, attendance figures for the 1958–59 drama season (i.e. in the early days of the new *Municipale*) were seen as very promising for the cultural authorities: 'The most obvious proof of

Playwright	Nationality	Century	Play(s) Staged in Reggio
Brecht, Bertholt	German	Twentieth	*Mother Courage and Her Children; The Life of Galileo; I, Bertholt Brecht; Rise and Fall of the City of Mahagonny*
Chekhov, Anton	Russian	Nineteenth	*Uncle Vanya*
Dostoyevsky, Fyodor	Russian	Nineteenth	*White Nights*
Goldoni, Carlo	Italian	Eighteenth	*Mine Hostess; The Servant of Two Masters; The Tyrants; The Lovers; Il Campiello*
Ionesco, Eugène	French	Twentieth	*Exit the King*
Mayakowsky, Vladimir	Russian	Twentieth	*The Bathhouse; The Bedbug*
Middleton, Thomas	English	Early seventeenth	*A Mad World, My Masters*
Miller, Arthur	American	Twentieth	*Death of a Salesman; A View from a Bridge*
Molière	French	Seventeenth	*The Imaginary Invalid*
O'Neill, Eugene	American	Twentieth	*Long Day's Journey into Night*
Osborne, John	English	Twentieth	*Luther*
Pinter, Harold	English	Twentieth	*The Homecoming; No Man's Land*
Pirandello, Luigi	Italian	Early twentieth	*Six Characters in Search of an Author; Henry IV; Right You Are (If You Think So); The Mountain Giants; Liolà; Man, Beast and Virtue; All for the Best*
Sartre, Jean-Paul	French	Twentieth	*Lucifer and the Lord*
Shaffer, Peter	English	Twentieth	*Black Comedy*
Shakespeare, William	English	Late sixteenth early seventeenth	*Twelfth Night; Romeo and Juliet; Hamlet (in English); Macbeth; The Merchant of Venice; A Midsummer Night's Dream; King John; The Tragedy of King Richard II*
Simon, Neil	American	Twentieth	*Plaza Suite*
Wilder, Thornton	American	Twentieth	*Our Town*

Figure 6.4: Plays staged in Reggio between the late 1950s and the late 1970s

the audience's positive response can be found in the statistics for this period ... with a total of 5,876 tickets for seven events, or an average attendance of 839 people.'[41]

Other figures available for the 1976–77 season confirm this steady attendance, with 50 drama events attracting 32,844 spectators, an average of 657 per event[42] – a relatively high number for a town the size of Reggio. In fact, these figures seem to have compared favourably with national attendance figures. Thus, in the 1975–76 drama season, the *Municipale* sold an average of 17 theatre tickets per 100 inhabitants of the province of Reggio, compared to 13 on average for the whole of Italy.[43] In fact, most figures available show that, in regional terms, Reggio came second only to Bologna, a town renowned for its university and intellectual life where one would therefore expect healthy attendance figures.

This study of drama in Reggio prompts the tentative conclusion that the cultural policy set up in the late 1950s was both innovative in artistic terms (see, for instance, the Living Theatre) and pluralist in the choice of the plays featured. As in the case of the Panizzi Library, the communist municipality seems to have been successful in attracting a comparatively high proportion of its population to the theatre, through the provision of quality and reasonably priced events, and the ideological dimension of this drama policy seems to have been very low. A brief examination of ballet and opera in Reggio confirms this conclusion.

Ballet and opera in Reggio

As part of its policy of public management of the *Municipale*, the municipality of Reggio decided to use this building to stage an increasing number of ballets and operas, a decision which was seen by some as a courageous one given that ballet and opera were both considered as expensive and exclusive artistic genres usually restricted to bourgeois audiences.[44] Accordingly, this decision was motivated by the desire to widen access to these traditionally exclusive performing arts, and significant resources were deployed in these fields. Thus, 31 ballet performances were staged in the years 1960–69 (inclusive), 55 in the years 1970–79 (inclusive), and the trend continued in the 1980s, with 120 performances in the years 1980–86 (inclusive).[45]

As in the case of drama, diversity and quality seem to have been the key characteristics of ballet dancing in Reggio. Indeed, the ballets were taken from the classical repertoire (e.g. *Les Sylphides*, music by Chopin, choreography by Fokine, *The Crystal Palace*, music by Bizet, choreography by Balanchine), as well as from the modern one (*Rhapsody in Blue*, music by Gershwin), with a fair number of ballets by Russian composers (Tchaikovsky, Prokoviev, Stravinsky) which have become classics of the genre.

A very noticeable feature of ballet dancing in Reggio was the number of ballet companies coming from the Eastern bloc and Yugoslavia: in 1960–69, out of the 31 ballet events in Reggio, 21 involved companies from socialist countries, six from Western countries and four from Italy. A total of 11 events (over a third of all performances) were staged by Yugoslav companies, a particularly strong link having been established with the Ljubljana dance company. In the 1970s, out of a total of 55 performances, 29 companies came from socialist countries, with Soviet companies staging 12 performances.[46]

This predominance of ballet companies from socialist countries can be explained by a number of factors. The simplest explanation might be that, as a communist municipality, it seemed logical for Reggio to opt for companies coming from the countries of 'really existing socialism' in order to strengthen its links with these countries, and maybe to use the quality of the ballet companies as a basis to draw more general conclusions on the contribution of socialism in the field of culture, and so on.

However, such an explanation does not seem entirely convincing: why would Reggio have given priority to ballet from the socialist countries and not – far from it – done the same in the fields of drama and opera? Why have this preference for Yugoslav companies in the early 1960s? After all, during the Cold War, the former Yugoslavia and its ruler Tito had been attacked by the Soviet Union and many orthodox communist parties as a dangerous 'deviation' (or worse) from the socialist model embodied by the Soviet Union, and, even after Khrushchev's public apologies to Tito and his country in 1955, Yugoslavia was not always seen as the best possible partner in the international communist movement.

Therefore, other factors are needed to explain this preference. First, despite the fact that the Soviets and their Eastern satellites promoted and used their ballet companies in what could be called the 'cultural Cold War' in order to demonstrate their self-proclaimed superiority as a socio-economic model (see, for instance, the role of the Bolshoi), it is a commonly acknowledged fact that Russia's contribution to twentieth-century ballet dancing is a major one, with choreographers such as Michel Fokine (1880–1942), who revolutionised ballet dancing before leaving Russia in 1918, or Vaslav Nijinski (1890–1950).

Building on and continuing this pre-Soviet expertise in ballet, Soviet ballet established itself at the forefront of this genre, and strongly encouraged socialist countries, including Yugoslavia before the 1948 rift, to follow in its path. Thus, the preference for companies coming from socialist countries could be explained by the desire to invite to Reggio some high-quality ballet companies. It was also motivated by financial factors, as recalled in the 1978 publication on the theatre.[47] It could indeed be argued that, all things being equal, it was much cheaper to invite, for instance, the National Slovenian Ballet (Ljubljana) than it would have been to invite the London-based Royal Ballet.

Thus, pragmatism and emphasis on quality and reasonable costs were probably the key factors in the choice of ballet companies, and this was reflected in the success of ballet in Reggio. Indeed, it seems that over the years ballet performances attracted increasing numbers of people, from an average of about 500 spectators per event in the first years (1957–65) to an average of 1,000 spectators per event in the late 1970s.[48] As in the case of drama, these figures compare very favourably with average audiences in other Italian towns and in the whole of Italy.[49] This particular aspect of cultural planning was described emphatically by a dance critic writing for *Paese Sera*, an Italian daily, in 1975:

> As regards ballet, Reggio is by far better than Rome. An audience made up not only of adults but also of a number of children from the schools in Reggio has seen, in the last three seasons and at a very modest price, an incredible range of companies of the highest level and a lot of the most important ballets in the classic and modern repertoires staged and interpreted with a talent which was always outstanding, sometimes extraordinary.[50]

A brief examination of the opera seasons strongly confirms this emphasis on quality and diversity, with 101 opera performances staged between 1957 and 1977, including 57 by classic Italian composers (e.g. Bellini, Puccini, Verdi) and 44 by foreign composers (e.g. Mozart, Purcell, Gounod, Borodin).

THE INSTITUTE FOR THE HISTORY OF THE RESISTANCE (ISTORECO)

A key dimension of the cultural policy of Reggio and other Emilian towns lies in their efforts to create and/or strengthen Party symbols and identity. The concepts of 'living memory', 'historical memory' and 'collective memory', borrowed from Lavabre's seminal work on the memory of French communists (see Chapter 4), will be used in this section as a basis to answer the following questions: has the PCI succeeded in creating a strong sense of identity centred on a collective memory shared by all its activists and sympathisers in Emilia? What were the main symbols used in this 'identity-making' process?

The Institute for the History of the Resistance and the War of Liberation (Istituto per la Storia della Resistenza e della Guerra di Liberazione) was first created in 1965, and was renamed in 1994 the Institute for the History of the Resistance and Contemporary Society (Istituto per la Storia della Resistenza e della Società Contemporanea) or ISTORECO.

The ISTORECO was established following a nationwide impetus from the National Association of Italian Partisans (ANPI in Italian), and similar institutes were created in most cities of northern Italy, where the Resistance had been very active. This network of local institutes was headed at the national level by the National Institute for the History of the Resistance, based in Milan, and at the regional level by the Bologna Institute.

The ISTORECO is a public, non-profit-making association. In its early days, it operated on a strictly voluntary basis, but its work and resources were enhanced by a law passed in 1967 allowing Italian civil servants, and teachers in particular, to be seconded as full-time employees in these associations while remaining on school payrolls. For example, Antonio Zambonelli, the director of the ISTORECO in Reggio, used to work as a primary school teacher before becoming the Institute's full-time scholar and administrator.[51]

From a political point of view, the Institute gathered historians and teachers from various political families. In fact, its creation had been undertaken by many former Emilian partisans representing all the political forces which had taken part in the Resistance: the PCI, the PSI (Partito Socialista Italiano, or Italian Socialist Party), the Christian democrats, and the Action Party (Partito d'Azióne). This was a political party which had its origins in the Justice and Liberty movement founded in France in 1929 by the Rosselli brothers and other anti-fascist exiles to combat Mussolini's dictatorship from abroad. The Action Party was founded in January 1943 by a number of intellectuals and politicians representing various political factions and traditions such as the reformist socialists, the radical democrats and the republicans. Its chief goals were the liberation of northern Italy from Nazi occupation, the overthrowing of the fascist regime and the implementation of a republic. The Action Party soon became one of the biggest Resistance organisations in occupied Italy, second only to the PCI.[52]

In fact, the first-ever President of ISTORECO, Vittorio Pelizzi, came from the Action Party, which seems to indicate that the Institute was always keen to maintain the united spirit of the Resistance, and was not just a communist think-tank, but a genuine research institute.[53]

The ISTORECO is funded from three main sources:

- the Italian Ministry for Education, which pays the only full-time member of the Institute;
- the local authorities, that is to say the province of Reggio Emilia, the municipality of Reggio (which provides a fifteenth-century building at a very low rent), and 26 small communes in the periphery of Reggio, all administered by the PCI;
- subscribers to the Institute's journal, *Ricerche Storiche* (Historical Research), most of them being school teachers or intellectuals close to the PCI.

The financial structure of the ISTORECO does not differ from that of any other public association, and the fact that the Italian government acknowledged the work of such associations by passing a law granting secondment to some of its teachers could be seen as an indication as to the cultural usefulness of the ISTORECO. It is indeed doubtful that a DCI-dominated state would have agreed to fund full-time jobs in recognised communist think-tanks. So far, it appears that the Institute, although it might be argued that it was dominated by the PCI and by communist municipalities, played the card of unity and co-operation with non-communists. What was, however, its role in the cultural scene of Reggio-Emilia?

Originally, the Institute's main remit was the study of the Resistance movements in the province of Reggio and the collection of local archives, but it also undertook the task of disseminating information and publications about anti-fascism and the partisan movements in the area. One concern of the ISTORECO was – and still is – that younger generations might forget about those years in particular, or underestimate the significance of historical knowledge in general. This concern for youth education led to the widening of the Institute's remit, as illustrated by its renaming in 1994, and also stimulated the redesigning of the Institute's journal, *Ricerche Storiche*, to include an educational section comprising articles on the way history should be taught at school, advice for history teachers, etc.

It could be argued that, given the influence of the PCI within local authorities and within ISTORECO itself, the Party used the Institute and its chief medium, *Ricerche Storiche*, to indoctrinate young people, to disseminate the official communist version of historic events or to relay orthodox Marxist views on historical processes. However, a close examination of the ideological and political contents of a number of ISTORECO printed materials does not support this view.

In 1975, on the occasion of the 30th anniversary of the Liberation of Italy, the ISTORECO published a pamphlet aimed at high-school pupils, written by Antonio Zambonelli.[54] Scrutiny of this pamphlet strongly suggests that ISTORECO publications were quite different from the orthodox communist historiography of the PCF in the same period found for instance in Ivry (see Chapter 5).

In its 43 pages, the emphasis was clearly put on the parallel themes of the need for the unity of all anti-fascist movements in the struggle against fascism and Nazism, of the unconditional fidelity to democratic values (in the liberal, Western sense of the word) and to post-war institutions (the Constitution and the Republic). In fact, it can be argued that a number of elements of historical analysis contained in this pamphlet did not echo the orthodox interpretations found in the PCF historiography of the time.

On the first page of the document, Zambonelli insists that he is the main author, but he acknowledges that he has greatly benefited from suggestions and advice dispensed by members of the Institute 'belonging to the various political forces of the Resistance'.[55]

In the opening sections of the pamphlet, in the passage where he discusses the reasons for the victory of fascism in the early 1920s, Zambonelli insists that the argument put forward by fascists that the country had to be saved from the prospect of a Bolshevik-style revolution was entirely unfounded, because, he argues: 'a revolution of the Russian type [was] unthinkable in the Italian context'.[56] This statement, which is clearly reminiscent of Gramsci's interpretation of the post-First World War situation in Italy, can be seen as an effort to legitimise the democratic nature of PCI strategy of *via italiana al socialismo*. The implication of this analysis was that the PCI had never been a party seeking to emulate the Bolshevik Party by seizing power through a violent, revolutionary process.

On the same page, one of the factors put forward by the author to explain the rise of Mussolini and his accession to power is 'the fact that the various parties were not united in the fight against fascist subversion'.[57] One could have expected, in an orthodox Marxist–Leninist analytical framework, that a single cause would have been identified, that is to say the responsibility of the bourgeoisie and of the industrialists who funded fascist squads. Zambonelli, while rejecting some of the blame heaped on the conservative forces of post-First World War Italy, shifts the emphasis towards the lack of unity of anti-fascist parties. What stems from this analysis is that the PCI was also to blame for not having sought an alliance with other anti-fascist forces.

On the subject of the Resistance movements, Zambonelli emphasises the united nature of the Liberation struggle by reminding his readership that the Liberation Committees had been formed by representatives from the PCI, the PSI, the DCI, the Liberal Party, and the Action Party.[58] This insistence on the joint merits of various political parties (unlike the hagiographic monopoly claimed by the PCF on Resistance martyrdom in

France) was even stronger in the passages on the Reconstruction period: 'De Gasperi, Togliatti, Nenni, Parri, Croce were some of the major protagonists of the political choices of this period [the years 1944–48].'[59]

This list clearly reflects the author's intention to acknowledge the contributions of most anti-fascist parties to the birth of the Italian Republic, irrespective of their relationship to the PCI. Alcide De Gasperi (1881–1954) was the principal founder of the Italian Christian Democratic Party, the main political rival of the PCI. As Premier of Italy between 1945 and 1953, he expelled the communists and socialists from the coalition government in May 1947 and consequently became the first political target of the PCI at the peak of the Cold War (1947–53).[60]

Pietro Nenni (1891–1980) was the main socialist leader of the post-war era and his PSI was allied to the PCI until 1956.[61] Ferruccio Parri (1890–1981) was one of the founders of the Action Party and a key organiser of Italian Resistance,[62] and Benedetto Croce (1866–1952), often presented as 'the most influential Italian philosopher of the twentieth century', was an advocate of political liberalism also famous for his writings on the 'birth and death of Marxism in Italy', which had generated heated controversies with PCI leaders and intellectuals.[63]

One of the most revealing passages of this pamphlet, however, is to be found in the section on the Cold War. Once again, one could have expected an orthodox presentation of American imperialism against the Soviet commitment to peace and equality among the peoples of the world, but the two superpowers are in fact introduced in the following terms:

> [There are] two blocs: on the one hand the Western countries (including Italy), subjected, *to a certain extent* [emphasis added], to American tutelage, and on the other hand the Eastern countries, the *people's democracies* [*sic*], in turn subjected to Soviet tutelage.[64]

In this passage, not only is the responsibility for the Cold War shared between the USA and the USSR, but it also appears that American tutelage might have been looser (note the qualifying 'to a certain extent', '*in un certo senso*' in Italian) than the Soviet one. Also, the use of italics (*democrazie popolari*) seems to imply a degree of criticism, i.e. that these countries were not democracies in the Italian sense of the word as endorsed by the PCI. When compared with the PCF literature of the 1970s, with its apology of the Soviet model, this pamphlet seems to indicate that Emilian communists had already gone a long way from the traditional pillars of Marxist–Leninist orthodoxy, which confirms the contrast between PCI and PCF historiographies highlighted by Lazar and noted in Chapter 1.[65]

This evidence suggests that the ISTORECO has fulfilled a crucial function in the production/dissemination of the symbols of the Resistance (unity of anti-fascist forces, commitment to democratic and republican values), to the extent that these themes seemed by the early 1970s to have relegated the internationalist credo (fealty to the kingdom of 'really existing socialism', superiority of the Soviet model, commitment to a Bolshevik-style revolution) to a secondary role in the symbolic universe of the Reggians.

The Institute has been successful in doing so for two reasons: first of all, the PCI did not claim any political monopoly on the legacy of the Resistance. All the anti-fascist parties were involved in the life and working of the ISTORECO, and the PCI, unlike the PCF with its myth of the *75,000 fusillés*, did not seek to exercise any sort of emotional monopoly on sacrifice and martyrdom, but sought, on the contrary, to make a genuine contribution to the progress of historical knowledge. Secondly, it can be argued that the ISTORECO contributed to the creation of a dynamic collective memory centred on the Resistance and its symbols of unity and anti-fascism in Reggio. The historical memory produced by communist historians has easily merged with the living memory of the Reggians, that is to say the familial memories of the struggle against fascism since the very early 1920s and of the political emigration of Reggian anti-fascists.

In other words, it can be argued that the PCI did not attempt to operate a transplant of a foreign model (Soviet-style socialism) in post-Second World War Reggio. On the contrary, its success was due to the fact that the Party historiography deliberately built on a pre-existing Emilian substratum or subculture. In fact, the PCI nurtured this subculture in order to transform its identity as a reformist party in the 1960s, to justify its strategies of *via italiana* and 'historic compromise'.

The power of this communist collective memory was still highly noticeable in the 1990s. At the *Fiesta de l'Unità* in Reggio in September 1995, the sheer enthusiasm of thousands of young Emilians for the values of the Resistance, which are nowadays disseminated through local rock songs and concerts, was highly visible. On the occasion of the 50th anniversary of the Liberation, the local authorities (province and municipality) commissioned a number of local rock bands to record a CD featuring old partisan songs as well as new creations on the theme of anti-fascism. The album, *Materiale Resistente*, is a good illustration of the constant effort of PCI-run local authorities to ensure that the values of the Resistance are still disseminated among younger generations of Emilians.

In France, on the other hand, the Resistance is merely restricted to a ritual 14 July commemorative ceremony at which elder *maquisards* (partisans) are awarded the Légion d'honneur. The PCF abandoned the political use of most of the symbols of the Resistance in the late 1960s, when this era became highly embarrassing, especially with the rise to power of Georges Marchais (he officially became the PCF Secretary-General in 1972). His claims to have been the victim of compulsory work in Germany during the war were challenged in the 1970s in what became known as the 'Marchais affair'.[66]

THE BANFI INSTITUTE IN REGGIO

One of the key reasons behind the creation of an institute for philosophical research in Reggio was the existence of a widespread, negative image according to which there was a lack of intellectual life and research in the town due the fact that it had never had any university or higher education structure. In those years, as recalled by Ugo Benassi, Reggio was often described as a 'grey town', that is to say a provincial town whose contribution to the intellectual and philosophical life of Italy was virtually insignificant.[67] It was also thought that Reggio was suffering from the intellectual prestige of neighbouring towns such as Bologna, which could pride itself on having the oldest university in Europe and on being one of the most influential towns in Italian culture.

In an attempt to correct this situation and overcome Reggio's grey town reputation, a series of initiatives was launched by a small group of local, left-wing intellectuals, whose aim was to use the intellectual excellence of neighbouring universities (Bologna in particular, but also Modena, Milan and Florence) to Reggio's advantage by organising joint colloquia and/or research projects with academics coming from these research centres and by trying to encourage scholars and postgraduate students to conduct some activities in Reggio. The first of these initiatives took place in May 1967, when a colloquium was organised to explore the main aspects of the philosophy of Antonio Banfi.[68] The choice of this philosopher by local intellectuals had a clear political significance.

Antonio Banfi was a Marxist philosopher who joined the PCI in 1941 and became a member of its Central Committee after the war, before he was elected to the Italian Senate in 1948 and 1953.[69] Although he was a friend of Togliatti and a member of the Party apparatus, he was never considered a dogmatic, orthodox Party intellectual, committed to the defence of a particular line. In fact, he was vigorously criticised on several occasions during the Cold War. For example, as a member of the Central Committee and director of the PCI-controlled journal *Studi Filosofici*, he was involved in a fierce controversy with Luigi Longo, an eminent PCI leader, in 1948.

This controversy followed immediately the publication in France of Jean Kanapa's *L'Existentialisme n'est pas un humanisme*, a book in which the PCF's main propagandist had launched, in his most typical Zhdanovist style, a series of violent and gross attacks on Sartre's philosophy. In a review of this pamphlet published in *Studi Filosofici*, one of Banfi's colleagues reacted with indignation to the vituperative style with which Kanapa was trying to dismiss existentialism. A few weeks later, in a meeting of the Party leadership, Longo publicly disapproved of the fact that a journal directed by a Central Committee member should have criticised the PCF's contribution to the ideological warfare of the time.[70]

Although, according to Ajello, this was not the only reason for the scrapping of Banfi's journal by the PCI in 1949, a clear parallel can be drawn between the fate of *Studi Filosofici* and that of Vittorini's *Il Politecnico* (see Chapter 4), namely that they had both refused the Party's imprimatur.[71] Thus, the choice of Banfi's legacy by the founders of the philosophical institute of Reggio in the late 1960s to early 1970s had a clear, symbolic dimension: it meant that the new Institute was to be a pluralist forum open to dialogue with various philosophical traditions, and not just an orthodox Marxist outpost.

The organisation and funding of the first Banfian colloquium, held in 1967, attracted considerable support from the provincial administration, which also secured the co-operation of scholars from the universities of Bologna and Milan. The proceedings of the colloquium were published in 1969 under the title *Antonio Banfi ed il pensiero contemporaneo*. Two groups of protagonists had prompted the success of the colloquium, which had attracted 40 contributors. First, there was a small academic community made up of old friends and colleagues of the late Banfi, gathered around Professor Felice Battaglia from the University of Bologna, himself a disciple of Banfi.

Second, there was a funding and administrative structure based upon the commitment of the local authorities (the province and the municipality) to promoting philosophical research in Reggio and to perpetuating the work and ideas of Antonio Banfi. After the success of the first colloquium, these two groups joined forces again to create a permanent centre for philosophical research in Reggio.

In November 1968, Banfi's widow Maria Malaguzzi and son Rodolfo offered to donate the philosopher's archives, letters and manuscripts to the municipality of Reggio, and explained their gesture in a letter addressed to the President of the province. In fact, they wanted the work of Banfi to be explored and continued by other philosophers. However, they indicated that their donation would only be made if the municipality and the province agreed to the establishment of a permanent research centre in Reggio, with a mission to foster philosophical meetings. The local authorities accepted the deal, and the Banfi Centre was inaugurated in October 1969.

The first years of the life of the Banfi Centre have been described as difficult years, mostly for financial and administrative reasons. This can be illustrated by the fact that it took the Institute nearly five years to relaunch *Studi Filosofici*, the journal first created by Banfi during the Second World War. This initiative was quickly followed by the funding of four postgraduate bursaries for young scholars intending to embark on doctoral projects in one of the following areas: the history of philosophy, education theories, and the history of Marxism.[72]

After this modest debut, a major reorganisation of the Centre was initiated in 1978, when the Centre was renamed Istituto Banfi. This new structure comprised a board of administrators and a scientific advisory board, and its financial resources were increased by the local authorities. The following year, the Institute organised a conference on the subject of 'Reason and Irrationality'. In the following years, the activities of the Institute expanded considerably to include colloquia on numerous and various topics, such as aesthetics, the philosophy of science, religions, history, and literature and economic and social sciences.[73] In other words, the remit of the Institute was widened in order to include most aspects of the humanities and the arts, to the detriment of the earlier restricted focus on Italian Marxism and Banfi.

The Banfi Institute also adopted a new format for its activities, with at their core a series of seminars for postgraduate students coming from many different Italian universities to present and discuss their research projects in philosophy and related areas, in a pluralist fashion. Indeed, many Christian and non-Marxist philosophers were invited to contribute to the seminars and colloquia organised by the Institute in the late 1970s and early 1980s.[74]

This process of change initiated in the late 1970s prompts the question of whether it reflected a tactical watershed in the political function of the Institute as defined by the PCI during this period. It could be argued by many that the Banfi Institute resembled in its early years a typical 'Gramscian' think-tank, with the aim of establishing the PCI's intellectual hegemony in Reggio and its province. Several aspects substantiate such an argument.

First of all, the nucleus of intellectuals behind the creation of the Centre could be described as a group of typical PCI 'organic intellectuals',[75] a term first used by Gramsci to describe Party intellectuals who had to disseminate the Marxist credo in order to seek to secure hegemony in civil society. Indeed, they all claimed to have inherited their political and intellectual commitment from Antonio Banfi, who, notwithstanding the point made earlier, had himself been a Party philosopher advocating fairly conventional Marxist and/or Soviet views. Some examples of Banfi's political commitment can be cited to illustrate this. For example, in an article entitled 'Ideas and Actions', Banfi claimed that philosophers had to work towards the creation of a philosophy aimed at action, namely what Marxists usually call a philosophy of 'praxis':

> Our task is to organise the world of mankind and not the reign of God, the world of every man, in a common effort and creation; this is a task which is open-ended and infinite, and it is therefore necessary to identify and implement the concrete conditions for this world to exist.[76]

This philosophy of praxis was quite clearly reminiscent of Gramsci's, and of Marx's famous eleventh *Thesis on Feuerbach* in which he criticised philosophers for what he saw as their purely speculative work ('idealism') and their lack of commitment to social change.

In the same vein, Banfi wrote: 'the field of ideologies is the field of concrete conflicts, conflicts which are unavoidable'.[77] This was an echo of the orthodox Marxist notion of philosophy as a struggle, which was found several years later in the writings of the PCF philosopher Louis Althusser, who defined philosophy as 'class struggle in the field of theory'.[78]

Moreover, Banfi was also involved in the PCI struggle for peace during the Cold War years. In December 1955, he advocated universal peace and the sharing of all nuclear technologies between the superpowers in order to guarantee peace through equal technological mastery.[79] These views were fairly orthodox ones promoted in the 1950s by the Soviet Union through the world peace movement.

On the other hand, it could also be argued that in the 1960s Banfi's followers tended to emphasise the pluralist, less orthodox side to Banfi's political life discussed earlier, and that they harnessed Banfi's legacy in Reggio in a way similar to the way the PCI used Gramsci at the national level to give intellectual and philosophical support to its changing strategy. This was done to emphasise the national dimension of Italian Marxism – and therefore of Italian communism – by establishing a clear distinction between it and the orthodox Marxism–Leninism credo of the Soviet model.

An Emilian intellectual who played a crucial role in this process was Ennio Scolari. He was intellectually and politically involved on three fronts. First of all, he was a professor of aesthetics at the University of Bologna. Secondly, he contributed to several left-wing journals of literary criticism, such as *Malebolge*, an influential, Bologna-based journal edited by Umberto Eco, the eminent semiotician. Scolari was therefore an active contributor to the debate on culture which dominated Italy's intellectual life in the 1960s. Thirdly, he was in charge of the cultural commission of the PCI in the province of Reggio.[80]

Committed to all these activities, Scolari was constantly engaging in a series of debates with non-Marxist thinkers, and it could be suggested that his protean commitment influenced the PCI in Reggio more than the Party controlled his activities as a scholar. In other words, one cannot simply describe an intellectual such as Scolari in the terms one would use to describe a French communist intellectual submitted to the strict supervision of the Party. Scolari was in fact an autonomous intellectual, insofar as his livelihood did not depend on PCI stipends.

It could, moreover, be suggested that, in the 1970s, the emphasis of the work of the intellectuals revolving around the Banfi Centre shifted from a mere commemoration of the works and life of Banfi – who was presented as an Emilian equivalent to Gramsci – to a genuine intellectual debate with many philosophers representing various schools of thought, and most of all Catholic philosophers. This strategy of debate or dialogue (*confronto* in Italian) obviously matched the political strategy of 'historic compromise' advocated by Berlinguer in the 1970s. A clear illustration of this focus on dialogue and promotion of research in many areas can be found in the second half of Article 1 of the new statutes of 1978, which gave birth to the Banfi Institute:

> The Institute's mission is to pay tribute to the works and teachings of the eminent philosopher, by promoting cognitive and operative activities of research, consultation and information in the following fields: history of philosophy, history of ideas, philosophy of science, pedagogy, economic theories, contemporary history.[81]

The emphasis of this article was clearly on the method chosen to honour Banfi's memory – the *confronto* – and not so much on a sterile study of the philosophical legacy of Banfi as such. This suggests that the Institute was not intending to indulge in the hagiography of Banfi and his contribution to Italian Marxism, but rather that it was committed to promoting knowledge and research through debates and pluridisciplinary encounters.

This shift in the role of the Institute can be confirmed by a brief examination of the list of topics selected by the Institute for its conferences and seminars in the years that followed. Between 1979 and 1984 (inclusive), out of 26 conferences and/or seminars organised by the Institute, only two were directly concerned with the work of Banfi. Many others dealt with a very wide range of topics: 'Science and philosophy in positivist culture' (1980), 'Unity of knowledge and scientific traditions in the first half of the eighteenth century', 'Autonomy and heteronomy in the field of the arts' (1981), 'Contemporary philosophy and religious experience' (1982), 'The influence of rhetoric in literary and philosophical culture between the sixteenth and the seventeenth centuries' (1982), 'Italian philosophy from 1870 to 1914' (1983), 'The boundaries of knowledge' (1983), 'Roland Barthes' Mythologies' (1984), 'Theoretical problems in the field of translation' (1984).[82]

In fact, this examination of the topics and disciplines covered by the Institute between 1979 and the mid-1980s suggests that the Banfi Institute looked like the philosophy department of a traditional university much more than an orthodox Marxist think-tank. Moreover, the high academic level of the debates enhanced the Institute's reputation for intellectual quality, which can be illustrated by the participation of famous contemporary thinkers in its activities. Thus, Umberto Eco came twice, in 1983 and in 1984, the French sociologist Jean Baudrillard attended the conference on Barthes in 1984, Michel Butor, a leading French novelist, critic and translator, came to talk about translation, as did Meschonnic and Ladmiral, two French academics known for their work in translation theory. There was also a cohort of professors from the universities of Bologna, Modena and Milan, who contributed the bulk of the Institute's work.[83]

This study of the work of the Banfi Institute suggests that, even if some could argue that at its creation the Banfi Centre looked like a traditional ideological instrument used by orthodox PCI intellectuals to disseminate the Marxist credo, the Banfi Institute rapidly lost its teleological dimension and became an academic forum characterised by the following aspects: an evident willingness to open Italian Marxism to a whole range of ideas and trends in a variety of disciplines; a wide range of conference topics and contributors; and a positive effort to provide the provincial town of Reggio with a quality academic centre for the study of humanities.

Thus, with its postgraduates and its many academic collaborators, the Banfi Institute contributed to the demise of Reggio's negative, 'grey' and provincial image. It proved to the rest of Italy that a provincial town too small to justify the opening of a university by the State could nevertheless equip itself with a centre of excellence in the field of philosophical research. As in the case of the library, this emphasis on quality and recognition was the real 'revolution' achieved by the Reggian communists, even if it was to the detriment of the orthodox indoctrination of the intellectual population of the province.

THE STRENGTHENING OF COMMUNIST IDENTITY IN RURAL EMILIA-ROMAGNA: THE CERVI MUSEUM NEAR REGGIO

A number of observers of Italian communism have proposed the idea that one of the major strengths of the PCI in mostly rural regions such as Emilia-Romagna, Umbria or Tuscany was its success in creating and disseminating a communist identity drawing on a pre-existing socio-political subculture.

For example, Geoffrey Pridham, in his case study on communism in Tuscany, underlines the weight of the traditional socialist subculture of rural Tuscany, based on two historical pillars, agrarian socialism and anticlericalism, both dating back from the second half of the nineteenth century. According to Pridham, and many other scholars, this subculture had its origins in the social base of Tuscany, that is to say the prevalence of sharecropping as a social and economic organisation of agricultural life.[84]

This sharecropping system, known as the *mezzadria* in Italian, was based on a few elementary rules: the land was the property of a few wealthy landowners who divided it in small parcels which were cultivated by *mezzadri* or sharecroppers, who had to pay their rent by relinquishing 50 per cent of their annual harvest to the landowner. This system was deemed highly unfair to the sharecroppers who often remained in a state of poverty, if not misery, and who resented the paternalistic or semi-feudal relationship binding them to the landowners. In a 1976 interview with a communist sharecropper, Marcelle Padovani still found evidence of this resentment, when the interviewee recalled the utter state of poverty that had characterised his life until the early 1970s – substantiated by his yearly account books and by the fact that his household could only afford their first bathroom in 1973 – and the organisation of mass demonstrations in the early 1950s against the medieval custom of *regalia*, that is to say gifts in kind (hens, cockerels, etc.) which had to be respectfully presented every Christmas to the landowners.[85]

This traditional agricultural system gave birth, in the nineteenth century, to aspirations for an agrarian revolution aimed at a redistribution of the land from the big landowners to the small sharecroppers and/or the creation of co-operatives run by farmers in their common interest. Also, since most of the big landowners of these areas were traditionally allied to the Catholic Church, which had been impoverished by the expropriation and selling of ecclesiastic goods undertaken by the State in the 1870s, a vast majority of sharecroppers became strong advocates of anticlerical views:

151

[From] the end of that century, socialism became virtually synonymous with anticlericalism, thus lending the latter greater political impact, so that in areas of socialist strength in particular party adhesion was an act simultaneous with a break with the Church. Anticlericalism therefore took root in Tuscany for a number of social and political reasons, although it never reached the vibrant form it assumed in Emilia-Romagna.[86]

Thus, these socio-economic developments which also took place in Emilia-Romagna explain the creation of a socialist stronghold in this region at the end of the nineteenth century. Indeed, the PSI, which came to power in Reggio in the 1890s, had mostly focused its political programme on the agrarian question.

One of the main figures of pre-1914 Emilian socialism was Camillo Prampolini, who has since become a quasi-legendary figure in the local pantheon: after the Liberation of Italy in 1945, his name was given to the main square in Reggio Emilia, and his statue at the entrance of the city hall still reminds passers-by of this subculture of commitment to social and political change. Prampolini's ideas on agrarian reforms – he was one of the originators of the co-operative movement in Emilia which was to become widespread after the Second World War – and on popular culture were to be harnessed by the Emilian communists in the post-war era to create a strong tradition of rural communism based on the symbolic character of the sharecropper, embodied by the Cervi family in the province of Reggio.

In the first pages of her book *La Longue Marche*, Marcelle Padovani emphasises the importance of the Emilian sharecropper in the creation of a strong rural communist identity, and describes this central character as 'a rationalist and a scientist, an "enlightened" peasant', deeply aware of the benefits of progress and scientific advances and 'hungry for all aspects of knowledge'.[87] This character, she goes on, is symbolically epitomised by Alcide Cervi, whose story is in many respects 'exemplary'.[88]

Alcide Cervi was born in 1875 and was the youngest in a family of Emilian *mezzadri*. With his wife Genoveffa, whom he married in 1899, he had nine children, two daughters and seven sons, all born between 1901 and 1921, who were to become part of the Cervi legend 50 years later. Politically, Alcide Cervi was for a number of years an activist in the Italian Popular Party.[89] This party, the ancestor of the DCI, was founded in 1918 and proposed a platform of social legislation and agrarian reforms.[90] During the fascist regime (1922–43), the Cervi sons were to adopt various political stances. It is known, for instance, that Aldo Cervi had publicly criticised the Concordat of 1929 and disagreed with one of his army superiors, an act of insubordination which got him three years' imprisonment. On his return home, Aldo Cervi adhered to the clandestine PCI and soon became one of its local leaders. In the course of the years that followed, the whole family, which had first reluctantly accepted Aldo's new political commitment, followed in his footsteps and joined the PCI. During the Second World War, the Cervi estate became a focal point in the organisation of the local Resistance, providing food and shelter for numerous partisans, and the Cervi sons became active protagonists of the struggle against fascism.[91]

The tragic epilogue of the Cervi saga took place on 25 November 1943, when the seven Cervi brothers, together with their father and a local partisan, were captured by the local fascists and sent to jail in Reggio Emilia. Whereas the old Cervi was released shortly afterwards, his seven sons and the local partisan were executed on 28 December 1943, in retaliation for the assassination of a local fascist leader by partisans a few hours earlier.[92] From this moment, the Cervi brothers left the realm of tragic history to enter that of martyrdom and legend, and the name Cervi has become the most emotional embodiment of heroism and anti-fascism in the province of Reggio Emilia.

It has often been noted that one of the strengths of communist parties was their ability to harness historical events and to use them to strengthen their identity by the creation of powerful political symbols suited to their strategic needs. In his *Politics and Symbols*, David Kertzer emphasises the central role played by this 'symbol-creating' function of the PCI in the creation of a strong, quasi-religious communist sense of belonging, especially in the regions controlled by the Party. Kertzer writes: 'we cannot understand the Party's appeal without understanding its successful construction of history'.[93] It should be noted that, when studying history construction at work, this section will distinguish between the concepts of 'mythologisation' (the making of myths, such as anti-fascist unity) and 'ritualisation' (the propagation of myths through the production of rites, e.g. concrete events such as commemorating marches, partisans' meetings, and so on) which are found in Kertzer.[94]

The process of harnessing the history of the Cervi was at first a rather diffuse process and started with the erection of commemorative markers in Poligno di Tiro, the place where the seven Cervi brothers had been shot, and with the generalisation of ritual events, such as the annual commemoration by the local branch of the ANPI of the anniversary of the tragedy. However, thousands of visitors, most of them locals, spontaneously generated in the late 1940s the rite of the 'Cervi pilgrimage' by paying a short visit to the by-then-retired Alcide Cervi, the sole survivor of the family – his wife had died of illness in 1944.[95]

Meanwhile, a more organised mythologisation process was taking place with the writing of the official history of the family undertaken by

Alcide Cervi himself, assisted by a local historian of communist allegiance called Renato Nicolai. The result of this work was a book entitled *I miei sette figli* (My Seven Sons), first published in 1955, which soon became a major best-seller throughout Italy, and was reissued in 1973 and 1981. It was also translated in many languages, including Russian and the other languages of the people's democracies, and met with huge success with many communist activists and/or backers in the rest of Europe.

As a result of this success, more and more visitors made the trip to the Emilian countryside to pay tribute to the Old Cervi (*Papa Cervi*, or *Il vecchio Cervi* in Italian) until his death in 1970. Plans were then put forward to hold a Cervi collection and to convert the farm into a public museum. In 1972, the local authority (provincial administration of Reggio) and the ANPI gathered the funds to create a Cervi Institute (Istituto Cervi), situated in Reggio and dedicated to the study of the rural world. This was followed in 1975 by the renaming of the Cervi House, which became the Cervi Museum, situated approximately 20 kilometres from Reggio.[96]

The Cervi Institute, according to its statutes, was created to promote and organise academic and cultural work in the field of the study of agriculture and the rural world, in their historical, economic, legal, literary and artistic dimensions. It functions mostly as a research centre specialising in the history of the rural world, and its main output consists of articles, journals and brochures on various aspects of this history. The Cervi Institute of Reggio is in fact part of a wider structure, the national Cervi Institute, based in Rome, which manages the Emilio Sereni library, also based in Rome, specialising in the collection of archives and other documents related to rural history. Other PCI-linked organisations and centres are connected to the Cervi Institute and have donated collections to the Sereni library, like for instance the National Alliance of Farmers (Alleanza Nazionale Contadini) and the FNMC–CGIL, the Federazione Nazionale Mezzadri e Coloni – CGIL which is the branch of the left-wing CGIL union relating to sharecroppers and agricultural workers.[97]

It could be argued that the Cervi Institute formed part of a vast network of PCI-controlled associations, and that its function was to contribute to the dissemination of PCI symbols in the rural world. In fact, a number of the political symbols disseminated and ritualised by the Cervi Museum can be seen at work in the guide to the Museum which has been regularly reprinted since the 1970s.[98]

The first and foremost theme present in the guide and represented in the actual Museum is of course the theme of anti-fascist Resistance in the Emilian countryside, and the living-room is emotionally filled with documents and relics reminding the visitor of the family's tragic involvement in the struggle against local fascists. The collections gathered in this room, from family photographs to Soviet medals and early editions of Cervi's *My Seven Sons*, are a poignant reminder of fascist oppression and of the personal tragedy which struck the family in 1943. In a way, this acts as what French historian Pierre Nora called a *lieu de mémoire*, that is to say a place filled with memories of historical events and tragedies. The Museum can therefore be seen as a ritualistic complement to the more academic side of history production undertaken in Reggio by the ISTORECO and by the Cervi Institute.

Another theme highlighted by the history of the Cervi family as presented in the Museum is the close relationship between communism and Catholic values in the Emilian countryside. Far from insisting on the traditional anticlerical stance characteristic of the socialist subculture, the Museum introduces the visitor to a more complex reality in which some of the Catholic values and communist ideas can coexist in the same family. The early political involvement of Alcide Cervi with the Popular Party and his wife's lifelong Christian devotion are thus mentioned in a positive manner, as if to show that Catholicism and communism were compatible. This was a clear expression of the desire by the PCI to establish and maintain a dialogue between communists and Christians. This also seems to substantiate the claim by Marcelle Padovani that the Italian Communist Party is not an anticlerical party because it always strove to promote understanding and to avoid conflicts and invectives between communists and Catholics.[99]

Another theme of interest in the displays of the Museum and in the works of the Institute is the history of agricultural tools and techniques, with its strong emphasis on the innovative contribution of the Cervi family to the area of farming. These technological innovations included the acquisition of a tractor in 1939, the first in the area, a new type of fireproof grain storage unit in 1943, and the introduction of various techniques. In a few words, the farm run by the Cervi family became a local model of rational agriculture based on scientific advances and opposed to the traditional model of pauperism and the bare survival of the *mezzadri*. The Cervi family, who were also *mezzadri*, saw themselves and were portrayed as entrepreneurs whose aim was to better their conditions of living through the use of science and knowledge.[100]

However, it can be contended that technological progress was by no means an end *per se*: it had, in the way it was used and ritualised by the local PCI, a political aim, that is to say the economic and social emancipation of local farmers. The Cervi family, as they are depicted in the Museum, were keen to challenge the feudalistic system of share-cropping based on the poor level of education of the *mezzadri*. This was quite reminiscent of the old left-wing idea that technological mastery and knowledge for the 'exploited classes' was to be a first step in their political emancipation.

The symbols produced and ritualised by the Cervi Institute and Museum can be subsumed under two categories: the Resistance – already found at the heart of the remit of the ISTORECO – and modernity. This combination of symbols aimed at strengthening PCI identity in the rural surroundings of Reggio and played a powerful role in rooting the Party in an area which underwent tremendous socio-economic change in the 1950s and after. By turning the Cervi farm into a model which promoted such values as 'rationalism', 'modernisation' and 'emancipation' through the adoption of modern agricultural techniques, the PCI was keen to be seen to manage or at least encourage this process of change in the rural world of Emilia, and its continued electoral success in those areas would indicate that the Party was successful in the production and dissemination of these symbols. It could therefore be argued that the Cervi Museum played a useful role in the strengthening of the societal dimension of Emilian communism.

CONCLUSION

This study of some of the institutions of the cultural policy implemented by the PCI in Reggio Emilia between the early 1960s and the late 1970s prompts a series of conclusions.

First of all, it appears clear that the set of policies implemented under the mayorships of Renzo Bonazzi and Ugo Benassi was not highly ideological in content. In fact, it could be argued that the PCI's primary aim was not to disseminate Marxist–Leninist dogma in order to pave the way for a violent revolution led by the 'vanguard of the proletariat'. Instead, it was geared towards the provision of a series of public, municipal services designed to be accessible to a wide majority of the Reggian population, as shown by the success of the Panizzi Library and of the Municipal Theatre, which both attracted a relatively high proportion of the local population.

The second conclusion of this case study is that some aspects of the cultural policy of Reggio can be seen as a medium to reinforce the legitimacy of the PCI as a governing party committed to good public administration and to democracy in Italy in the 1960s and 1970s. Indeed, even what could be described as the most Gramscian or 'hegemony-producing' of Reggio's cultural institutions, the Banfi Institute, can also be depicted as an authentic academic forum for philosophical debate and dialogue and as a tool used to legitimate Italian Marxist thinkers, especially Antonio Banfi, who could be considered as the Emilian equivalent to Gramsci, against imported Leninist doctrines. In other words, this Institute was used as part of a national drive launched by Togliatti in the 1950s to assert the PCI's ideological independence from the Soviet Union.

Moreover, the Banfi Institute can be analysed as a tool in the communists versus anti-communists game, for it is clearly an illustration of the eagerness of the PCI intellectuals to engage in intellectual dialogue with non-Marxist philosophers in general and with Catholic ones in particular. Hence, it can be argued that the PCI in Reggio, by engaging in dialogue with non-Marxist thinkers, was hoping to demonstrate to the Emilian intelligentsia that it was not a totalitarian, dogmatic party, but rather a tolerant, broad-minded force seeking to enrich its theories and to keep in touch with contemporary ideas and theories.

This argument can be strengthened when one considers the existence and active role of the ISTORECO and the Cervi Museum, which were analysed using concepts borrowed from political sociology and anthropology (Kertzer, Lavabre). This case study suggests that, by putting so much emphasis on the Resistance in the period studied, the PCI was intent on rooting a set of democratic values in the local collective memory. Indeed, the work of the ISTORECO has firmly established the equation anti-fascism = PCI = democracy and commitment to the defence of democratic values as a major cornerstone of communist identity in Emilia.

In fact, this widespread emphasis on local Resistance has contributed – and still contributes – to creating the image of a patriotic, democratic PCI in the eyes of thousands of Emilians. In other words, one could argue that the Resistance folklore and mythology, which is firmly based upon many genuine cases of martyrdom (see the famous case of Alcide Cervi's sons), has progressively replaced the imported constituents of Italian communism (Leninism and fealty to the socialist countries) at the local level.

NOTES

[1] Lazar, *Maisons rouges*, p. 215.
[2] Ginsborg, *A History of Contemporary Italy*, p. 296.
[3] Author's interview with Mr Renzo Bonazzi, former Mayor (1962–76), 9 September 1995.
[4] Ibid.
[5] See U. Benassi, *Piazza Grande: Il mestiere di sindaco* (Reggio Emilia: Edizioni Analisi/Tecnostampa, 1989).
[6] Author's interview with Mr Ugo Benassi, former Mayor (1976–87), 15 September 1995.
[7] Author's interview with Renzo Bonazzi, 9 September 1995.

[8] Author's interview with Ugo Benassi, 15 September 1995.

[9] Ibid.

[10] Minutes of the steering committee of the local PCI, 12 November 1979. Agenda: 'Istituto Cervi e iniziative collegate al decennale della morte di Alcide Cervi'.

[11] Author's interview with Mr Antonio Zambonelli, Director, ISTORECO, 8 September 1995.

[12] See M. La Falce, 'The Communist Party in Emilia-Romagna: Party Institutionalisation and Organisational Changes in the Period 1970–1990' (PhD dissertation Bristol University, 1994), Ch. 2, pp. 80–127.

[13] Lazar, Maisons rouges, p. 223.

[14] G. Pridham, The Nature of the Italian System: A Regional Case Study (London: Croom Helm, 1981), pp. 84–90.

[15] Data regarding the history of the library in Reggio are extracted from Panizzi Library (Reggio Emilia), La Biblioteca Panizzi di Reggio Emilia (Reggio Emilia: Tecnostampa, 1989).

[16] V. Masoni, Correggio: Cinque secoli di politica culturale (Bologna: Edizioni Analisi, 1982), pp. 186–7.

[17] Author's interview with Dr Maurizio Festanti, Director, Panizzi Library, 13 September 1995.

[18] Ibid.

[19] Ibid.

[20] Ibid.

[21] Panizzi Library (Reggio Emilia), La Biblioteca Panizzi di Reggio Emilia, p. 8.

[22] I. Grossi and G. Sacchini, Iscritti, lettori e letture alla Panizzi di Reggio Emilia (Bologna: Mongolfiera, 1990), pp. 51–8.

[23] Ibid., p. 59.

[24] Panizzi Library (Reggio Emilia), La Biblioteca Panizzi di Reggio Emilia, p. 8.

[25] Gundle, Between Hollywood and Moscow, p. 151.

[26] Most of the data used in this section are extracted from Reggio Emilia, Vent'anni di teatro pubblico, 1957–1977 (Reggio Emilia: Tecnostampa, 1978).

[27] Ibid., p. xi.

[28] Ibid., pp. 6–7.

[29] J. Ralite, Complicités avec Jean Vilar–Antoine Vitez (Paris: Tirésias, 1996), p. 127.

[30] Ibid., p. 50.

[31] Bonazzi is quoted in Reggio Emilia, Living Theatre in Reggio Emilia (Reggio Emilia: Tecnostampa, 1995), p. 10.

[32] Ibid., p. 11.

[33] See, for instance, the article on Artaud in J. Julliard and M. Winock (eds), Dictionnaire des intellectuels français (Paris: Le Seuil, 1996), pp. 90–1.

[34] Reggio Emilia, Living Theatre in Reggio Emilia, pp. 22–3.

[35] A number of reviews are reproduced in Reggio Emilia, Living Theatre in Reggio Emilia, pp. 42–56.

[36] Ibid., pp. 47–8.

[37] Ibid., p. 51.

[38] Ibid.

[39] The lists of companies and events in Figure 6.4 are based on data extracted from Reggio Emilia, Vent'anni di teatro pubblico.

[40] Data extracted from Reggio Emilia, Nota sulla gestione dei teatri di Reggio Emilia (Reggio Emilia: Tecnostampa, 1984), Appendix 6.

[41] Reggio Emilia, *Vent'anni di teatro pubblico*, p. 112.

[42] Reggio Emilia, *Nota sulla gestione dei teatri di Reggio Emilia*, Appendix 7.

[43] Ibid., p. 12.

[44] Reggio Emilia, *Vent'anni di teatro pubblico*, pp. 7–10.

[45] Ibid., pp. 61–81.

[46] Ibid., pp. 61–81.

[47] Ibid., p. 63.

[48] Ibid., pp. 64–6.

[49] Reggio Emilia, *Nota sulla gestione dei teatri di Reggio Emilia*, Appendix 6.

[50] V. Ottolenghi, *Paese Sera*, 21 January 1975, is quoted in Reggio Emilia, *Vent'anni di teatro pubblico*, p. 62.

[51] Most data on the ISTORECO were gathered during the author's interview with Mr Antonio Zambonelli, Director of the Institute, held on 8 September 1995.

[52] See the article on the Action Party in P. Cannistraro (ed.), *Historical Dictionary of Fascist Italy* (Westport, CT: Greenwood Press, 1982), pp. 399–400.

[53] Author's interview with Antonio Zambonelli, 8 September 1995.

[54] A. Zambonelli, *Fascismo, Resistenza, Repubblica (Dagli Anni Venti agli Anni Settanta)* (Reggio Emilia: Istituto per la Storia della Resistenza et della Guerra di Liberazione, 1975).

[55] Ibid., p. 2.

[56] Ibid., p. 11.

[57] Ibid., p. 11.

[58] Ibid., p. 27.

[59] Ibid., p. 33.

[60] See, for instance, the article on De Gasperi in F. Coppa (ed.), *Dictionary of Modern Italian History* (Westport, CT: Greenwood Press, 1985), pp. 116–18.

[61] Ibid., pp. 290–1.

[62] Ibid., pp. 318–19.

[63] Ibid., pp. 104–7.

[64] Zambonelli, *Fascismo, Resistenza, Repubblica*, p. 36.

[65] Lazar, *Maisons rouges*, p. 18.

[66] A good summary of the controversy surrounding Marchais' whereabouts during the Second World War can be found in a recent biography of the late PCF leader: T. Hofnung, *Georges Marchais: L'inconnu du Parti communiste français* (Paris: L'Archipel, 2001), pp. 45–62.

[67] See Benassi, *Piazza Grande*, pp. 118–19.

[68] Most of the data used in this section were gathered during the author's interview with Dr Maurizio Brioni, director of the Banfi Institute, on 16 September 1995.

[69] A brief account of Banfi's political career and work can be found in Ajello, *Intelletuali e PCI*, pp. 289–93.

[70] Ibid., p. 291.

[71] Ibid., pp. 292–3.

[72] Banfi Institute, *Annali, 1986–1987* (Modena: Mucchi, 1988), p. 71.

[73] Ibid., pp. 71–3.

[74] Ibid., pp. 75–82.

[75] Ibid., p. 69.

[76] Banfi is quoted in Banfi Institute, *Annali, 1986–1987*, p. 29.

[77] Ibid., p. 19.

[78] L. Althusser, *Réponse à John Lewis* (Paris: Maspéro, 1973), p. 13.

[79] Banfi is quoted in Banfi Institute, *Annali, 1986–1987*, p. 35.

[80] Ibid., p. 70.

[81] Ibid., p 147.

[82] Ibid., pp. 75–82.

[83] Ibid., pp. 75–82.

[84] Pridham, *The Nature of the Italian System*, pp. 29–112. For a very useful, recent synthesis on the political subculture of Tuscany, see also M. Caciagli, 'Toscanes rouges: du PSI au PCI, du PCI au PDS', in D. Cefaï, (ed.), *Cultures politiques* (Paris: Presses Universitaires de France, 2001), pp. 299–316.

[85] Padovani, *La Longue Marche*, p. 37.

[86] Pridham, *The Nature of the Italian System*, pp. 32–3.

[87] Padovani, *La Longue Marche*, p. 9.

[88] Ibid., p. 9.

[89] Cervi Institute, *Museo Cervi: Guida alla visita* (Reggio Emila: Centro Stampa, 1991), p. 13.

[90] See the article on the Italian Popular Party in Coppa (ed.), *Dictionary of Modern Italian History*, pp. 209–10.

[91] Cervi Institute, *Museo Cervi: Guida alla visita*, pp. 13–14.

[92] Ibid., p. 15.

[93] Kertzer, *Politics and Symbols*, p. 16.

[94] Ibid., pp. 16–40.

[95] Cervi Institute, *Museo Cervi: Guida alla visita*, p. 15.

[96] Ibid., p. 6.

[97] Author's interview with Dr Antonio Canovi, historian, Cervi Institute, Reggio Emilia, 15 September 1995.

[98] See Cervi Institute, *Museo Cervi: Guida alla visita*.

[99] Padovani, *La Longue Marche*, pp. 81–114.

[100] Cervi Institute, *Museo Cervi: Guida alla visita*, pp. 17–29.

7

Revisiting the Contrast between the PCF and PCI: The Prevalence of International Factors

Having in the previous chapters confirmed on the ground, at the micro-political level, the validity of the universally postulated contrast between the French and Italian Communist Parties, this final chapter aims to review and revisit the main explanatory factors underpinning this much-contrived divergence.[1] The task of identifying causal factors is not an easy one, given the complex, multiform nature of communist parties. A possible approach, however, is to reproduce the two-dimensional model (societal/teleological) of communist parties proposed by Courtois and Lazar (see Chapter 1).

Thus, the next two sections of this chapter identify a number of factors pertaining to the two dimensions of the PCF and the PCI, in an attempt to identify differences which could account for the contrast between these parties. While it is argued here that the contrast emerged from a combination of national and international factors, the contention in this chapter is that, in the last instance, the emergence of the contrast and its magnitude were mostly determined by international factors.

CONTRASTING THE PCF AND THE PCI: 'THE UNBEARABLE HEAVINESS OF NATIONAL REALITIES'?

In a 1984 article whose title, 'PCI–PCF: l'insoutenable pesanteur des réalités nationales', was a stylistic variation on Milan Kundera's *Unbearable Lightness of Being*, Italian political scientist Stefano Bartolini strongly argued that the contrast between the two parties was primarily attributable to national factors such as the relations between Party and society in both countries.[2]

In fact, this is a view which is commonly found in the literature, and a number of national factors have been singled out to account for the contrast. Among these, one of the most frequently invoked to explain the specific nature of post-Second World War Italian communism and its tendency to become fully integrated into Italian society and politics is the traumatic legacy of the fascist era (1922–43). This is an argument mostly made by proponents of the PCI as a primarily national phenomenon. For instance, Joan Barth Urban contends that what she calls Togliatti's 'commitment to this moderate line' (the democratic, reformist strategy of broad political alliances followed by the PCI after 1944) stemmed from the fact that: 'initially his concern centred on internal Italian political elements, those that had welcomed the rise of Mussolini and profited from fascist rule until the bitter reckoning of military defeat in World War II'.[3]

Thus, according to Urban, 'the potential clout and ruthlessness of domestic reaction was, for Togliatti, the basic lesson to be learned from Italy's fascist ordeal'.[4] This was a threat which, together with the lessons drawn from the Spanish Civil War – namely the perils of external intervention by Hitler and Mussolini – and the crushing by British troops of the Greek communist Resistance's bid for control of Athens, 'contributed mightily' to Togliatti's formulation of PCI strategy of backing the creation of a constitutional democracy: 'this was a strategy that was rooted in Italy's fascist experience'.[5]

If one follows this line of argument, the PCI's commitment to constitutional democracy and broad alliances can be seen as stemming primarily from the traumatic experience of fascism and from the long-lasting threat of neo-fascism or authoritarian solutions in post-war Italy. This argument can be further substantiated by an analysis of Berlinguer's strategy, in the 1970s, of 'historic compromise' (a wide-ranging alliance including the Christian democrats) as a reaction to the events of 1973 in Chile, that is to say General Pinochet's coup which overthrew the left-wing government of Salvador Allende, and to a context of terrorism in Italy.

Moreover, even scholars more critical of the outlook of the PCI as a primarily national force acknowledge that the fascist era had influenced its post-war strategy to a certain extent. This is the case, for instance, of Marc Lazar, who argues that, while there were no substantial differences in the post-war strategies of the PCI and the PCF in the years 1944–56, minor nuances slowly emerged between the two parties. Thus, Togliatti's genuine desire to play the constitutional game and to secure a parliamentary democracy in Italy – albeit, as argued by Lazar, in a long-term bid to achieve a socialist transformation of Italy and not for the sake of parliamentary democracy *per se* – came from a political priority, namely to prevent any resurgence of a fascist regime.[6]

In a similar vein, in a study of the PCI in the Comintern years (1921–43) in which his overall argument was that there existed a cast-iron link between the PCI and the Soviet Union,[7] Aldo Agosti, an Italian expert on the Comintern and author of a biography of Togliatti, claims that the failure of the PCI leadership to analyse the success of fascism in the 1920s was to become significant in the subsequent formulation of PCI strategy:

> This close interdependence between the birth and establishment of the communist movement, on the one hand, and the affirmation of the fascist dictatorship, on the other, left an indelible mark in the genetic inheritance of Italian communists: the problem of analysing fascism and of the fight against it dominated their horizons without interruption and conditioned their relations with the Communist International in a determinant way.[8]

Thus, fascism and its traumatic experience undoubtedly left a mark on post-war PCI strategies, and anti-fascism was a key feature of its discourse and policies, as seen on the ground in the case of Reggio (see Chapter 6). This does not mean to say that the PCI was the only communist party to play this card, of course. On the contrary, in his stimulating history of the communist idea in the twentieth century, François Furet clearly argues that anti-fascism became a key constituent of the identity of all communist parties after the Second World War: 'Anti-fascism: this word encompassed everything that ensured the radiance of communism in the post-war era. Communists, as a result, understood this very well when they constantly referred to this emblem, which they preferred to any other.'[9]

What is argued, however, is that, to many Italian communists, fascism had been a concrete reality which had shaped Italian life for twenty years, and which subsequently fuelled their political thinking. To French communists, on the other hand, fascism became in the 1950s a rhetorical tool, a political label used to denigrate political opponents. For example, the PCF equated de Gaulle's return to power in 1958 to a military, authoritarian coup, and de Gaulle himself was labelled a fascist.

A second domestic factor which could help explain the contrast between the two parties is the history of the left in France and in Italy. It could indeed be argued that, in Italy, the split between socialists and communists was never as pronounced as in France, where it appeared irrevocable. In fact, there is evidence that, even in the aftermath of the Leghorn Congress which resulted in the creation of the PCI in 1921, a small number of communist leaders, including Gramsci and Tasca, envisaged a reunification with the PSI.[10] Similarly, in the years 1947–56, there was between the PCI and the PSI a pact for unity of action (a unique situation in western Europe), and the reunification of the two parties was once again discussed, whereas in France the PCF and the SFIO (the

Section Française de l'Internationale Ouvrière, the ancestor of today's French Socialist Party) fiercely opposed each other.

This situation was reflected at the level of trade unions: while the French CGT (Confédération Générale du Travail – General Workers' Confederation) underwent a major split in 1947, which gave birth to the socialist-led CGT–FO (nowadays known as Force Ouvrière), the Italian CGIL (Confederazione Generale Italiana del Lavoro – Italian General Workers' Confederation) remained united to include a strong minority of socialists.

It could be argued that this desire on the part of Italian communists not to burn all their bridges between their party and the socialists, and to maintain a strong, united trade union movement, was a moderating factor, especially in the highly conflictual Cold War years. In fact, in his biography of Togliatti, which emphasises the international dimension of Italian communism, Giorgio Bocca argues that, in 1956, Togliatti was afraid of the political isolation that would result from a split with the PSI. He also states that Togliatti's famous interview in *Nuovi Argomenti*, in which he wrote about 'polycentrism' and reiterated his desire to achieve the *via italiana*, was written, in part, with Italian socialists in mind, in an attempt to reassure them about the democratic credentials of the PCI.[11] By the same token, the failure of the PCI to prevent the split with the PSI in 1956–57 and the subsequent process of *rapprochement* between the PSI and the DCI, which led to the creation of a centre-left governmental coalition in 1963, strengthened among PCI leaders the desire to leave the 'infernal ditch of permanent opposition' (Togliatti).[12]

In a few words, this argument would suggest that the differences in the histories of the left in France and in Italy meant that the PCF, which was isolated at most times, was tempted to resort to sectarianism and to fall back on its teleological dimension, whereas the PCI was keen to avoid isolation and to seek alliances with other forces, hence its political moderation. Thus, this national factor strengthens the point made about anti-fascism and the alliance-building obsession of PCI leaders.

A third explanatory factor undoubtedly lies in the influence of the Roman Catholic Church in Italy, which can also be seen as a moderating factor. In fact, the role of the Church is probably a crucial factor, for it is at the junction of the national and international dimensions of Italian communism. Since this section is primarily concerned with national aspects, however, the international dimension of this factor, namely the desire on the part of the Soviet bloc to promote an image of dialogue with the Vatican, will be discussed in the next section.

In Italy, the Catholic Church is omnipresent not only in civil society but also in the political life of the country, and the Christian democrats were in government between 1945 and 1994. The role of the Church meant that the PCI always felt an absolute need to maintain a dialogue with Christians at all times, in spite of some periods of bitter conflict between the two forces, such as in the late 1940s, when the Vatican threatened to excommunicate the communists *en masse*. This kind of dialogue with Christians was of course not specific to Italy (it was part of an international communist strategy, especially in the 1960s), but it acquired a crucial relevance there. This is illustrated for instance by the fact that the PCI voted in favour of the inclusion of the Lateran Concordat (a compromise between Mussolini and the Church dating from 1929) in the Italian Constitution of 1948, and by the constant search for compromise with Christians on the part of the PCI. According to Lazar, this *rapprochement* was best illustrated by Berlinguer, whose moral integrity and austerity 'embodied the symbiosis [between Church and PCI]'.[13] Further illustrations of this point can be found in the fact that Berlinguer's wife was a regular churchgoer, and that a high-ranking communist such as Franco Rodano, who acted as a special adviser to both Togliatti and Berlinguer, was well known as a devout Catholic.[14]

In France, on the other hand, the role of the Church in politics has been very restricted since the beginning of the twentieth century (see the laws of 1906 on the separation of the Church and the State), and the Christian democrats only played a minor political role, with the possible exception of the MRP (Mouvement Républicain Populaire – Popular Republican Movement) in the late 1940s. This strong, lay republican framework meant that the PCF did not have the constant need to moderate its policies to appeal to a Christian population or to compromise with a prevalent Christian democratic force.

Another set of domestic factors which can be mentioned here pertains to the respective political cultures of France and Italy into which both parties arguably inserted themselves, in the 1930s in the case of the PCF and after 1945 in the case of the PCI.

As regards France, it can be argued that politics is characterised by a long tradition of radicalism stemming from the Revolution of 1789, with such emblematic symbols of political radicalism as the *sans-culotte* or Maximilien Robespierre, one of the revolutionaries who orchestrated the *Terreur* of the years 1792–94. It is therefore tempting to claim that the PCF fitted perfectly into this national tradition. This is an argument mainly found in the works of the proponents of French communism as a reality rooted in French history, such as PCF historian Roger Martelli. In his *Le Rouge et le bleu*, he writes that what he calls 'le stalinisme à la française' was partly the result of the legacy of a political culture of 'popular and revolutionary origins [which] characterises in the long term, in France, the history of the subordinate classes'.[15]

This class war dimension of French communism, which led to the creation of a 'counter-society', in which communism was a besieged fortress, was further compounded by the might of the French state, which fought fiercely any political or social force which challenged its power ('in France, the state is not inclined towards conciliation with those who threaten ... its power'[16]), and by a post-war political spectrum focused around two strongly antagonistic poles, communism and Gaullism, which both benefited from this 'system of controlled, mutual aggression'. All these factors meant that the PCF found itself in a ghetto, which suited its prevailing teleological dimension.[17]

In Italy, on the other hand, the political culture inherited from the *Risorgimento* is one of compromise between parties, called *trasformismo*. In an 1876 electoral speech, left-wing leader Agostino Depretis had advocated a transformation of Italian parties in an attempt to merge the right and the left in an ambivalent synthesis. This prompted a number of Italian politicians to apply the term *trasformismo*, in a pejorative fashion, to their colleagues who had renounced their political ideals to become advocates of a pragmatic approach to politics through the constant search for broad government coalitions.[18] This pattern of *trasformismo* became a key political tradition in the twentieth century,[19] and could be seen as a characteristic of PCI behaviour in the post-war era.

Even if the Italian communists were never really in government in the period 1947–95, they did play the game of *trasformismo*, for example by adopting a highly positive constitutional role in the years 1945–48, and a generally constructive legislative role. Thus, communist MPs voted in favour of a majority of the acts and bills discussed in parliament in the years throughout the post-war era, even in the years 1948–53, 'when the Christian democrats and communists were engaged in outright ideological warfare'.[20]

This non-conflictual, moderate behaviour was also possible because of the almost legendary weakness of the Italian state, which left substantial room for the nurturing of other forces: 'the existence of true social and political spheres has enabled the PCI to put down very deep roots in Italian society without having to fight the state in a systematic fashion'.[21]

So far, attention has focused on the main domestic factors (history and the legacy of fascism, political configuration, the role of the Church and political cultures or traditions) which could contribute to a better understanding of the contrast between the PCF and the PCI. Among other factors sometimes found are the party membership and electorate, the PCF being depicted as 'the most dogmatically proletarian in its approach',[22] the PCI on the other hand being more *interclassista*, as Italians would say. In other words, the PCI was held to be more open to agricultural workers and employees. This difference was found at the level of the national leaderships of the parties. Thus, PCF leaders were, by and large, former workers proud of their working-class background – even if in many cases they did not spend very many years in mines or factories before becoming professional apparatchiks – whose formal education was often limited, even if some became cultured autodidacts. The most typical example of such a leader was Maurice Thorez who prided himself on his mining background before learning Latin in his fifties.[23]

A number of PCI leaders, on the other hand, were from a more bourgeois social background and had the opportunity to study at university. This was the case of Thorez's Italian counterpart, Togliatti, whose father was a civil servant and who grew up to have a profound respect for humanistic, bourgeois culture and universities.[24] Similarly, Enrico Berlinguer was an educated, middle-class man whose style was diametrically opposed to Georges Marchais', who played up his working-class origins and speech to the point of caricature.[25]

Moreover, it could be argued that, in the field of Marxist doctrine, the PCI had in Gramsci a real theoretician who left a rich and protean legacy which was available for as astute a leader as Togliatti to harness in the 1950s and 1960s, thus gaining some degree of ideological independence from Soviet orthodoxy (see Chapter 4).

In fact, the issue of leadership appears to be a crucial one, because it lies clearly at the junction of the national and international dimensions of French and Italian communism. Indeed, the two historical leaders of the PCF and the PCI, Thorez and Togliatti, gained their positions in the crucial, formative years of the Comintern (1919–43). It is therefore necessary, in any tentative explanation of the contrast between these two parties, to go beyond the national factors and to examine the international ones which made it possible for this divergence to emerge and increase at a later stage (1950s–1960s).

EXPLAINING THE ORIGINS OF THE CONTRAST: SOME CRUCIAL INTERNATIONAL FACTORS

The legacy of the Comintern is vital in many respects. First of all, it is a legacy which is common to the PCF, the PCI and all the other communist parties, which all became bolshevised first, in the 1920s, and stalinised after Stalin's victory over his political rivals in the Soviet Union in 1928. This strong, imposed allegiance has now been clearly established in the case both of the PCF, with for example Kriegel and Courtois' *Eugen Fried*,[26] and of the PCI, with the work of Aga-Rossi and Zavlasky,[27] both studies providing ample evidence from recently disclosed Comintern archives based in Moscow. This implies that any claim that the PCI started to become independent from Moscow in those years has little support from this historical evidence.

Therefore, if one admits that both parties were fully bolshevised and compliant with Stalin's directives after 1928, and that, to pursue Lazar's metaphor of the two satellites, the Comintern era was their common 'launching pad',[28] the question which arises here is that of the origins of the subsequent, post-war contrast. In other words, what was the difference in the launching process of these two satellites which provoked their trajectories to diverge at a later stage? It is argued here that a key explanatory factor is the respective positions of Thorez and Togliatti in the Comintern, and vis-à-vis Stalin.

Maurice Thorez, who became the Secretary-General of the PCF in the early 1930s, only played a minor role in the Comintern apparatus, and it could be argued that he was little more than a mere executor of the Comintern directives who always remained under strict Soviet control for at least three reasons. First, he clearly owed his position to Stalin and to the Comintern who chose him as PCF leader during the restructuring of the PCF of 1930–31, which resulted in a series of purges of other leaders (Barbé and Célor, for instance).[29] Second, throughout the 1930s, he was closely watched and supervised by the shadowy Eugen Fried, a Comintern representative residing in Paris.[30]

A key episode illustrates this allegiance and dependence of Maurice Thorez. In early 1931, a depressed Maurice Thorez, facing external (Comintern) criticisms as well as internal dissent, with the stalinisation of the Party still ongoing, went to see his mentor Fried, gave him a letter of resignation, asked him to send it to the executive of the Comintern and informed him that he would only inform the Political Bureau of the PCF after he had received a reply from the Comintern.[31] As a perfect mentor, Fried gave Thorez full reassurance about the trust that the Comintern had placed in him, urged him not to resign, promised him that he would not send the resignation letter to the Comintern executive and proceeded to send a detailed report with a copy of Thorez's letter to Moscow! To any student of communism, this is a highly revealing episode, which probably explains why it remained secret until the 1990s. It is revealing because it is an irrefutable illustration of the fact that Thorez knew very well that he owed his position to Moscow: he did not present his resignation to his French comrades, but intended to send it directly to the Comintern.

A third possible reason pertains to the use by the Comintern and later by the Soviet Union of the biographies of communist leaders and activists worldwide to secure their allegiance, especially when these biographies were not entirely beyond criticism.[32] A number of unsavoury 'errors' found in Thorez's biography would have included the fact that in 1925–26 he had been a friend of Boris Souvarine, himself a friend of Trotsky, who was to become one of the first anti-Stalinists in the 1930s[33] (not to mention Thorez's aborted resignation of 1931). Thus, Thorez appeared like a leader who, if he was not devoid of certain political abilities and skills, had very little or no room for manoeuvre in the 1930s, which meant that he was not equipped subsequently to break the Stalinist mould of his formative years.

Palmiro Togliatti, on the other hand, made a very impressive career in the apparatus of the Comintern in parallel to his rise in the PCI leadership. In the Comintern, first of all, Ercoli (Togliatti's pseudonym) rose very quickly: one of his biographers, Giorgio Bocca, writes that by the autumn of 1926 (that is, before Stalin had triumphed over Trotsky and Bukharin), he was already a 'rising star' in the Communist International.[34] Less than ten years later, in 1934–35, Togliatti effectively became number two in the Comintern hierarchy, after Dimitrov, when he was selected to become Secretary for central European countries.[35] He then played a key role in 1937–39 when he was sent to Spain to co-ordinate the action of the International Brigades during the Civil War, this time using the pseudonym 'Alfredo'.[36] In 1940, he was arrested and jailed in France, and apparently escaped from prison following a deal between the French secret police and the NKVD (the forebear of the KGB),[37] which would suggest that Stalin himself had intervened in favour of Ercoli.

Togliatti's very impressive career triggers a few questions: how did the leader of what was then a small party of activists in jail or in exile (the PCI) make it to the top of the Comintern? What was his relationship with Stalin? How did he manage to survive the great purges of 1937–38 which decimated the Comintern apparatus as well as the Soviet one?

A key factor in understanding Togliatti's success lies in his personal abilities. Referring to his rise in the Comintern apparatus in the second half of the 1920s, at the time of a bitter struggle for power in the Soviet leadership, Giorgio Bocca writes:

> The new [Comintern] leaders were shaped through hard struggles and dramatic choices. In this process, Togliatti was in his element: he was not and would never be a slow mover, and he knew how to mediate between opposing positions, he knew how to produce documents which were acceptable to all parties, he mastered the forms and the regulations; he was, as Trotsky once said, 'the lawyer' of the Comintern.[38]

These mediating skills, echoed by other scholars (Middlemas, for instance, writes about Togliatti's 'subtle diplomacy'[39]), enabled Togliatti to earn Stalin's respect: 'With Stalin, he always played the card of patience and astuteness, and he was admired by Stalin who saw in him a cunning and patient man.'[40] In other words, what could be argued here is that Togliatti was one of the very few communists who knew how to handle Stalin, which is probably why he survived – both metaphorically and physically – at the top of the Comintern until its dissolution in 1943. This could also partly explain why Stalin turned to Togliatti in 1950 when he invited the PCI leader to become the new head of the Cominform, although there might have been other reasons behind this offer.

Togliatti's ability to understand and negotiate with Stalin, however, should not be seen as a sign of his independence, and any serious dissent from him was out of the question: as a cynical, astute *Realpolitiker*, Togliatti knew full well that he had to obey Stalin's international directives at all times, and 'on most occasions, he remained Stalin's mouthpiece'.[41] This meant for instance that, in order to survive the great purges of 1937–38, Ercoli had to play the role of a 'public prosecutor' in a number of ideological trials: he himself admitted, after the war, that he had held a significant responsibility in the purge which had led to the physical elimination of the entire Polish leadership in those years.[42] He also knew how to keep a very quiet profile and how to be very cautious in difficult times: when a number of PCI exiles were arrested in Moscow in those terrible years, he never attempted to intervene in their favour, for he knew that it would have cost him dearly.

Thus, historical evidence suggests that Togliatti, far from being a kind of mythological free agent, was in fact a very ambivalent, cunning leader, who managed to establish what Middlemas called a 'privileged position with Stalin',[43] which had crucial repercussions for the PCI. Indeed, because he was respected by Stalin and enjoyed this privileged position, Togliatti was given a degree of licence when it came to running the PCI domestically in post-war Italy.

This is where the origins of the divergence between the two satellites probably lie: whereas Thorez was a leader who owed everything to Stalin and never played a crucial international role, Togliatti earned his position in the Comintern and in the PCI thanks to his astuteness and also earned Stalin's respect in the process. This was to have vital repercussions in the post-war years, as illustrated by the following key episode.

It has been suggested that, in the early 1950s, Stalin attempted to attract and keep both Thorez and Togliatti in Russia, ostensibly for their own safety.[44] Whatever Stalin's true reasons, what is significant is that, in the case of Thorez, Stalin took advantage of a health breakdown (in 1950, Thorez had a stroke which left him with hemiplegia) to invite the PCF leader to spend some time convalescing in the Soviet Union, and managed to keep him there for three years. It was only after Stalin's death (March

1953) that Thorez was able to return to France, and it is probable that he stayed for such a long period in the Soviet Union with some reluctance.[45] In the case of Togliatti, however, Stalin's ruse was quite different: he attempted to lure the Italian by offering him, at the end of 1950, the presidency of the Cominform. After lengthy and cunning negotiations, however, Togliatti managed to avoid Stalin's trap and returned to Italy in early 1951.[46]

Another explanatory factor strengthening the difference in ranking between Thorez and Togliatti can be found in the respective positions of the two parties in the list of priorities of the Comintern, especially in the 1930s. In fact, it could be argued that the PCI, after the advent of fascism in Italy in 1922 and the ban on all opposition parties in 1926, became a small sect of exiles or clandestine leaders, a relatively insignificant tool which offered very little scope for the Comintern's strategy. On the other hand, especially after the accession to power of Hitler in 1933 and the ban on the German Communist Party, which had been until then the largest and, in strategic terms, most promising European communist party, the PCF became the largest party and the highest priority for the Comintern. This could explain why much stricter means of control were needed in the case of the French Party (see Fried) than in the case of the Italian one, which was of little interest to Moscow.[47]

This contrast between the importance of the PCF and the PCI in the eyes of Moscow leads to another crucial explanatory factor, the respective positions of France and Italy on the international scene and their relevance to Soviet foreign policy goals, especially after 1945. This point is well summarised by Lazar:

> The appreciation by the CPSU [Communist Party of the Soviet Union] of the importance of a given communist party depends not only on the inner strength of this party, but also on the country concerned and on the position of this country on the regional or international scene. The Soviets maintained a tight supervision of the PCF because France interested them, and they willingly relaxed their grip on the PCI because Italy, with the exception of the 1930s, played a relatively marginal role in international relations.[48]

A few historical factors substantiate this argument. First, France had a large colonial empire which offered considerable scope in geopolitical terms, and the PCF contributed to the creation and training of communist parties and activists in northern and central Africa and in Indochina. Italy, on the other hand, was not a colonial power, in spite of Mussolini's repeated attempts in the 1930s to establish Italian colonies in Africa (Ethiopia and Libya, in particular). In any case, Italy was stripped of its

171

colonial possessions at the end of the Second World War. In 1945, France was on the side of victorious countries and obtained a permanent seat on the Security Council of the United Nations, alongside Britain, the USA, the USSR and China, as well as occupation zones in Germany and Berlin. Italy, on the other hand, was a defeated country whose international ambitions had clearly faltered with the fascist regime.

More importantly still, France had in General de Gaulle a post-war leader who in 1944–45, as well as in the 1960s, played a diplomatic 'game of balance' between Moscow and Washington, a game which was of the utmost interest for Stalin and his successors, all the more since de Gaulle's successors as Presidents of France in the 1970s, Pompidou (1969–74) and even more so Giscard d'Estaing (1974–81), were keen to maintain good relations with the Soviet Union.[49] Italy, on the other hand, was clearly and irrevocably aligned with the United States,[50] and therefore offered little of geopolitical interest to the USSR.[51]

Another key geopolitical factor here is the interest that the Soviets increasingly took in securing good relations with the Vatican. This process of *rapprochement*, frequently referred to as the 'communist–Christian dialogue' at the highest level, started in the 1960s and was the result of two concomitant international factors. First, it formed an integral part of the Soviet policy of *détente* and 'peaceful coexistence'. Thus, a series of encounters between Marxist and Christian philosophers broke out simultaneously in several western European countries, such as France, Italy and the Federal Republic of Germany, but also in Czechoslovakia and Yugoslavia.[52] From the viewpoint of the Vatican, the dialogue was largely made possible by the change of attitude towards communism which characterised the papacy of John XXIII (1958–63). Thus, whereas his predecessors had since the 1920s adopted a vociferous anti-communist stance which had culminated in the 1949 edict of excommunication against Catholics who voted for communist parties or sympathised with their doctrine,[53] John XXIII adopted a much more tolerant stance towards communism and shared Khrushchev's notion of 'peaceful coexistence', as illustrated in his encyclical *Pacem in Terris*.[54]

In this process, one could speculate that the Soviets were keen to encourage good relations between Italian communists and Christian democrats as a token of good will to the Vatican. Thus, international Soviet goals converged with the PCI's national interest, which was to show itself as a moderate, non-dogmatic political force (see above). This convergence of international (Soviet) and national (PCI) interests make the presence of the Church in Italy a very potent explanatory factor.

For all these reasons, the PCF had to be maintained under strict supervision, whereas the PCI, as long as it followed and echoed the general themes of international Soviet propaganda (peace, disarmament, third world emancipation, and so on), was given much more latitude in domestic affairs.

CONCLUSION

After this review of possible explanatory factors, it can be argued that what made it possible for the contrast between the PCF and the PCI to emerge and increase in the 1950s and 1960s was not the fact that Togliatti was less Stalinist than Thorez or that the PCI was inherently more national, societal or centrifugal from its early days than its French counterpart. On the contrary, an apparent paradox is that what rendered this contrast possible was that Togliatti was in the 1930s much closer – geographically and politically – to Stalin than Thorez, which enabled the former to win a degree of licence in the conduct of PCI affairs after the Second World War and even more so after Stalin's death. Moreover, this growing independence of the PCI after Stalin's death happened in an international context in which France played a significant role in the eyes of Moscow, whereas Italy was considered a secondary power. Therefore, it seems that the PCI was only able to prioritise its national, societal dimension primarily because of international factors such as the geopolitics of the Soviet Union.

NOTES

[1] An earlier version of this chapter was recently published in article form: C. Guiat, 'Revisiting the Historical Contrast Between the French and Italian Communist Parties: The Prevalence of International Factors', *Totalitarian Movements and Political Religions*, 2, 2 (2001), pp. 18–38.

[2] S. Bartolini, 'PCI–PCF: l'insoutenable pesanteur des réalités nationales', *Politique aujourd'hui*, 7, Nov.–Dec. (1984), pp. 22–35.

[3] Urban, *Moscow and the Italian Communist Party from Togliatti to Berlinguer*, p. 345.

[4] Ibid., p. 345.

[5] Ibid., p. 345.

[6] Lazar, *Maisons rouges*, pp. 54–5. A very similar argument can be found in Gundle, *Between Hollywood and Moscow*, p. 14.

[7] See A. Agosti, 'The Comintern and the Italian Communist Party in light of new documents, 1921–1940', Chapter 7 in T. Rees and A. Thorpe (eds), *International Communism and the Communist International, 1919–1943* (Manchester: Manchester University Press, 1998), pp. 103–16.

[8] Ibid., p. 104.

[9] Furet, *Le Passé d'une illusion*, p. 573.

[10] Agosti, 'The Comintern and the Italian Communist Party', p. 104.

[11] G. Bocca, *Palmiro Togliatti* (Milan: Mondadori, 1991), pp. 585–7. For a discussion of Togliatti's interview in *Nuovi Argomenti*, see, for instance, Lazar, *Maisons rouges*, pp. 94–5.

[12] Lazar, *Maisons rouges*, p. 291.

[13] Ibid., p. 267.

[14] For a brief account of the political career and philosophical outlook of Franco Rodano and other Catholics who became PCI activists in the post-war era, such as Lucio Lombardo Radice, see, for instance, L. Swidler and E. Grace (eds), *Catholic–Communist Collaboration in Italy* (Lanham, MD: University Press of America, 1988), pp. 38–44. On Rodano, see also R. Mulazzi Giammanco, *The Communist–Catholic Dialogue in Italy* (New York: Praeger, 1989), p. 72.

[15] Martelli, *Le Rouge et le bleu*, p. 111.

[16] Lazar, *Maisons rouges*, p. 296.

[17] Ibid., p. 297.

[18] On the concept of *trasformismo* and the historical context of its emergence, see, for instance, S. Romano, *Histoire de l'Italie du Risorgimento à nos jours* (Paris: Le Seuil, 1977), pp. 71–9.

[19] Ibid., p. 74. See also Spotts and Wieser, *Italy, a Difficult Democracy*, pp. 113–15.

[20] Ibid., p. 113.

[21] Lazar, *Maisons rouges*, p. 298.

[22] McInnes, *The Communist Parties of Western Europe*, p. 60.

[23] On the construction of the much-contrived image of Thorez as a working-class hero, see in particular the remarkable book by French historian Stéphane Sirot: S. Sirot, *Maurice Thorez* (Paris: Presses de la FNSP, 2000).

[24] Bocca, *Palmiro Togliatti*, pp. 21–2.

[25] See, in particular, Georges Marchais' most recent biography: Hofnung, *Georges Marchais*.

[26] See the remarkable Kriegel and Courtois, *Eugen Fried*.

[27] See Aga-Rossi and Zaslavsky, *Togliatti e Stalin*.

[28] Lazar, *Maisons rouges*, p. 53.

[29] On this particular purge, see, for instance, Courtois and Lazar, *Histoire du PCF*, pp. 104–6. See also Dreyfus, *PCF, crises et dissidences*, pp. 41–51.

[30] Fried was in fact Thorez's mentor for the best part of the 1930s. This is the main contention of Kriegel and Courtois, *Eugen Fried*.

[31] Ibid., pp. 133–6.

[32] On the function of PCF activists' biographies in their political career, see, for instance, Robrieux, *La Secte*, pp. 38–53.

[33] In the 1930s, Boris Souvarine wrote the first critical biography of Stalin, published in France. On the life and political commitment of Souvarine, see Panné, *Boris Souvarine*.

[34] Bocca, *Palmiro Togliatti*, p. 121.

[35] P. Huber, 'Structure of the Moscow apparatus of the Comintern and decision-making', in Rees and Thorpe, *International Communism and the Communist International*, p. 50.

[36] On Togliatti's shadowy and effective role during the Spanish Civil War, see Bocca, *Palmiro Togliatti*, pp. 263–95.

[37] Ibid., p. 7.

[38] Ibid., p. 122.

[39] Middlemas, *Power and the Party*, p. 90.

[40] Bocca, *Palmiro Togliatti*, p. 11.

[41] Middlemas, *Power and the Party*, p. 90.

[42] Bocca, *Palmiro Togliatti*, pp. 245–58. See also Aga-Rossi and Zaslavsky, *Togliatti e Stalin*, p. 32.

[43] Middlemas, *Power and the Party*, p. 90.

[44] On this episode, see Lazar, *Maisons rouges*, pp. 79–80.

[45] See Courtois and Lazar, *Histoire du PCF*, p. 265.

[46] Bocca, *Palmiro Togliatti*, pp. 491–500.

[47] Lazar, *Maisons rouges*, p. 308.

[48] Ibid., p. 309.

[49] On President Giscard d'Estaing's foreign policy towards the USSR, see particularly J.J. Becker, *Crises et alternances, 1974–1994*, Vol. 19 of the *Nouvelle Histoire de la France contemporaine* (Paris: Le Seuil, 1998), pp. 203–10.

[50] On this question, see, for instance, J. Harper, 'Italy and the World since 1945', in McCarthy (ed.), *Italy since 1945*, pp. 97–101.

[51] See S. Pons, 'La place de l'Italie dans la politique extérieure de l'URSS (1943–1944)', *Communisme*, 49–50 (1997), pp. 91–105.

[52] See, for instance, Swidler and Grace (eds), *Catholic–Communist Collaboration in Italy*, pp. 7–16.

[53] Mulazzi Giammanco, *The Communist–Catholic Dialogue in Italy*, p. 4.

[54] Swidler and Grace (eds), *Catholic–Communist Collaboration in Italy*, p. 7.

Conclusion

The detailed, 'focused comparison'[1] of the cultural policies implemented by the French and Italian Communist Parties in Ivry-sur-Seine and Reggio Emilia between the early 1960s and the early 1980s, which forms the core of this study, tends to confirm that the contrast between these two parties, identified and presented in general terms at the end of Chapter 1, was very visible on the ground, that is to say at the micro-political level.

On the one hand, the case study on Ivry (Chapter 5) establishes that the cultural policy of the PCF was mostly determined by ideological factors, such as the attempted indoctrination of the local population, the defence of the myth of the superiority of the Soviet model, and the clientelisation of a number of artists whose work was used for propaganda purposes. By creating and strengthening what has been described as a bastion culture or a 'counter-society' in Ivry, the PCF asserted its identity as a Leninist revolutionary force irrevocably linked to international communism and largely external to the French socio-political system. This emphasis on what Courtois and Lazar call the 'teleological dimension' of the PCF does not mean that the societal dimension of communism in Ivry was insignificant.

In fact, a key factor in explaining the long-lasting political success of the PCF in strongholds such as Ivry was its ability to canvass and meet a number of expectations emanating from the local population in terms of welfare and cultural provision, as illustrated in Ivry by the successful examples of such facilities as the Conservatoire or the cinema. What the case study shows is that, of the two dimensions of French communism, teleological and societal, that were found in Ivry, the teleological one remained prevalent throughout the period studied here. This finding confirms the view held by Courtois and Lazar and presented at the end of Chapter 1, namely that the PCF was first and foremost a party shaped by its strong ties with the Soviet model.

On the other hand, the case study on Reggio (Chapter 6) establishes that the cultural policy implemented by the PCI in this town was primarily geared towards the provision of quality facilities and services and the creation and strengthening of a communist identity focusing on pillars such as anti-fascism and the defence of the constitution and democratic institutions of contemporary Italy. This substantiates the commonly held view that the Reggian PCI had by the early 1970s become a political force fully integrated into the Italian political system and that it was capable of managing a city efficiently and in the interest of the local population.

The findings of these case studies also tend to corroborate a widespread contention pertaining to the relationship between the local/regional administrators and the national leadership within each of these two parties. Thus, in the case of Ivry, policy-making at the local level was a faithful reflection of the national strategy of the French communists, as argued in Chapter 4, and does not seem to have departed from or had any influence on PCF policy and strategy formulation. On the other hand, careful examination of policy-making in Reggio Emilia prompts the following questions: was the national strategy of the PCI influenced by the reformist approach to policy-making visible at the regional/grassroots level? Or did the national leadership choose to turn a blind eye to such blatant reformism? On this issue, Stephen Gundle suggests a positive answer to the former question when it comes to cultural policy-making in the 1970s:

> It was largely through the activities of left-wing city administrations in the cultural sphere that new techniques were pioneered, old positions and approaches were attacked and discredited, and the way was prepared for the adoption of more flexible and limited cultural policies.[2]

If we move beyond the local/national debate, however, the emphasis placed in Reggio on national, Italian values does not imply a total neglect by the Emilian PCI of its relationship with the international communist movement, as illustrated by the fact that a significant number of eastern European and Soviet ballet companies were invited to perform in Reggio until at least the late 1970s. Thus, the thorough examination of the cultural policy of Reggio tends to confirm the view that Italian communism never totally severed its links with Moscow.[3] Moreover, some aspects of this policy were not politically unequivocal, as was shown by the example of the Banfi Institute which had arguably a clear 'hegemonic' purpose, in Gramscian terms, in the late 1960s and early 1970s.

It would therefore be simplistic to claim that the PCI had by then abandoned all its revolutionary pretensions, or that its teleological dimension had been jettisoned altogether. In fact, the politically motivated vision of a systematic contrast between a PCF that would have remained an internationalist, revolutionary counter-society committed to Soviet-style regimes and a PCI that would have become in the 1960s to 1970s a fully independent, societal force bears little validity on the ground, for it appears that both the PCF and the PCI remained at the junction of their teleological and societal dimensions.

What emerges from this study is that, in the case of the PCF in Ivry, the teleological dimension always prevailed, whereas in the case of the PCI in Reggio we have reasons to argue that the societal dimension became the priority in the 1960s to 1970s, relegating its teleological dimension to a secondary role. In other words, to come back to Lazar's metaphor of the two satellites discussed earlier in this book, the two parties were clearly in different orbits by the 1970s.[4]

The historical origins of this contrast, however, as contended in Chapter 7, can in the last instance be attributed to a series of international factors such as the crucial role of the formative years of the Comintern in shaping the post-war teleological future of both parties and the geopolitics of the USSR in the years 1944–80.

This contention would ultimately suggest that the magnitude and significance of the contrast between the two largest western European communist parties need to be put into new perspective. In fact, it implies that the widespread myth of an attractive PCI 'naturally' committed to finding its own, independent reformist strategy since its early days needs to make way for a much more dispassionate approach to this political force, as advocated in a small number of studies.[5] By the same token, any claim that the PCI was in its very essence a party which was different from its French counterpart as early as in the Comintern years (1920–43) or the Liberation (1944–45) has to be qualified: it was only in the late 1940s and early 1950s that the PCI and the PCF started to enter diverging orbits. This increasing contrast became visible on the ground in the late 1950s and early 1960s, as established in this study. In spite of this evident contrast, it could be argued that the two parties remained comparable phenomena, similar to satellites revolving around the same planet. Therefore, the over-inflated, term-for-term, 'dramatic' contrast between these two parties often found in the literature needs to be replaced by a more relative approach.

CONCLUSION

NOTES

[1] George, 'Case Studies and Theory Development: The Method of Structured, Focused Comparison', pp. 43–68.

[2] Gundle, *Between Hollywood and Moscow*, p. 181.

[3] Gundle, 'The Italian Communist Party: Gorbachev and the End of "Really Existing Socialism"', pp. 15–30.

[4] To pursue Lazar's metaphor: Lazar, *Maisons rouges*, p. 53.

[5] See particularly Aga-Rossi and Zaslavsky, *Togliatti e Stalin*, pp. 7–23, and Lazar, *Maisons rouges*, p. 21.

References

Aga-Rossi, E. and Zaslavsky, V., *Togliatti e Stalin: Il PCI e la politica estera staliniana negli archivi di Mosca* (Bologna: Il Mulino, 1997).

Agosti, A., 'The Comintern and the Italian Communist Party in light of new documents, 1921–1940', Chapter 7 in T. Rees and A. Thorpe (eds), *International Communism and the Communist International, 1919–1943* (Manchester: Manchester University Press, 1998), pp. 103–16.

Ajello, N., *Intelletuali e PCI, 1944–1958* (Bari: Laterza, 1979).

Allum, P., *Politics and Society in Post-War Naples* (Cambridge: Cambridge University Press, 1973).

Almond, G. and Verba, S., *The Civic Culture: Political Attitudes and Democracy in Five Nations* (Princeton, NJ: Princeton University Press, 1963).

Althusser, L., *Réponse à John Lewis* (Paris: Maspéro, 1973).

Amyot, G., *The Italian Communist Party: The Crisis of the Popular Front Strategy* (London: Croom Helm, 1981).

Aragon, L., *La Culture et les hommes* (Paris: Editions Sociales, 1947).

Ashford, D. (ed.), *Financing Urban Government in the Welfare State* (London: Croom Helm, 1980).

Badie, B. and Hermet, G., *Politique comparée* (Paris: Presses Universitaires de France, 1990).

Banfi Institute, *Annali, 1986–1987* (Modena: Mucchi, 1988).

Bartolini, S., 'PCI–PCF: l'insoutenable pesanteur des réalités nationales', *Politique aujourd'hui*, 7, Nov.–Dec. (1984), pp. 22–35.

Becker, J.J., *Le Parti communiste veut-il prendre le pouvoir? La stratégie du PCF de 1930 à nos jours* (Paris: Le Seuil, 1981).

Becker, J.J., *Crises et alternances, 1974–1994*, Vol. 19 of the *Nouvelle Histoire de la France contemporaine* (Paris: Le Seuil, 1998).

Bell, D.S. (ed.), *Western European Communists and the Collapse of Communism* (Oxford: Berg, 1993).

Bell, D.S. and Criddle, B., *The French Communist Party in the Fifth Republic* (Oxford: Clarendon Press, 1994).

Belloin, G., *Nos rêves, camarades* (Paris: Le Seuil, 1979).

Benassi, U., *Piazza Grande: Il mestiere di sindaco* (Reggio Emilia: Edizioni Analisi/Tecnostampa, 1989).

Bernard, J.P., *Le PCF et la question littéraire, 1921–1939* (Grenoble: Presses Universitaires de Grenoble, 1972).

Bernard, J.P., *Paris rouge, 1944–1964: Les communistes français dans la capitale* (Seyssel: Champ Vallon, 1991).

Berthet, D., *Le PCF, la culture et l'art (1947–1954)* (Paris: La Table Ronde, 1990).

Bertrand, O., 'Trois vies dédiées à Ivry-la-Rouge', *Libération*, 19–20 December (1998), pp. 10–11.

Besson, J. (ed.), *Sociologie du communisme en Italie* (Paris: Armand Colin/Presses de la FNSP, 1974).

Billoux, F., *Quand nous étions ministres* (Paris: Editions Sociales, 1972).

Blackmer, D., *Unity in Diversity: Italian Communism and the Communist World* (Cambridge, MA: MIT Press, 1968).

Blackmer, D., 'Continuity and Change in Postwar Italian Communism', in D. Blackmer and S. Tarrow (eds), *Communism in Italy and France* (Princeton, NJ: Princeton University Press, 1977), pp. 21–68.

Blackmer, D. and Kriegel, A., *The International Role of the Communist Parties of Italy and France* (Cambridge, MA: Harvard University, Center for International Affairs, 1975).

Blackmer, D. and Tarrow, S. (eds), *Communism in Italy and France* (Princeton, NJ: Princeton University Press, 1977).

Bocca, G., *Palmiro Togliatti* (Milan: Mondadori, 1991).

Bon, F. (ed.), *Le Communisme en France* (Paris: Armand Colin, 1969).

Bosworth, R., *The Italian Dictatorship: Problems and Perspectives in the Interpretation of Mussolini and Fascism* (London: Arnold, 1998).

Bourderon, R. (ed.), *Le PCF, étapes et problèmes, 1920–1972* (Paris: Editions Sociales, 1981).

Bradby, D., *Modern French Drama, 1940–1980* (Cambridge: Cambridge University Press, 1984).

Burles, J., Martelli, R. and Wolikow, S., *Les Communistes et leur stratégie: Réflexions sur une histoire* (Paris: Messidor/Editions Sociales, 1981).

Buton, P., *Les Lendemains qui déchantent: Le Parti communiste français à la Libération* (Paris: Presses de la FNSP, 1993).

Caciagli, M., 'Une analyse comparative de trois municipalités communistes en Italie, France et Espagne', *Communisme*, 22–3 (1989), pp. 73–93.

Caciagli, M., 'Toscanes rouges: du PSI au PCI, du PCI au PDS', in D. Cefaï (ed.), *Cultures politiques* (Paris: Presses Universitaires de France, 2001), pp. 299–316.

Cannistraro, P. (ed.), *Historical Dictionary of Fascist Italy* (Westport, CT: Greenwood Press, 1982).

Caute, D., *The Fellow-Travellers: A Postscript to Enlightenment* (London: Weidenfeld & Nicolson, 1973).

Ceretti, G., *A l'ombre des deux T: 40 ans avec Palmiro Togliatti et Maurice Thorez* (Paris: Julliard, 1973).

Cervi Institute, *Museo Cervi: Guida alla visita* (Reggio Emilia: Centro Stampa, 1991).

Chambaz, B., 'L'implantation du Parti Communiste Français à Ivry', in J. Girault (ed.), *Sur l'implantation du Parti communiste français dans l'entre-deux-guerres* (Paris: Editions Sociales, 1977), pp. 147–77.

Chemin, A., 'L'histoire du communisme redevient un enjeu politique', *Le Monde*, 9–10 November 1997, p. 7.

Chubb, J., *Patronage, Power and Poverty in Southern Italy: A Tale of Two Cities* (Cambridge: Cambridge University Press, 1982).

Clarke, M., *Antonio Gramsci and the Revolution that Failed* (New Haven, CT: Yale University Press, 1977).

Coeuré, S., *La Grande Lueur à l'Est: Les Français et l'Union Soviétique, 1917–1939* (Paris: Le Seuil, 1999).

Coppa, F. (ed.), *Dictionary of Modern Italian History* (Westport, CT: Greenwood Press, 1985).

Copsey, N., 'A Comparison between the Extreme Right in Contemporary France and Britain', *Contemporary European History*, 1, 6 (1997), pp. 101–16.

Courtois, S., *Le PCF dans la guerre: De Gaulle, la Résistance, Staline …* (Paris: Ramsay, 1980).

Courtois, S. (ed.), *Le Livre noir du communisme: Crimes, terreur, répression* (Paris: Laffont/Bouquins, 1998).

Courtois, S. and Lazar, M., *Histoire du PCF* (Paris: Presses Universitaires de France, 1995).

Courtois, S. and Peschanski, D., 'From Decline to Marginalization: The PCF Breaks with French Society', in M. Waller and M. Fennema (eds), *Communist Parties in Western Europe: Decline or Adaptation?* (Oxford: Basil Blackwell, 1988), pp. 47–68.

Daix, P., *Aragon, une vie à changer* (Paris: Le Seuil, 1975).

Daix, P., *J'ai cru au matin* (Paris: Laffont, 1976).

D'Attorre, P.P. (ed.), *I comunisti in Emilia-Romagna: Documenti e materiali* (Bologna: Gramsci Institute, 1981).

De Felice, R., *Les Rouges et les noirs: Mussolini, la République de Salo et la Résistance, 1943–1945* (Geneva: Georg Editeur, 1999).

De Jouvenel, R., *Confidences d'un ancien sous-marin du PCF* (Paris: Julliard, 1980).

Delbrêl, M., *Ville marxiste: Terre de mission* (Paris: Le Cerf, 1970).

Desanti, D., *Les Staliniens: Une expérience politique, 1944–1956* (Verviers: Marabout, 1976).

Desanti, D., *Les Aragonautes: Les cercles du poète disparu* (Paris: Calmann-Lévy, 1997).

De Sédouy, A. and Harris, A., *Voyage à l'intérieur du Parti communiste* (Paris: Le Seuil, 1974).

De Villefosse, L., *L'Oeuf de Wyasma* (Paris: Julliard, 1962).

Djian, J.M., *La Politique culturelle* (Paris: Le Monde-Editions, 1997).

Donneur, A. and Padioleau, J., 'Local Clientelism in Post-Industrial Society: The Example of the French Communist Party', *European Journal of Political Research*, 10, 1 (1982), pp. 71–82.

Dreyfus, M., *PCF, crises et dissidences* (Brussels: Complexe, 1990).

Duggan, C. and Wagstaff, C. (eds), *Italy in the Cold War: Politics, Culture and Society, 1948–1958* (Oxford: Berg, 1995).

Eckstein, H., 'Case Study and Theory in Political Science', in F. Greenstein and N. Polsby (eds), *Handbook of Political Science*, Vol. 7 (Reading, MA: Addison-Wesley, 1975), pp. 79–137.

Elleinstein, J., *Le PC* (Paris: Grasset, 1976).

Estèbe, P. and Remond, E., *Les Communes au rendez-vous de la culture: Pour des politiques culturelles municipales* (Paris: Syros, 1983).

Fajon, E., *Ma vie s'appelle liberté* (Paris: Laffont, 1976).

Fauvet, J., *Histoire du Parti communiste français (vol. 2): Vingt-cinq ans de drames, 1939–1965* (Paris: Fayard, 1965).

Fejtö, F., *Histoire des démocraties populaires* (Paris: Le Seuil, 1979).

Feldman, E., *Concorde and Dissent: Explaining High Technology Project Failures in Britain and France* (Cambridge: Cambridge University Press, 1985).

Fontana, B., *Hegemony and Power: On the Relation between Gramsci and Machiavelli* (Minneapolis, MN: University of Minnesota Press, 1993).

Forgacs, D., *A Gramsci Reader: Selected Writings, 1916–1935* (London: Lawrence & Wishart, 1988).

Fourcaut, A., *Bobigny, banlieue rouge* (Paris: Editions Ouvrières/Presses de la FNSP, 1986).

Fourcaut, A. (ed.), *Banlieue rouge, 1920–1960, Années Gabin, années Thorez: Archétype du populaire, banc d'essai des modernités* (Paris: Autrement, 1992).

Frei, M., *Italy: The Unfinished Revolution* (London: Mandarin, 1997).

Furet, F., *Le Passé d'une illusion: Essai sur l'idée communiste au XXe siècle* (Paris: Le Livre de Poche, 1996).

George, A., 'Case Studies and Theory Development: The Method of Structured, Focused Comparison', in P.G. Lauren (ed.), *Diplomacy: New Approaches in History, Theory and Policy* (New York: Free Press, 1979), pp. 43–68.

Gérôme, N. and Tartakowsky, D., *La Fête de l'Humanité: Culture communiste, culture populaire* (Paris: Messidor/Editions Sociales, 1988).

Ginsborg, P., *A History of Contemporary Italy: Society and Politics, 1943–1988* (Harmondsworth: Penguin, 1990).

Girault, J. (ed.), *Sur l'implantation du Parti communiste français dans l'entre-deux-guerres* (Paris: Editions Sociales, 1977).

Greene, T., 'The Communist Parties of Italy and France: A Study in Comparative Communism', *World Politics*, 21 (Oct. 1968 – July 1969), pp. 2–25.

Grossi, I. and Sacchini, G., *Iscritti, lettori e letture alla Panizzi di Reggio Emilia* (Bologna: Mongolfiera, 1990).

Guiat, C., 'Revisiting the Historical Contrast Between the French and Italian Communist Parties: The Prevalence of International Factors', *Totalitarian Movements and Political Religions*, 2, 2 (2001), pp. 18–38.

Gundle, S., 'The Italian Communist Party: Gorbachev and the End of "Really Existing Socialism"', in D.S. Bell (ed.), *Western European Communists and the Collapse of Communism* (Oxford: Berg, 1993), pp. 15–30.

Gundle, S., *I comunisti italiani tra Hollywood e Mosca: la sfida della cultura di massa (1943–1991)* (Florence: Giunti, 1995).

Gundle, S., 'The Legacy of the Prison Notebooks: Gramsci, the PCI and Italian Culture in the Cold War Period', in C. Duggan and C. Wagstaff (eds), *Italy in the Cold War: Politics, Culture and Society, 1948–1958* (Oxford: Berg, 1995), pp. 131–47.

Gundle, S., *Between Hollywood and Moscow: The Italian Communists and the Challenge of Mass Culture (1943–1991)* (Durham, NC: Duke University Press, 2000).

Haraszti, M., *L'Artiste d'Etat: De la censure en pays socialiste* (Paris: Fayard, 1983).

Harper, J., 'Italy and the World since 1945', in P. McCarthy (ed.), *Italy since 1945* (Oxford: Oxford University Press, 2000), pp. 95–118.

185

Hastings, M., *Halluin-la-Rouge, 1919–1939: Aspects d'un communisme identitaire* (Lille: Presses Universitaires de Lille, 1991).

Hatim, B. and Mason, I., *The Translator as Communicator* (London: Routledge, 1997).

Hellman, S., *Italian Communism in Transition: The Rise and Fall of the Historic Compromise in Turin, 1975–1980* (Oxford: Oxford University Press, 1988).

Hofnung, T., *Georges Marchais: L'inconnu du Parti communiste français* (Paris: L'Archipel, 2001).

Huber, P., 'Structure of the Moscow apparatus of the Comintern and decision-making', in T. Rees and A. Thorpe (eds), *International Communism and the Communist International* (Manchester: Manchester University Press, 1998), pp. 41–64.

Hughes, A. and Reader, K. (eds), *Encyclopedia of Contemporary French Culture* (London: Routledge, 1998).

Ivryculture, monthly newsletter dedicated to cultural affairs in Ivry-sur-Seine, 1983–88.

Ivry-ma-Ville, monthly newsletter published by the municipality of Ivry-sur-Seine since the 1960s.

Jäggi, M., Müller, R. and Schmid, S., *Red Bologna* (London: Writers and Readers, 1977).

Jeambar, D., *Le PC dans la maison* (Paris: Calmann-Lévy, 1984).

Judt, T., '"The Spreading Notion of the Town": Some Recent Writings on French and Italian Communism', *The Historical Journal*, 28, 4 (1985), pp. 1011–21.

Julliard, J. and Winock, M. (eds), *Dictionnaire des intellectuels français* (Paris: Le Seuil, 1996).

Kehayan, N. and J., *Rue du prolétaire rouge: Deux communistes français en URSS* (Paris: Le Seuil, 1978).

Kertzer, D., *Comrades and Christians: Religion and Political Struggle in Communist Italy* (Cambridge: Cambridge University Press, 1980).

Kertzer, D., *Politics and Symbols: The Italian Communist Party and the Fall of Communism* (New Haven, CT: Yale University Press, 1996).

Kesselman, M., *The Ambiguous Consensus: A Study of Local Government in France* (New York: Knopf, 1967).

Kriegel, A., *Aux origines du communisme français* (Paris: Flammarion, 1969).

Kriegel, A., *The French Communists: Profile of a People*, trans. E. Halperin (Chicago: University of Chicago Press, 1972).

Kriegel, A., 'The French Communist Party and the Fifth Republic', in D. Blackmer and S. Tarrow (eds), *Communism in Italy and France* (Princeton, NJ: Princeton University Press, 1977), pp. 69–86.

Kriegel, A. and Courtois, S., *Eugen Fried: Le grand secret du PCF* (Paris: Le Seuil, 1997).

Kuper, A., *Culture: The Anthropologists' Account* (Cambridge, MA: Harvard University Press, 1999).

Lacorne, D., *Les Notables rouges: La construction municipale de l'union de la gauche* (Paris: Presses de la FNSP, 1980).

La Falce, M., 'The Communist Party in Emilia-Romagna: Party Institutionalisation and Organisational Changes in the Period 1970–1990' (PhD dissertation, Bristol University, 1994).

Lange, P. and Vannicelli, M. (eds), *The Communist Parties of Italy, France and Spain: Postwar Change and Continuity* (London: Allen & Unwin, 1981).

Lavabre, M.C., *Le Fil rouge: Sociologie de la mémoire communiste* (Paris: Presses de la FNSP, 1994).

Lavau, G., 'Le Parti communiste dans le système politique français', in F. Bon (ed.), *Le Communisme en France* (Paris: Armand Colin, 1969), pp. 7–81.

Lavau, G., 'L'historiographie communiste, une pratique politique', in P. Birnbaum and J.M. Vincent (eds), *Critique des pratiques sociales* (Paris: Gallimard, 1978), pp. 121–64.

Lavau, G., *A quoi sert le Parti communiste français?* (Paris: Fayard, 1981).

Lavau, G., 'Les partis communistes en France et en Italie', *Etudes*, June (1982), pp. 756–72.

Lazar, M., *Maisons rouges: Les Partis communistes français et italien de la Libération à nos jours* (Paris: Aubier, 1992).

Lazar, M., 'Le réalisme socialiste aux couleurs de la France', in M. Winock (ed.), *Le Temps de la guerre froide* (Paris: Le Seuil, 1994), pp. 191–210.

Lazar, M., 'Le communisme est-il soluble dans l'histoire?', *L'Histoire*, 223 (1998), pp. 70–2.

Leonardini, J.P., *Profils perdus d'Antoine Vitez* (Paris: Messidor, 1990).

Lerolle, H., 'De certaines coutumes électorales du PCF: le cas d'Ivry-sur-Seine', *Communisme*, 18–19 (1988), pp. 19–32.

Leroy, R., *La Culture au présent* (Paris: Editions Sociales, 1972).

Lijphart, A., 'Comparative Politics and the Comparative Method', *American Political Science Review*, 65, 3 (1971), pp. 682–93.

Lijphart, A., 'The Structure of Inference', in G. Almond and S. Verba (eds), *The Civic Culture Revisited* (Boston, MA: Little, Brown and Company, 1980), pp. 37–56.

Looseley, D., *The Politics of Fun: Cultural Policy and Debate in Contemporary France* (Oxford: Berg, 1995).

McCarthy, P. (ed.), *Italy since 1945* (Oxford: Oxford University Press, 2000).

McInnes, N., *The Communist Parties of Western Europe* (Oxford: Oxford University Press, 1975).

Machin, H. (ed.), *National Communism in Western Europe: A Third Way for Socialism?* (London: Methuen, 1983).

Mammarella, G., *Il partito comunista italiano, 1945–1975* (Florence: Vallechi, 1976).

Marchais, G., *Le Défi démocratique* (Paris: Grasset, 1973).

Martelli, R., *Le Rouge et le bleu: Essai sur le communisme dans l'histoire française* (Paris: Editions de l'Atelier, 1995).

Martin, J., 'Gramsci and Political Analysis: Hegemony and Legitimacy' (PhD dissertation, Bristol University, 1993).

Masoni, V., *Correggio: Cinque secoli di politica culturale* (Bologna: Edizioni Analisi, 1982).

Mayer, L., *Redefining Comparative Politics: Promise versus Performance* (London: Sage, 1989).

Mény, Y., 'Financial Transfers and Local Government in France: National Policy Despite 36,000 Communes', in D. Ashford (ed.), *Financing Urban Government in the Welfare State* (London: Croom Helm, 1980), pp. 142–57.

Mény, Y., 'France', in E. Page and M. Goldsmith (eds), *Central and Local Government Relations: A Comparative Analysis of West European Unitary States* (London: Sage, 1987), pp. 88–106.

Middlemas, K., *Power and the Party: Changing Faces of Communism in Western Europe* (London: André Deutsch, 1980).

Mieli, R. (ed.), *Il PCI allo specchio* (Milan: Rizzoli, 1983).

Miles, M., 'Qualitative Data as an Attractive Nuisance: The Problem of Analysis', *Administrative Science Quarterly*, 24 (1979), pp. 590–601.

Montaldo, J., *Les Finances du parti communiste* (Paris: Albin Michel, 1977).

Montaldo, J., *La France communiste* (Paris: Albin Michel, 1978).

Mulazzi Giammanco, R., *The Communist–Catholic Dialogue in Italy* (New York: Praeger, 1989).

Neri Serneri, S., 'A Past to be Thrown Away? Politics and History in the Italian Resistance', *Contemporary European History*, 4, 3, November (1995), pp. 367–81.

Nizan, P., *Pour une nouvelle culture* (Paris: Grasset, 1971).

Ory, P., *La Belle Illusion: Culture et politique sous le signe du Front populaire, 1935–1938* (Paris: Plon, 1994).

Padovani, M., *La Longue Marche: Le PC italien* (Paris: Calmann-Lévy, 1976).

Page, E. and Goldsmith, M. (eds), *Central and Local Government Relations: A Comparative Analysis of West European Unitary States* (London: Sage, 1987).

Paggi, L. and D'Angelillo, M., *I comunisti italiani e il riformismo* (Turin: Einaudi, 1986).

Pajetta, G., *Le crisi che ho vissuto: Budapest, Praga, Varsovia* (Rome: Editori Riuniti, 1982).

Panizzi Library (Reggio Emilia), *La Biblioteca Panizzi di Reggio Emilia* (Reggio Emilia: Tecnostampa, 1989).

Panné, J.L., *Boris Souvarine, le premier désenchanté du communisme* (Paris: Laffont, 1993).

Parmelin, H., *Libérez les communistes* (Paris: Stock, 1979).

Pasquino, G., 'Mid-Stream and under Stress: The Italian Communist Party', in M. Waller and M. Fennema (eds), *Communist Parties in Western Europe: Decline or Adaptation?* (Oxford: Basil Blackwell, 1988), pp. 26–46.

Pavone, C., *Una guerra civila: saggio storico sulla moralità nella Resistenza* (Turin: Bollati Boringhieri, 1991).

PCF, *Histoire du Parti communiste français (Manuel)* (Paris: Editions Sociales, 1964).

PCF, *Le PCF dans la Résistance* (Paris: Editions Sociales, 1967).

Pellicani, L., *Gramsci, Togliatti e il PCI: Dal moderno principe al post-comunismo* (Rome: Armando Editore, 1990).

Plissonnier, G., *Une vie pour lutter* (Paris: Messidor, 1984).

Pons, S., 'La place de l'Italie dans la politique extérieure de l'URSS (1943–1944)', *Communisme*, 49–50 (1997), pp. 91–105.

Porcu, S., 'Le PCI et l'administration locale à Bologne (1945–1977)', *Revue française de science politique*, 29, 1 (1979), pp. 33–52.

Prenant, M., *Toute une vie à gauche* (Paris: Encre Editions, 1980).

Pridham, G., *The Nature of the Italian System: A Regional Case Study* (London: Croom Helm, 1981).

Pronier, R., *Les Municipalités communistes* (Paris: Balland, 1983).

Przeworski, A. and Teune, H., *The Logic of Comparative Social Inquiry* (New York: Wiley, 1970).

Pudal, B., *Prendre Parti: Pour une sociologie historique du PCF* (Paris: Presses de la FNSP, 1989).

Putnam, R., *The Beliefs of Politicians: Ideology, Conflict and Democracy in Britain and Italy* (New Haven, CT: Yale University Press, 1973).

Putnam, R., *Making Democracy Work: Civic Traditions in Modern Italy* (Princeton, NJ: Princeton University Press, 1993).

Ralite, J., *Complicités avec Jean Vilar–Antoine Vitez* (Paris: Tirésias, 1996).

Ranger, J., 'L'évolution du vote communiste en France depuis 1945', in F. Bon (ed.), *Le Communisme en France* (Paris: Armand Colin, 1969), pp. 211–54.

Ranger, J., 'Le déclin du Parti communiste français', *Revue française de science politique*, 36, 1 (1986), pp. 46–63.

Reale, E., *Avec Jacques Duclos au banc des accusés à la réunion constitutive du Cominform à Szklarska Poreba* (Paris: Plon, 1958).

Rees, T. and Thorpe, A. (eds), *International Communism and the Communist International, 1919–1943* (Manchester: Manchester University Press, 1998).

Reggio Emilia, *Vent'anni di teatro pubblico, 1957–1977* (Reggio Emilia: Tecnostampa, 1978).

Reggio Emilia, *Nota sulla gestione dei teatri di Reggio Emilia* (Reggio Emilia: Tecnostampa, 1984).

Reggio Emilia, *Living Theatre in Reggio Emilia* (Reggio Emilia: Tecnostampa, 1995).

Robrieux, P., *Maurice Thorez, vie secrète et vie publique* (Paris: Fayard, 1975).

Robrieux, P., *Histoire intérieure du Parti communiste* (Paris: Fayard, 1980–84. Four vols).

Robrieux, P., *Histoire intérieure du Parti communiste: Biographies; Chronologie; Bibliographie*, Vol. 4 (Paris: Fayard, 1984).

Robrieux, P., *La Secte* (Paris: Stock, 1985).

Romano, S., *Histoire de l'Italie du Risorgimento à nos jours* (Paris: Le Seuil, 1977).

Ronai, S., 'Comment conserver une municipalité communiste: observations de terrain', *Communisme*, 22–23 (1989), pp. 93–105.

Rosette, M., *La Gestion municipale dans l'action* (Paris: Editions Sociales, 1977).

Ruscoe, J., *The Italian Communist Party (1976–1981) on the Threshold of Government* (London: Macmillan, 1982).

Sanantonio, E., 'Italy', in E. Page and M. Goldsmith (eds), *Central and Local Government Relations: A Comparative Analysis of West European Unitary States* (London: Sage, 1987), pp. 107–29.

Sassoon, D., *The Strategy of the Italian Communist Party from the Resistance to the Historic Compromise* (London: Pinter, 1981).

Schain, M., *French Communism and Local Power: Urban Politics and Political Change* (London: Pinter, 1985).

Scot, J.P., 'Stratégie et pratiques du PCF, 1944–1947', in R. Bourderon (ed.), *Le PCF, étapes et problèmes, 1920–1972* (Paris: Editions Sociales, 1981), pp. 227–90.

Serfaty, S. and Gray, L. (eds), *The Italian Communist Party Yesterday, Today and Tomorrow* (London: Aldwych Press, 1981).

Shore, C., *Italian Communism: The Escape from Leninism* (London: Pluto Press, 1990).

Shore, C., 'Ethnicity as Revolutionary Strategy: Communist Identity Construction in Italy', in S. Macdonald (ed.), *Inside European Identities: Ethnography in Western Europe* (Oxford: Berg, 1993), pp. 27–53.

Sirot, S., *Maurice Thorez* (Paris: Presses de la FNSP, 2000).

Soulet, J.F., *Histoire comparée des Etats communistes de 1945 à nos jours* (Paris: Armand Colin, 1996).

Spire, A. and Chancel, J. (eds), *La Culture des camarades* (Paris: Autrement, 1992).

Spire, A. and Viala, J.P., *La Bataille du livre* (Paris: Editions Sociales, 1976).

Spotts, F. and Wieser, T., *Italy, a Difficult Democracy* (Cambridge: Cambridge University Press, 1986).

Spriano, P., *Storia del partito comunista italiano* (Turin: Einaudi, 1967–75. Five vols).

Swidler, L. and Grace, E. (eds), *Catholic–Communist Collaboration in Italy* (Lanham, MD: University Press of America, 1988).

Tannahill, R., *The Communist Parties of Western Europe: A Comparative Study* (Westport, CT: Greenwood Press, 1978).

Tarrow, S., *Between Centre and Periphery: Grassroots Politicians in Italy and France* (New Haven, CT: Yale University Press, 1977).

Thorez, M., *Fils du peuple* (Paris: Editions Sociales, 1937).

Thorez, P., *Une voix, presque mienne* (Paris: Gallimard, 1986).

Tiersky, R., *French Communism, 1920–1972* (New York: Columbia University Press, 1974).

Tiersky, R., *Ordinary Stalinism: Democratic Centralism and the Question of Communist Political Development* (London: Allen & Unwin, 1986).

Tillon, C., *Un 'Procès de Moscou' à Paris* (Paris: Le Seuil, 1971).

Trigon, M., *Retour aux sources: Lettres à mon fils* (Paris: Le Temps des Cerises, 1994).

Urban, J.B., *Moscow and the Italian Communist Party from Togliatti to Berlinguer* (London: I.B. Tauris, 1986).

Verba, S., 'Some Dilemmas in Comparative Research', *World Politics*, 20, Oct. (1967), pp. 111–27.

Verba, S., Nie, N. and Kim, J., *Participation and Political Equality: A Seven-Nation Comparison* (Cambridge: Cambridge University Press, 1978).

Verdès-Leroux, J., *Au service du Parti: Le Parti communiste, les intellectuels et la culture (1944–1956)* (Paris: Fayard/Minuit, 1983).

Verdès-Leroux, J., *Le Réveil des somnambules: Le Parti communiste, les intellectuels et la culture (1956–1985)* (Paris: Fayard/Minuit, 1987).

Verdès-Leroux, J., 'Qui a signé l'Appel de Stockholm?', in Winock, M. (ed.), *Le Temps de la guerre froide* (Paris: Le Seuil, 1994), pp. 114–19.

Verdès-Leroux, J., *Refus et violences: Politique et littérature à l'extrême droite des années 1930 aux retombées de la Libération* (Paris: Gallimard, 1996).

Vitez, A., *De Chaillot à Chaillot* (Paris: Hachette, 1981).

Vittoria, A., *Togliatti e gli intelletuali: Storia dell'Istituto Gramsci negli anni cinquanta e sessanta* (Rome: Editori Riuniti, 1992).

Waller, M. and Fennema, M. (eds), *Communist Parties in Western Europe: Decline or Adaptation?* (Oxford: Basil Blackwell, 1988).

Weber, H., *Le Parti communiste italien: aux sources de l'eurocommunisme* (Paris: Christian Bourgois, 1977).

Werth, N., *Histoire de l'Union Soviétique* (Paris: Presses Universitaires de France, 1999).

Winock, M. (ed.), *Le Temps de la guerre froide* (Paris: Le Seuil, 1994).

Winock, M., *Le Siècle des intellectuels* (Paris: Le Seuil, 1999).

Wolikow, S., 'Le PCF et le Front populaire', in R. Bourderon (ed.), *Le PCF, étapes et problèmes, 1920–1972* (Paris: Editions Sociales, 1981), pp. 99–197.

Wurmser, A., *Fidèlement vôtre: Soixante ans de vie politique et littéraire* (Paris: Grasset, 1979).

Yin, R., 'The Case Study Crisis: Some Answers', *Administrative Science Quarterly*, 26 (1981), pp. 58–65.

Zambonelli, A., *Fascismo, Resistenza, Repubblica (Dagli Anni Venti agli Anni Settanta)* (Reggio Emilia: Istituto per la Storia della Resistenza et della Guerra di Liberazione, 1975).

Further Reading

COMPARATIVE STUDIES OF WESTERN COMMUNIST PARTIES, INCLUDING THE PCF AND THE PCI

Almond, G., *The Appeals of Communism* (Princeton, NJ: Princeton University Press, 1954).

Bartolini, S., 'PCI–PCF: l'insoutenable pesanteur des réalités nationales', *Politique aujourd'hui*, 7, Nov.–Dec. (1984), pp 22–35.

Bartolini, S., 'Per un analisi dei rapporti tra partiti socialisti e comunisti in Italia e in Francia', *Rivista Italiana di Scienza Politica*, 3, Dec. (1987), pp. 439–80.

Bell, D.S. (ed.), *Western European Communists and the Collapse of Communism* (Oxford: Berg, 1993).

Blackmer, D. and Kriegel, A., *The International Role of the Communist Parties of Italy and France* (Cambridge, MA: Harvard University, Center for International Affairs, 1975).

Blackmer, D. and Tarrow, S. (eds), *Communism in Italy and France* (Princeton, NJ: Princeton University Press, 1977).

Caciagli, M., 'Une analyse comparative de trois municipalités communistes en Italie, France et Espagne', *Communisme*, 22–3 (1989), pp. 73–93.

Ceretti, G., *A l'ombre des deux T: 40 ans avec Palmiro Togliatti et Maurice Thorez* (Paris: Julliard, 1973).

Gotovitch, J., Delwit, P. and Dewaele, J.M., *L'Europe des communistes* (Brussels: Complexe, 1992).

Greene, T., 'The Communist Parties of Italy and France: A Study in Comparative Communism', *World Politics*, 21 (Oct. 1968 – July 1969), pp. 2–25.

Guiat, C., 'Revisiting the Historical Contrast between the French and Italian Communist Parties: The Prevalence of International Factors',

Totalitarian Movements and Political Religions, 2, 2 (2001), pp. 18–38.

Judt, T., '"The Spreading Notion of the Town": Some Recent Writings on French and Italian Communism', *The Historical Journal*, 28, 4 (1985), pp. 1011–21.

Kriegel, A., *Un autre communisme?* (Paris: Hachette, 1977).

Lange, P. and Vannicelli, M. (eds), *The Communist Parties of Italy, France and Spain: Postwar Change and Continuity* (London: Allen & Unwin, 1981).

Lazar, M., 'PCF, PCI, euromissiles et lutte pour la paix, 1979–1987', *Communisme*, 18–19 (1988), pp. 139–61.

Lazar, M., '"Affinités électives", "convergences parallèles" et "déchirements fratricides": les relations entre partis communistes et socialistes en France et en Italie', *Pouvoirs*, 50 (1989), pp. 151–68.

Lazar, M., *Maisons rouges: Les Partis communistes français et italien de la Libération à nos jours* (Paris: Aubier, 1992).

McInnes, N., *The Communist Parties of Western Europe* (Oxford: Oxford University Press, 1975).

Machin, H. (ed.), *National Communism in Western Europe: A Third Way for Socialism?* (London: Methuen, 1983).

Middlemas, K., *Power and the Party: Changing Faces of Communism in Western Europe* (London: André Deutsch, 1980).

Portelli, H., 'La voie nationale des PC français et italien', *Projet*, 106, June (1976), pp. 659–72.

Reale, E., *Avec Jacques Duclos au banc des accusés à la réunion constitutive du Cominform à Szklarska Poreba* (Paris: Plon, 1958).

Tannahill, R., *The Communist Parties of Western Europe: A Comparative Study* (Westport, CT: Greenwood Press, 1978).

Tiersky, R., *Ordinary Stalinism: Democratic Centralism and the Question of Communist Political Development* (London: Allen & Unwin, 1986).

Timmerman, H., 'National Strategy and International Autonomy: The Italian and French Communist Parties', *Studies in Comparative Communism*, 5, Aug. (1972), pp. 258–76.

Waller, M. and Fennema, M. (eds), *Communist Parties in Western Europe: Decline or Adaptation?* (Oxford: Basil Blackwell, 1988).

METHODOLOGICAL ISSUES (COMPARATIVE POLITICS AND CASE STUDIES)

Almond, G. and Verba, S., *The Civic Culture: Political Attitudes and Democracy in Five Nations* (Princeton, NJ: Princeton University Press, 1963).

Ashford, D. (ed.), *Comparing Public Policies: New Concepts and Methods* (Beverly Hills, CA: Sage, 1978).

Badie, B. and Hermet, G., *Politique comparée* (Paris: Presses Universitaires de France, 1990).

Copsey, N., 'A Comparison between the Extreme Right in Contemporary France and Britain', *Contemporary European History*, 1, 6 (1997), pp. 101–16.

Eckstein, H., 'Case Study and Theory in Political Science', in F. Greenstein and N. Polsby (eds), *Handbook of Political Science*, Vol. 7 (Reading, MA: Addison-Wesley, 1975), pp. 79–137.

Feldman, E., *Concorde and Dissent: Explaining High Technology Project Failures in Britain and France* (Cambridge: Cambridge University Press, 1985).

George, A., 'Case Studies and Theory Development: The Method of Structured, Focused Comparison', in P.G. Lauren (ed.), *Diplomacy: New Approaches in History, Theory and Policy* (New York: Free Press, 1979), pp. 43–68.

Hatim, B. and Mason, I., *The Translator as Communicator* (London: Routledge, 1997).

Lijphart, A., 'Comparative Politics and the Comparative Method', *American Political Science Review*, 65, 3 (1971), pp. 682–93.

Mayer, L., *Redefining Comparative Politics: Promise versus Performance* (London: Sage, 1989).

Miles, M., 'Qualitative Data as an Attractive Nuisance: The Problem of Analysis', *Administrative Science Quarterly*, 24 (1979), pp. 590–601.

Putnam, R., *Making Democracy Work: Civic Traditions in Modern Italy* (Princeton, NJ: Princeton University Press, 1993).

Tarrow, S., *Between Centre and Periphery: Grassroots Politicians in Italy and France* (New Haven, CT: Yale University Press, 1977).

Verba, S., 'Some Dilemmas in Comparative Research', *World Politics*, 20, Oct. (1967), pp. 111–27.

Yin, R., 'The Case Study Crisis: Some Answers', *Administrative Science Quarterly*, 26 (1981), pp. 58–65.

Yin, R., *Applications of Case Study Research* (Newbury Park, CA: Sage, 1993).

STUDIES OF THE FRENCH COMMUNIST PARTY

General and Historical Studies

Azéma, J.P., Prost, A. and Rioux, J.P. (eds), *Le Parti communiste français des années sombres, 1938–1941* (Paris: Le Seuil, 1986).

Becker, J.J., *Le Parti communiste veut-il prendre le pouvoir? La stratégie du PCF de 1930 à nos jours* (Paris: Le Seuil, 1981).

Bell, D.S. and Criddle, B., *The French Communist Party in the Fifth Republic* (Oxford: Clarendon Press, 1994).

Belloin, G., *Nos rêves, camarades* (Paris: Le Seuil, 1979).

Bon, F. (ed.), *Le Communisme en France* (Paris: Armand Colin, 1969).

Bourderon, R. (ed.), *Le PCF, étapes et problèmes, 1920–1972* (Paris: Editions Sociales, 1981).

Burles, J., Martelli, R. and Wolikow, S., *Les Communistes et leur stratégie: Réflexions sur une histoire* (Paris: Messidor/Editions Sociales, 1981).

Buton, P., *Les Lendemains qui déchantent: Le Parti communiste français à la Libération* (Paris: Presses de la FNSP, 1993).

Chemin, A., 'L'histoire du communisme redevient un enjeu politique', *Le Monde*, 9–10 November 1997, p. 7.

Coeuré, S., *La Grande Lueur à l'Est: Les Français et l'Union Soviétique, 1917–1939* (Paris: Le Seuil, 1999).

Courtois, S., *Le PCF dans la guerre: De Gaulle, la Résistance, Staline ...* (Paris: Ramsay, 1980).

Courtois, S., 'PCF: le parti de Moscou', *L'Histoire*, 223, July–Aug. (1998), pp. 42–49.

Courtois, S. and Lazar, M., *Histoire du PCF* (Paris: Presses Universitaires de France, 1995).

Dreyfus, M., *PCF, crises et dissidences* (Brussels: Complexe, 1990).

Elleinstein, J., *Le PC* (Paris: Grasset, 1976).

Fajon, E., *Ma vie s'appelle liberté* (Paris: Laffont, 1976).

Fauvet, J., *Histoire du Parti communiste français (vol. 1): De la guerre à la guerre, 1917–1939* (Paris: Fayard, 1964).

Fauvet, J., *Histoire du Parti communiste français (vol. 2): Vingt-cinq ans de drames, 1939–1965* (Paris: Fayard, 1965).

Girault, J. (ed.), *Sur l'implantation du Parti communiste français dans l'entre-deux-guerres* (Paris: Editions Sociales, 1977).

Girault, J. (ed.), *Les Ouvriers en banlieue, XIXe-XXe siècle* (Paris: Editions de l'Atelier/Editions Ouvrières, 1998).

Harris, A. and De Sédouy, A., *Voyage à l'intérieur du Parti communiste* (Paris: Le Seuil, 1974).

Hincker, F., *Le Parti communiste au carrefour* (Paris: Albin Michel, 1979).

Hincker, F., 'La lecture de la Révolution française par le Parti communiste français', *Communisme*, 20–21 (1988), pp. 101–10.

Hofnung, T., *Georges Marchais: L'inconnu du Parti communiste français* (Paris: L'Archipel, 2001).

Jeambar, D., *Le PC dans la maison* (Paris: Calmann-Lévy, 1984).

Jenson, J. and Ross, G., *The View from Inside: A French Communist Cell in Crisis* (Berkeley, CA: University of California Press, 1984).

Kehayan, N. and J., *Rue du prolétaire rouge: Deux communistes français en URSS* (Paris: Le Seuil, 1978).

Kriegel, A., *Aux origines du communisme français* (Paris: Flammarion, 1969).

Kriegel, A., *The French Communists: Profile of a People*, trans. E. Halperin (Chicago: University of Chicago Press, 1972).

Kriegel, A., *Communismes au miroir français* (Paris: Gallimard, 1974).

Kriegel, A. and Courtois, S., *Eugen Fried: Le grand secret du PCF* (Paris: Le Seuil, 1997).

Lavabre, M.C., *Le Fil rouge: Sociologie de la mémoire communiste* (Paris: Presses de la FNSP, 1994).

Lavau, G., 'Le Parti communiste dans le système politique français', in F. Bon (ed.), *Le Communisme en France* (Paris: Armand Colin, 1969), pp. 7–81.

Lavau, G., 'L'historiographie communiste, une pratique politique', in P. Birnbaum and J.M. Vincent (eds), *Critique des pratiques sociales* (Paris: Gallimard, 1978), pp. 121–64.

Lavau, G., *A quoi sert le Parti communiste français?* (Paris: Fayard, 1981).

Lazar, M., 'Le communisme est-il soluble dans l'histoire?', *L'Histoire*, 223 (1998), pp. 70–2.

Lecoeur, A., *La Stratégie du mensonge* (Paris: Ramsay, 1980).

Martelli, R., *Le Rouge et le bleu: Essai sur le communisme dans l'histoire française* (Paris: Editions de l'Atelier, 1995).

Montaldo, J., *Les Finances du parti communiste* (Paris: Albin Michel, 1977).

Montaldo, J., *La France communiste* (Paris: Albin Michel, 1978).

Panné, J.L., *Boris Souvarine, le premier désenchanté du communisme* (Paris: Laffont, 1993).

PCF, *Histoire du Parti communiste français (Manuel)* (Paris: Editions Sociales, 1964).

PCF, *Le PCF dans la Résistance* (Paris: Editions Sociales, 1967).

Platone, F., 'Les communistes au gouvernement: une expérience "complexe et contradictoire"', *Revue politique et parlementaire*, Jan.–Feb. (1985), pp. 28–49.

Plissonnier, G., *Une vie pour lutter* (Paris: Messidor, 1984).

Prenant, M., *Toute une vie à gauche* (Paris: Encre Editions, 1980).

Pudal, B., *Prendre Parti: Pour une sociologie historique du PCF* (Paris: Presses de la FNSP, 1989).

Ranger, J., 'Le déclin du Parti communiste français', *Revue française de science politique*, 36, 1 (1986), pp. 46–63.

Robrieux, P., *Maurice Thorez, vie secrète et vie publique* (Paris: Fayard, 1975).

Robrieux, P., *Histoire intérieure du Parti communiste* (Paris: Fayard, 1980–84. Four vols).

Robrieux, P., *Histoire intérieure du Parti communiste, 1920–1945*, Vol. 1 (Paris: Fayard, 1980).

Robrieux, P., *Histoire intérieure du Parti communiste, 1945–1972*, Vol. 2 (Paris: Fayard, 1981).

Robrieux, P., *Histoire intérieure du Parti communiste, 1972–1982*, Vol. 3 (Paris: Fayard, 1982).

Robrieux, P., *Histoire intérieure du Parti communiste: Biographies; Chronologie; Bibliographie*, Vol. 4 (Paris: Fayard, 1984).

Robrieux, P., *La Secte* (Paris: Stock, 1985).

Sirot, S., *Maurice Thorez* (Paris: Presses de la FNSP, 2000).

Spire, A., *Profession permanent* (Paris: Le Seuil, 1980).

Tartakowsky, D., *Une histoire du PCF* (Paris: Presses Universitaires de France, 1982).

Thorez, M., *Fils du peuple* (Paris: Editions Sociales, 1937).

Thorez, P., *Une voix, presque mienne* (Paris: Gallimard, 1986).

Tiersky, R., *French Communism, 1920–1972* (New York: Columbia University Press, 1974).

Tillon, C., *Un 'Procès de Moscou' à Paris* (Paris: Le Seuil, 1971).

Vigreux, J., *Waldeck Rochet: Une biographie politique* (Paris: La Dispute, 2000).

French Communism at the Local Level

Bertrand, O., 'Trois vies dédiées à Ivry-la-Rouge', *Libération*, 19–20 December (1998), pp. 10–11.

Brard, J.P., *Paroles d'un maire* (Paris: Syros, 1994).

Brunet, J.P., *Saint-Denis, la ville rouge: Socialisme et communisme en banlieue ouvrière, 1890–1939* (Paris: Hachette/Fayard, 1980).

Brunet, J.P., *Jacques Doriot: Du communisme au fascisme* (Paris: Balland, 1986).

Courtois, S., 'Les municipalités communistes en question', *Communisme*, 4 (1984).

Delbrêl, M., *Ville marxiste: Terre de mission* (Paris: Le Cerf, 1970).

Donneur, A. and Padioleau, J., 'Local Clientelism in Post-Industrial Society: The Example of the French Communist Party', *European Journal of Political Research*, 10, 1 (1982), pp. 71–82.

Duclos, J., 'Les communistes français dans les municipalités', *Nouvelle Revue Internationale* (February 1970).

Dupuy, F., *Etre maire communiste* (Paris: Calmann-Lévy, 1975).

Fourcaut, A., *Bobigny, banlieue rouge* (Paris: Editions Ouvrières/Presses de la FNSP, 1986).

Fourcaut, A. (ed.), *Banlieue rouge, 1920–1960, Années Gabin, années Thorez: Archétype du populaire, banc d'essai des modernités* (Paris: Autrement, 1992).

Hastings, M., *Halluin-la-Rouge, 1919–1939: Aspects d'un communisme identitaire* (Lille: Presses Universitaires de Lille, 1991).

Hérodote, Après les banlieues rouges, Special Issue, 43 (1986).

Lacorne, D., *Les Notables rouges: La construction municipale de l'union de la gauche* (Paris: Presses de la FNSP, 1980).

Lerolle, H., 'De certaines coutumes électorales du PCF: le cas d'Ivry-sur-Seine', *Communisme*, 18–19 (1988), pp. 19–32.

Pronier, R., *Les Municipalités communistes* (Paris: Balland, 1983).

Ronai, S., 'Comment conserver une municipalité communiste: observations de terrain', *Communisme*, 22–23 (1989), pp. 93–105.

Rosette, M., *La Gestion municipale dans l'action* (Paris: Editions Sociales, 1977).

Schain, M., *French Communism and Local Power: Urban Politics and Political Change* (London: Pinter, 1985).

Stovall, T., 'French Communism and Suburban Development: The Rise of the Paris Red Belt', *Journal of Contemporary History*, 24, 3 (1989), pp. 437–60.

Trigon, M., *Retour aux sources: Lettres à mon fils* (Paris: Le Temps des Cerises, 1994).

The PCF, Culture and Intellectuals

Aragon, L., *La Culture et les hommes* (Paris: Editions Sociales, 1947).

Bernard, J.P., *Le PCF et la question littéraire, 1921–1939* (Grenoble: Presses Universitaires de Grenoble, 1972).

Bernard, J.P., *Paris rouge, 1944–1964: Les communistes français dans la capitale* (Seyssel: Champ Vallon, 1991).

Berthet, D., *Le PCF, la culture et l'art (1947–1954)* (Paris: La Table Ronde, 1990).

Cohen-Solal, A., *Paul Nizan, communiste impossible* (Paris: Grasset, 1980).

Daix, P., *Aragon, une vie à changer* (Paris: Le Seuil, 1975).

Daix, P., *J'ai cru au matin* (Paris: Laffont, 1976).

Daix, P., *Tout mon temps: Mémoires* (Paris: Fayard, 2001).

De Jouvenel, R., *Confidences d'un ancien sous-marin du PCF* (Paris: Julliard, 1980).

Desanti, D., *Les Staliniens: Une expérience politique, 1944–1956* (Verviers: Marabout, 1976).

Desanti, D., *Les Aragonautes: Les cercles du poète disparu* (Paris: Calmann-Lévy, 1997).

De Villefosse, L., *L'Oeuf de Wyasma* (Paris: Julliard, 1962).

Figuères, L. (ed.), *Le Parti communiste français, la culture et les intellectuels* (Paris: Editions Sociales, 1962).

Garaudy, R., *Le Communisme et la renaissance de la culture française* (Paris: Editions Sociales, 1945).

Gérôme, N. and Tartakowsky, D., *La Fête de l'Humanité: Culture communiste, culture populaire* (Paris: Messidor/Editions Sociales, 1988).

Leduc, V., *Les Tribulations d'un idéologue* (Paris: Syros, 1986).

Leonardini, J.P., *Profils perdus d'Antoine Vitez* (Paris: Messidor, 1990).

Leroy, R., *La Culture au présent* (Paris: Editions Sociales, 1972).

Nizan, P., *Pour une nouvelle culture* (Paris: Grasset, 1971).

Parmelin, H., *Libérez les communistes* (Paris: Stock, 1979).

Ralite, J., *Complicités avec Jean Vilar–Antoine Vitez* (Paris: Tirésias, 1996).

Roy, C., *Somme toute* (Paris: Gallimard, 1976).

Spire, A. and Chancel, J. (eds), *La Culture des camarades* (Paris: Autrement, 1992).

Spire, A. and Viala, J.P., *La Bataille du livre* (Paris: Editions Sociales, 1976).

Verdès-Leroux, J., *Au service du Parti: Le Parti communiste, les intellectuels et la culture (1944–1956)* (Paris: Fayard/Minuit, 1983).

Verdès-Leroux, J., *Le Réveil des somnambules: Le Parti communiste, les intellectuels et la culture (1956–1985)* (Paris: Fayard/Minuit, 1987).

Vitez, A., *De Chaillot à Chaillot* (Paris: Hachette, 1981).

Winock, M. (ed.), *Le Temps de la guerre froide* (Paris: Le Seuil, 1994).

Wurmser, A., *Fidèlement vôtre: Soixante ans de vie politique et littéraire* (Paris: Grasset, 1979).

Materials Published by the Municipality of Ivry-sur-Seine

Ivry-ma-Ville, monthly newsletter, 1971–85.

STUDIES OF THE ITALIAN COMMUNIST PARTY

General and Historical Studies

Aga-Rossi, E. and Zaslavsky, V., *Togliatti e Stalin: Il PCI e la politica estera staliniana negli archivi di Mosca* (Bologna: Il Mulino, 1997).

Amyot, G., *The Italian Communist Party: The Crisis of the Popular Front Strategy* (London: Croom Helm, 1981).

Andreucci, F., 'Paolo Spriano et l'identité culturelle du communisme italien', *Communisme*, 20–21 (1988), pp. 55–9.

Barbagli, M. and Corbetta, P., 'After the Historic Compromise: A Turning Point for the PCI', *European Journal of Political Research*, 10, 3 (1982), pp. 213–39.

Belligni, S. (ed.), *La giraffa e il liocorno: Il PCI dagli anni '70 al nuovo decennio* (Milan: Franco Angeli, 1983).

Besson, J. (ed.), *Sociologie du communisme en Italie* (Paris: Armand Colin/Presses de la FNSP, 1974).

Blackmer, D., *Unity in Diversity: Italian Communism and the Communist World* (Cambridge, MA: MIT Press, 1968).

Bocca, G., *Palmiro Togliatti* (Milan: Mondadori, 1991).

Clarke, M., *Antonio Gramsci and the Revolution that Failed* (New Haven, CT: Yale University Press, 1977).

Di Loreto, P., *Togliatti e la doppiezza: Il PCI tra democrazia e insurrezione 1944–1949* (Bologna: Il Mulino, 1991).

Fiori, G., *Vita di Enrico Berlinguer* (Bari: Laterza, 1989).

Groppo, B., 'Les divergences entre Togliatti et Secchia et l'évolution politique du parti communiste italien, 1944–1954', *Communisme*, 9 (1986), pp. 35–51.

Groppo, B. and Riccamboni, G., 'Le Parti communiste italien face aux crises du "socialisme réel"', *Communisme*, 3 (1983), pp. 65–83.

Kertzer, D., *Comrades and Christians: Religion and Political Struggle in Communist Italy* (Cambridge: Cambridge University Press, 1980).

Kertzer, D., *Politics and Symbols: The Italian Communist Party and the Fall of Communism* (New Haven, CT: Yale University Press, 1996).

Lange, P., 'Crisis and Consent, Change and Compromise: Dilemmas of Italian Communism in the 1970s', *West European Politics*, 2, 3 (1979), pp. 110–32.

Levesque, J., 'Le Parti communiste italien, l'URSS et l'ordre international: Le cheminement du PCI depuis 1975', *Revue française de science politique*, 37, 2 (1987), pp. 141–80.

Mammarella, G., *Il partito comunista italiano, 1945–1975* (Florence: Vallechi, 1976).

Mieli, R. (ed.), *Il PCI allo specchio* (Milan: Rizzoli, 1983).

Padovani, M., *La Longue Marche: Le PC italien* (Paris: Calmann-Lévy, 1976).

Paggi, L. and D'Angelillo, M., *I comunisti italiani e il riformismo* (Turin: Einaudi, 1986).

Pajetta, G., *Le crisi che ho vissuto: Budapest, Praga, Varsovia* (Rome: Editori Riuniti, 1982).

Pellicani, L., *Gramsci, Togliatti e il PCI: Dal moderno principe al post-comunismo* (Rome: Armando Editore, 1990).

Ruscoe, J., *The Italian Communist Party (1976–1981) on the Threshold of Government* (London: Macmillan, 1982).

Sassoon, D., *The Strategy of the Italian Communist Party from the Resistance to the Historic Compromise* (London: Pinter, 1981).

Serfaty, S. and Gray, L. (eds), *The Italian Communist Party Yesterday, Today and Tomorrow* (London: Aldwych Press, 1981).

Shore, C., *Italian Communism: The Escape from Leninism* (London: Pluto Press, 1990).

Shore, C., 'Ethnicity as Revolutionary Strategy: Communist Identity Construction in Italy', in S. Macdonald (ed.), *Inside European Identities: Ethnography in Western Europe* (Oxford: Berg, 1993).

Spriano, P., *Storia del partito comunista italiano* (Turin: Einaudi, 1967–75. Five vols).

Spriano, P., *Storia del partito comunista italiano: Da Bordiga a Gramsci* (vol. 1) (Turin: Einaudi, 1967).

Spriano, P., *Storia del partito comunista italiano: Gli anni della clandestinità* (vol. 2) (Turin: Einaudi, 1969).

Spriano, P., *Storia del partito comunista italiano: I fronti popolari, Stalin, la guerra* (vol. 3) (Turin: Einaudi, 1970).

Spriano, P., *Storia del partito comunista italiano: La fine del fascismo; dalla riscossa operaia alla lotta armata* (vol. 4) (Turin: Einaudi, 1973).

Spriano, P., *Storia del partito comunista italiano: La Resistenza; Togliatti e il partito nuovo* (vol. 5) (Turin: Einaudi, 1975).

Trigilia, C., *Grandi partiti e piccole imprese: Comunisti e democristiani nelle regione a economia diffusa* (Bologna: Il Mulino, 1986).

Urban, J.B., *Moscow and the Italian Communist Party from Togliatti to Berlinguer* (London: I.B. Tauris, 1986).

Weber, H., *Le Parti communiste italien: aux sources de l'eurocommunisme* (Paris: Christian Bourgois, 1977).

Italian Communism at the Local Level

Allum, P., *Politics and Society in Post-War Naples* (Cambridge: Cambridge University Press, 1973).

Anderlini, F., *Terra rossa: Comunismo ideale socialdemocrazia reale; Il PCI in Emilia-Romagna* (Bologna: Gramsci Institute, 1990).

Benassi, U., *Piazza Grande: Il mestiere di sindaco* (Reggio Emilia: Edizioni Analisi/Tecnostampa, 1989).

Bologna, *Giuseppe Dozza a dieci anni dalla morte* (Bologna: Tecnostampa, 1985).

Caciagli, M., 'Toscanes rouges: du PSI au PCI, du PCI au PDS', in D. Cefaï (ed.), *Cultures politiques* (Paris: Presses Universitaires de France, 2001), pp. 299–316.

Cappelli, O., *Governare Napoli: Le sinistre alla prova nella capitale del Mezzogiorno* (Bari: De Donato, 1978).

Chubb, J., 'Naples under the Left: The Limits of Local Change', *Comparative Politics*, 13, 1 (1980), pp. 53–78.

Chubb, J., *Patronage, Power and Poverty in Southern Italy: A Tale of Two Cities* (Cambridge: Cambridge University Press, 1982).

D'Attore, P.P. (ed.), *I comunisti in Emilia-Romagna: Documenti e materiali* (Bologna: Gramsci Institute, 1981).

Hellman, S., *Italian Communism in Transition: The Rise and Fall of the Historic Compromise in Turin, 1975–1980* (Oxford: Oxford University Press, 1988).

Jäggi, M., Müller, R. and Schmid, S., *Red Bologna* (London: Writers and Readers, 1977).

La Falce, M., 'The Communist Party in Emilia-Romagna: Party Institutionalisation and Organisational Changes in the Period 1970–1990' (PhD dissertation, Bristol University, 1994).

Onofri, N., *Il triangolo rosso, 1943–1947: La verità sul dopoguerra in Emilia-Romagna attraverso i documenti d'archivio* (Rome: Sapere 2000, 1994).

Parker, S., 'Local Government and Social Movements in Bologna since 1945' (PhD dissertation, Cambridge University, 1992).

Porcu, S., 'Le PCI et l'administration locale à Bologne (1945–1977)', *Revue française de science politique*, 29, 1 (1979), pp. 33–52.

Pridham, G., *The Nature of the Italian System: A Regional Case Study* (London: Croom Helm, 1981).

Seidelman, R., 'Urban Movements and Communist Power in Florence', *Comparative Politics*, 13, 4 (1981), pp. 437–59.

Tarrow, S., *Peasant Communism in Southern Italy* (New Haven, CT: Yale University Press, 1967).

Travis, D., 'Communism in Modena: The Provincial Origins of the Partito Comunista Italiano (1943–1945)', *The Historical Journal*, 29, 4 (1986), pp. 875–95.

The PCI, Culture and Intellectuals

Ajello, N., *Intelletuali e PCI, 1944–1958* (Bari: Laterza, 1979).

Ajello, N., *Il lungo addio: Intelletuali e PCI dal 1958 al 1991* (Bari: Laterza, 1997).

Fontana, B., *Hegemony and Power: On the Relation between Gramsci and Machiavelli* (Minneapolis, MN: University of Minnesota Press, 1993).

Forgacs, D., *A Gramsci Reader: Selected Writings, 1916–1935* (London: Lawrence & Wishart, 1988).

Gundle, S., *I comunisti italiani tra Hollywood e Mosca: la sfida della cultura di massa (1943–1991)* (Florence: Giunti, 1995).

Gundle, S., 'The Legacy of the Prison Notebooks: Gramsci, the PCI and Italian Culture in the Cold War Period', in C. Duggan and C. Wagstaff (eds), *Italy in the Cold War: Politics, Culture and Society, 1948–1958* (Oxford: Berg, 1995).

Gundle, S., *Between Hollywood and Moscow: The Italian Communists and the Challenge of Mass Culture (1943–1991)* (Durham, NC: Duke University Press, 2000).

Martin, J., 'Gramsci and Political Analysis: Hegemony and Legitimacy' (PhD dissertation, Bristol University, 1993).

Masoni, V., *Correggio: Cinque secoli di politica culturale* (Bologna: Edizioni Analisi, 1982).

Miesler, N., *La via italiana al realismo: La politica culturale artistica del PCI dal 1944 al 1956* (Milan: Mazzota, 1975).

Vittoria, A., *Togliatti e gli intelletuali: Storia dell'Istituto Gramsci negli anni cinquanta e sessanta* (Rome: Editori Riuniti, 1992).

Materials published by the municipality of Reggio Emilia

Banfi Institute, *Annali, 1986–1987* (Modena: Mucchi, 1988).

Cervi Institute, *Museo Cervi: Guida alla visita* (Reggio Emilia: Centro Stampa, 1991).

Grossi, I. and Sacchini, G., *Iscritti, lettori e letture alla Panizzi di Reggio Emilia* (Bologna: Mongolfiera, 1990).

Panizzi Library, *La Biblioteca Panizzi di Reggio Emilia* (Reggio Emilia: Tecnostampa, 1989).

Reggio Emilia, *Vent'anni di teatro pubblico, 1957–1977* (Reggio Emilia: Tecnostampa, 1978).

Reggio Emilia, *Nota sulla gestione dei teatri di Reggio Emilia* (Reggio Emilia: Tecnostampa, 1984).

Reggio Emilia, *Living Theatre in Reggio Emilia* (Reggio Emilia: Tecnostampa, 1995).

Teatro Municipale Valli, *Trent' anni di balletto a Reggio Emilia (1956–'86)* (Reggio Emilia: Tecnostampa, 1986).

Zambonelli, A., *Fascismo, Resistenza, Repubblica (Dagli Anni Venti agli Anni Settanta)* (Reggio Emilia: Istituto per la Storia della Resistenza et della Guerra di Liberazione, 1975).

Index

INDEX